PERFORMANCE-ORIENTED REMEDIES IN EUROPEAN SALE OF GOODS LAW

Contractual remedies aimed at performance create a well-known rift between common law and civil law traditions, in one system existing in the shadow of damages, whilst in the other regarded as a generally enforceable right following from the contract. Developments in approximation of laws in Europe, in particular in consumer sales law, suggest however that a convergence of these approaches may be within reach. Putting the focus on the contract of sale—which, as the most common type of contract, may fulfill a leading role in the harmonisation process—this book aims to provide a model for further convergence of European sales laws, engaging along the way with issues of contract theory and comparative law lying at the heart of the process. Independently from this, the comparison between different systems is used in order to highlight particular problems in the remedial schemes of individual systems and to see whether a better solution may be borrowed from elsewhere. Weighing the interests of sellers and buyers as reflected in national laws as well as in uniform sets of rules such as CISG and the PECL, a plea is made for a primary position for performance-oriented remedies in the harmonisation of European sales law. In this context, special significance is attributed to the possibility of cure by the seller, which has both practical and conceptual links to the buyer's remedies aimed at performance.

Volume 10: Studies of the Oxford Institute of European and Comparative Law

Studies of the Oxford Institute of European and Comparative Law

Volume 1: The Harmonisation of European Contract Law: Implications for European Private Laws, Business and Legal Practice
Edited by Stefan Vogenauer and Stephen Weatherill

Volume 2: The Public Law/Private Law Divide
Edited by Mark Freedland and Jean-Bernard Auby

Volume 3: Constitutionalism and the Role of Parliaments
Edited by Katja Ziegler, Denis Baranger and A W Bradley

Volume 4: The Regulation of Unfair Commercial Practices under EC Directive 2005/29: New Rules and Techniques
Edited by Stephen Weatherill and Ulf Bernitz

Volume 5: Human Rights and Private Law: Privacy as Autonomy
Edited by Katja Ziegler

Volume 6: Better Regulation
Edited by Stephen Weatherill

Volume 7: Forum Shopping in the European Judicial Area
Edited by Pascal de Vareilles-Sommières

Volume 8: The Reform of Class and Representative Actions in European Legal Systems: A New Framework for Collective Redress in Europe
Christopher Hodges

Volume 9: Reforming the French Law of Obligations: Comparative Relections on the Avant-projet de réforme du droit des obligations et de la precription ('the Avant-projet Catala')
Edited by John Cartwright, Stefan Vogenauer and Simon Whittaker

Volume 10: Performance-Oriented Remedies in European Sale of Goods Law
Vanessa Mak

Performance-Oriented Remedies in European Sale of Goods Law

Vanessa Mak

·HART·
PUBLISHING

OXFORD AND PORTLAND, OREGON
2009

Published in North America (US and Canada) by
Hart Publishing
c/o International Specialized Book Services
920 NE 58th Avenue, Suite 300
Portland, OR 97213-3786
USA
Tel: +1 503 287 3093 or toll-free: (1) 800 944 6190
Fax: +1 503 280 8832
E-mail: orders@isbs.com
Web Site: www.isbs.com

Hart Publishing Ltd, 16c Worcester Place, Oxford, OX1 2JW
Telephone: +44 (0)1865 517530 Fax: +44 (0) 1865 510710
E-mail: mail@hartpub.co.uk
Website: http://www.hartpub.co.uk

British Library Cataloguing in Publication Data
Data Available

ISBN: 978-184113-893-0

Typeset by Hope Services (Abingdon) Ltd
Printed and bound in Great Britain by
CPI Antony Rowe, Wiltshire

Acknowledgments

The book in front of you is the updated version of a DPhil thesis by the same title, written in Oxford and defended in December 2006. It could not have come about without the generous support of my family, friends and colleagues to whom I would like to express my warmest thanks and gratitude. A number of people deserve special mention.

In Oxford, my greatest debt is to my academic supervisor, Professor Ewan McKendrick. Throughout the course of the project, his encouragement and insight were invaluable and have, many times, helped me to shape my ideas more clearly and to improve the text on important points. I am deeply grateful, furthermore, to Professor Sir Roy Goode. Working for him has been a great inspiration both during the writing of the thesis and in taking my first steps on the academic career ladder. On a personal note, I would like to thank him and his wife, Catherine, for their kindness and hospitality.

I would like to express gratitude, also, to Professor Hector MacQueen and Professor Stefan Vogenauer who, in their capacity of DPhil examiners, provided me with helpful feedback on the thesis and on the final manuscript of the book.

Of the Oxford Law Faculty, St Peter's College and Oriel College, I wish to thank the friends and fellow doctoral students who were there throughout and with whom I share many precious memories. Many names and faces remain in my heart and in my mind. I am especially grateful to: Alicia, Dorota, Ester, Jeff, Magda, Russ, Veronika, Ng, Carla, Nat and Tim—your friendship means the world to me and I hope to meet up again often in the different places and countries that we move to (or have moved to) from Oxford.

The updates on the manuscript were made during my stay as a visiting researcher at the Max Planck Institute for Comparative and International Private Law in Hamburg from the end of 2007 until Summer 2008. My warmest thanks go out to Professor Reinhard Zimmermann for his kind hospitality, and to the friends and colleagues who made me feel 'zuhause' in a new city: Dominik, Flo, Lili, Jens, Martin, Matt, Verena, Walter, Anatol, Eva, Kristin, Vera, and Eva. In Bremen, I would like to thank Professor Aurelia Colombi Ciacchi and Professor Peter Rott.

Thanks are due also to Richard Hart, who kindly agreed to publish this book in the series of the Oxford Institute of European and Comparative Law (OIECL). I am especially grateful for the fantastic job that he and his staff have done in correcting the text of the manuscript, and for their professional and kind cooperation in getting the book ready for publication.

The research could not have been carried out without generous financial support from the Oxford Law Faculty, St Peter's College, the Max Planck Institute in Hamburg, and the Prins Bernhard Cultuurfonds.

Finally, I would like to thank my family in the Netherlands, especially my parents and my sisters Elaine and Chantal. Your love and support has been, and continues to be, invaluable.

Vanessa Mak
Utrecht, September 2008

Contents

Table of Cases

France

Netherlands

United Kingdom

United States

Table of National Legislation

France

Germany

Netherlands

United Kingdom

Table of European Law

Directives

Treaties

Table of International Treaties and Conventions

1

Introduction

WHILE MURPHY'S LAW[1] does not apply universally, it is a common occurrence for things to go wrong in the execution of contracts. Unfortunately but inevitably, parties will not always be able to live up to the obligations that they have (voluntarily) undertaken towards their contracting partner. If they did, the courts would be significantly less burdened with cases than they currently are. An attenuation of the pain of defective or non-performance may, however, be found in the law of remedies. When difficulties are experienced in the execution of a contract, the parties may turn here to find a solution, a 'remedy' for the unsuccessful performance. It will determine what their rights are and who has to bear the burden of the unsatisfactory performance, and it may also suggest a solution as to whether and how the parties are able to continue their cooperation and fulfill the contract after all.

Whereas the majority of commentators put remedies at the end of the chain of elements that make up the law of contract (formation, contents, vitiating factors such as mistake, frustration and misrepresentation), their place appears to be more central in practice than this ordering suggests. It is only when things do not go according to plan that the contents of a contract are truly put to the test. If all goes well and the contract is executed as envisaged, the parties may never even look at the contract again and, so to speak, may leave it lying in a drawer somewhere. Where things do go wrong, however, it becomes important for the parties to find out (i) what their rights are under the contract, and (ii) whether they will be able to enforce them.[2] Remedies may have their main impact on the second question, but they appear to be of relevance to the first point as well. After all, parties may decide to what degree they want to be bound by contractual obligations on the basis of what remedies they will have to provide to the other party in the event that they are unable to live up to their promises.

Remedies, therefore, are of central importance to contracts and may influence a party's decision to enter into a contract, as well as on what terms to do so. As a consequence, where there is uncertainty as to the contents of the remedial scheme that governs a contract, it may discourage parties from entering into that contract. This may be the case not only when there are ambiguities in the remedies provisions found in the domestic law of the country in which a party

[1] The rule that everything that can go wrong, *will* go wrong.

[2] In relation to the second point, compare R Zakrzewski, *Remedies Reclassified* (Oxford, Oxford University Press, 2005).

is resident, but also where a party has insufficient information as to the substantive law of possible other systems that may govern the contract. For example, where the contracting parties are both resident in different countries, one party may (for practical reasons) be forced to accept the law of the other party's country as the governing law of the contract.[3] However, this may put him at a disadvantage because he is likely to be less familiar with the law of that country than with his own domestic law. Where this is likely to occur on a regular basis, it is thought that a case for harmonisation of laws may be made.

Harmonisation—but where to start and how to achieve it? This book aims to contribute to the approximation of contract laws in Europe by providing a model for the remedial scheme in the most common type of contract, the contract of sale. A comparison of domestic laws and international rules will be used as a basis to formulate some guidelines for possible harmonisation in this area. A second aim of the book, linked to the question of harmonisation but also valid independently from that, is to use the comparison between different systems in order to highlight particular problems in the remedial schemes of individual systems and to see whether a better solution may be borrowed from elsewhere.

The focus will in particular be on a type of remedy that in continental legal systems is generally available to an aggrieved buyer, but the availability of which in the English common law system is much more restricted: the remedy aimed at performance. Remedies that fit this category may, depending on the jurisdiction considered, include specific performance, repair, replacement, and even cure offered by the seller.[4] A reason to focus on these is that they go straight to the heart of the contractual interest which remedies for non-performance or breach seek to protect, namely the interest of the aggrieved party in obtaining the performance that he contracted for. This interest, now commonly referred to as the 'performance interest',[5] has long been recognised as the core of the remedial schemes in civil law jurisdictions, and in recent years appears to have gained prominence in the English common law system as well. What comes to the fore is not just the interest of the aggrieved party in obtaining a remedy that gives him the value of the performance which he expected to receive under the contract, but rather his interest in obtaining a remedy that gives him the actual performance that he would have received had the contract been performed satisfactorily.[6] Weighing the tension between performance-oriented remedies and other remedies that seek to protect this interest—in particular compensatory damages—in light of different approaches taken by civil law and common law systems in Europe, this book makes a plea for a primary position for performance-oriented remedies in the harmonisation of European sales law.

[3] This will often be the case where a weaker party (for example a consumer) can only obtain a contract if he agrees to the standard terms of business of the other party.

[4] For a more detailed classification of the performance-oriented remedies, see ch 3, p 52.

[5] A term first coined by D Friedmann, 'The Performance Interest in Contract Damages' (1995) 111 *Law Quarterly Review* 628 at 629.

[6] Compare E McKendrick, *Contract Law: Text, Cases and Materials*, 2nd edn (Oxford, Oxford University Press, 2005) 1048–49.

I. SCOPE OF THE PROJECT

The main part of the book will look at existing rules on performance-oriented remedies in several European jurisdictions, seeking to find a common core or to identify common principles that could lie at the basis of future harmonisation or review of domestic rules on remedies in European sale of goods laws. The scope of the project may be further defined, first, by setting out briefly which jurisdictions and other relevant sets of rules are taken into account and, secondly, by making some observations about the substantive scope of the comparison.

1. Jurisdictions and Legal Rules under Consideration

The comparison takes account of solutions found in English, Dutch and German law, and also considers how these systems have been influenced by existing European legislation (such as the Consumer Sales Directive).[7] The national jurisdictions were selected for several reasons. To begin with, since the main legal traditions represented in the EU are the common law and the civil law, a realistic picture of the possibilities for harmonisation will only be obtained by comparing systems that fall within either category. This is especially true in relation to performance-oriented remedies, where the approaches of common law and civil law systems, at least at first glance, appear to be markedly different. As to the choice of systems to compare within these traditions, English law naturally represents itself as the example of a common law system, since it is one of the few in Europe and, without a doubt, the most influential one. With regard to civilian systems, which make up the majority of legal systems in the EU, the choice is somewhat less straightforward. German and Dutch law were chosen for two reasons. First, these systems represent some of the most recent codifications of sales laws in Europe, German law recently having seen an extensive reform of the law of obligations and Dutch law having introduced a new Civil Code in 1992. In the re-codifications of sales law, both systems took account of international uniform rules on sales, such as CISG[8] and the Consumer Sales Directive. Therefore, not only are these sales laws up-to-date with recent developments, they also reflect international standards for sale of goods law that may form a basis for future harmonisation in Europe. Secondly, the Germanic tradition is widely represented in Europe and it therefore makes sense to focus on systems falling within this tradition in order to identify common underlying principles that could also further the goal of

[7] Directive 99/44/EC of the European Parliament and of the Council on certain aspects of the sale of consumer goods and associated guarantees [1999] OJ L171/12 (Consumer Sales Directive).

[8] UN Convention on Contracts for the International Sale of Goods (adopted 11 April 1980, entered into force 1 January 1988) 1489 UNTS 3 (CISG).

harmonisation. On this ground, it would have been interesting also to take account of the Romanist legal tradition, of which French law is the prime example. Regrettably, since the research was carried out in the course of a doctoral degree and therefore had to comply with time regulations as well as the constraints imposed by a maximum word limit, a choice had to be made to leave this system out of the comparison. For a comprehensive comparison of French and English law on remedies in contract law, I refer to Yves-Marie Laithier's dissertation on the subject, published in 2004.[9]

In addition to the comparison between English, Dutch and German law, where appropriate for illustrative purposes, reference will occasionally be made to Scots law. The Sale of Goods Act 1979 applies not only to England and Wales, but also to Scotland. While, because of the civil law influences found in the system, differentiations may be made for Scottish law, it is thought to be instructive in certain instances to compare the application of the Act in this system with its application in England and Wales. Examples can be found in the chapters on specific performance and cure.[10]

The comparison of domestic systems will be complemented by a comparison with several instruments of a European or international nature. Sets of rules that are taken into account in this context are CISG, the Principles of European Contract Law (PECL), the Unidroit Principles of International Commercial Contracts (PICC), and the Consumer Sales Directive. It is recognised that each of these instruments has a somewhat different scope, some restricted to either commercial or consumer contracts, others containing general rules of contract law. Moreover, unlike the other instruments, the PECL and the PICC are 'soft law' and therefore not binding on contracting parties unless expressly stipulated in the contract or otherwise found to be incorporated.[11] The aim of the comparison, however, is to determine if and to what extent each of these instruments may provide a basis for future harmonisation or review of sale of goods law in Europe, with a particular focus on remedies. Regardless of their official standing, it is thought that the content of these instruments could be a model for harmonisation, for example as proof of what would be an acceptable solution for international contractual dealings, or of the type of compromises that may be made between different legal systems within different (common law and civil law) traditions. The divergent scopes of these instruments, moreover, makes them relevant to the general aim of harmonisation projects relating to sale of goods law in Europe, which focus on commercial as well as consumer contracts in the domestic and in the cross-border context.

[9] Y-M Laithier, *Étude comparative des sanctions de l'inexécution du contrat* (Paris, LGDJ, 2004).

[10] See ch 4, pp 105–6; ch 6, pp 180 ff.

[11] See further ch 2, pp 32–4.

2. Limitations to the Substantive Scope of the Project

While the project relates to remedies for defective performance in a wide range of sales contracts, a choice has been made to limit its scope to contractual aspects of sale. Other areas that may have a bearing on remedies, such as personal property law or tort liability for defective products, have been left out of the present comparison for a number of reasons.

The main reason for this limitation is that the scope for performance-oriented remedies on the basis of tort or property claims is very limited. Tort-based claims for liability for defective products are aimed at securing compensation for individuals who have been harmed as a result of the defective functioning of a product. While a claim in damages based on this ground may—where there is a contract between the injured party and the supplier or manufacturer—be made in addition to a contractual claim for repair or replacement of the product, there is no direct link between the claims and they may be brought alongside each other. There may, of course, be instances of potential overlap where an injured buyer is able either to claim damages based on tort liability or damages for consequential loss. The question of damages for consequential loss, however, also has no direct bearing on the current project. After all, just as it may be possible to award damages for consequential loss on top of the losses suffered directly as a consequence of breach, it may be possible to award such damages in addition to an order for specific performance. As long as the damages award does not relate to the same interest that the specific performance order seeks to protect, nothing would normally stand in the way of such a judgment.[12]

Though, with regard to property claims, some overlap may exist with contractual remedies for non-delivery or non-conformity, the issue appears otherwise outside the scope of the current project. In cases where there is a defect in title preventing the passing of property in the goods to the buyer, this may be classified as a non-conformity to which the normal, contractual rules apply that also govern other non-conformities such as defects in description or quality.[13] A discussion of property claims in other cases does not seem warranted in the present context, since performance-oriented remedies such as specific performance, repair or replacement have little relevance outside situations where contractual liability for non-conformity or non-delivery exists. The question of passing of property, for example, may be relevant to determine the moment of passing of risk and so to determine whether the seller or the buyer shall bear the loss of goods being lost or destroyed, damaged or deteriorated.[14] In cases where the risk

[12] E Peel (ed), *Treitel on the Law of Contract*, 12th edn (London, Sweet & Maxwell, 2007) [20-034].

[13] Compare for English law s 12(1) of the Sale of Goods Act 1979; AG Guest (ed), *Benjamin's Sale of Goods*, 7th edn (London, Sweet & Maxwell, 2006) [4-006]. For Dutch law, see art 7:15 BW; J Hijma, *Asser V(I) Bijzondere Overeenkomsten. Koop en Ruil*, 6th edn (Deventer, WEJ Tjeenk Willink, 2001) [270]. In German law, § 433 I and § 437 BGB; D Reinicke and K Tiedtke, *Kaufrecht* (Munich, Luchterhand, 2004) [391].

[14] Compare *Benjamin's Sale of Goods* (n 13 above) [6-001].

lies on the seller and he fails to deliver goods, the buyer may be able to obtain replacement goods from the seller or, if the seller cannot effect this, a remedy in damages. In cases where goods are delivered and at the buyer's risk, however, a buyer may not be entitled to refuse to accept them if they are otherwise in conformity with the contract. In these circumstances, the buyer will not be entitled to specific performance or a related remedy such as repair or replacement.

The question of passing of risk may, however, be relevant to the current project in one respect: a number of legal systems ties the time of assessment of the conformity requirement to the moment of passing of risk. For example, a rule to this effect applies in German and in Dutch law,[15] and it may also be found in article 36(1) of CISG. However, though the time of passing of risk therefore may be relevant for determining at what point in time a conformity obligation—or rather the breach of it—gives rise to remedies for the buyer, there is no objective reason for tying the assessment of the conformity requirement to the question of risk. In the systems just mentioned, the time for passing of risk happens to coincide with that of delivery, which may also be a good time to assess conformity. In other systems, however, the time of passing of risk may be a different one. For example, in English law risk passes with the property,[16] which may be at the time of conclusion of the contract or of appropriation of unascertained goods to the contract.[17] But English law does not specify at which time the conformity requirement becomes effective. The fact that the two issues are not linked in this system suggests that they may be assessed independently from one another. It may well be that other factors, such as the agreed time for performance of the contract or the time of delivery (which in practice may well be the same thing), provide a better indicator than the time of passing of risk.[18] In light of this, issues of property and passing of risk have been left outside the scope of this book.

This is not to say that the issues of tort liability, property and the passing of risk should be left aside in the process of harmonisation of European contract and sales law. While there may not be enough overlap to necessitate discussion of them in the context of the current project, these issues are relevant in the wider harmonisation project and should be considered in this context. To pick certain topics for harmonisation whilst leaving other issues unregulated creates the risk of fragmentation, making parts of contract law subject to uniform rules whilst referring to (divergent) national rules in relation to issues outside the harmonising legislation.[19] The fact that tort and property issues in sales law have proved difficult to harmonise—as exemplified by CISG which for this reason

[15] Reinicke and Tiedtke, *Kaufrecht* (n 14 above) [390]; Hijma, *Asser V(I) Bijzondere Overeenkomsten* (n 13 above) [332].

[16] *Benjamin's Sale of Goods* (n 13 above) [6-002].

[17] *ibid*, [5-017], [5-067].

[18] See further ch 6, p 159.

[19] Compare M Loos, *Spontane harmonisatie in het contracten- en consumentenrecht* (Den Haag, Boom, 2006) 6; W van Gerven, 'A Common Law for Europe: The Future Meeting the Past?' (2001) 4 *European Review of Private Law* 485 at 490–91.

explicitly excludes them from its scope[20]—may, however, mean that harmonisation will take place at a slower pace than it may for the contractual rules on sale.[21]

II. BACKGROUND AND THEORETICAL FRAMEWORK

Having set out the scope of the project, another preliminary matter requires attention. In order to make a realistic assessment of the proximity of the different laws under consideration and the possibilities for harmonisation or review, it is necessary to set out the background against which the book should be read. On what grounds is harmonisation of sales law in Europe desirable? Is it feasible? And if so, how do we find common principles in systems that, at least in relation to performance-oriented remedies, appear to diverge radically in the ways that they tackle similar problems? Chapters two and three will deal with these issues in more detail. As an introductory point, however, it is thought helpful to set out the approaches to contract theory found in each of the jurisdictions under consideration, so as to determine a common angle from which the systems may usefully be studied. It will be seen that despite differences inherent to the different legal traditions, a promissory theory of contract may be used in each of the systems as a justification for the availability of performance-oriented remedies and as a starting point for determining the scope of the remedies.

1. The Civilian Tradition: German and Dutch Law

German and Dutch law, in this regard, may well be discussed together, since they are closely linked systems. Not only do they share similar foundations—both being members of the civil law tradition that developed in Western Europe since the Middle Ages, with roots going back to the classical law of the Roman Empire—but even today the content and structure of their civil codes bear striking similarities.[22] The drafters of the most recent re-codification of the Dutch civil code, the *Burgerlijk Wetboek* (BW), left behind the more loosely structured model of the previous code, which was Napoleonic in origin and closely linked to the French *code civile*. Instead, a layered structure was adopted, based on the

[20] CISG arts 4 and 5. Compare P Schlechtriem and I Schwenzer (eds), *Commentary on the UN Convention on the International Sale of Goods*, 2nd English edn (Oxford, Oxford University Press, 2005) 70.

[21] See ch 2, p 32.

[22] See generally K Zweigert and H Kötz, *Introduction to Comparative Law*, 3rd revised edn (Oxford, Oxford University Press, 1998) 75 ff, 132 ff. For the development of the rules on liability for non-conformity in sale of goods law from Roman times to modern, German law, see R Zimmermann, *The New German Law of Obligations* (Oxford, Oxford University Press, 2005) 82 ff.

German pandect tradition of legal scholarship. It imposed a more strongly defined framework of legal principles and concepts, with general rules laid down in earlier parts of the code permeating it throughout and providing the background against which to read more specific rules in other parts of the code. The content, also, was more firmly—and possibly more rigidly—determined, as new rules were introduced in the code that filled gaps in the earlier code and that reflected solutions developed in the case law of the courts.

The dogmatic, principle-based nature of the codes appears to be in line with the contents of the rules that they contain. Both German and Dutch law, starting from the principle of sanctity of contract or *pacta sunt servanda*, regard specific performance type remedies as central to the protection of contractual interests. This is reflected in the fact that the remedies aimed at performance are of general availability and, moreover, that they are given a primary position in relation to other remedies, such as damages or termination.[23] In this respect, the systems—at least at first sight—stand apart from English law, where a more reluctant attitude is adopted towards the availability of specific performance.[24] Painting with a broad brush, the civil law and common law traditions, on this particular point, may be contrasted on the basis of their tendency either to adhere to legal principle or to give preference to considerations of a more pragmatic nature. For German and Dutch law, the rules on remedies appear to be inspired by principle more than by pragmatism, in line with the dogmatic attitude found in the codes as well as in legal scholarship in these systems. The primary nature of performance-oriented remedies may be justified on the basis of one principle in particular—the binding nature of a promise.

As shown by Unberath in a comprehensive study of the philosophical foundations of remedies for breach of contract, German contract theory relies on two important premises: first, that contractual promises are binding; and secondly, that a promisee may protect his contractual interest in performance through an enforcement mechanism that gives him the actual performance that he contracted for (*Leistungszwang*).[25] Similar principles underlie the rules on remedies for breach of contract in the Dutch civil code.[26] The leading principle in both systems is *pacta sunt servanda*, that is, the principle that obligations are binding on the parties who have created them. Obligations, thus, are regarded as rights acquired by the promisee, so that he has an entitlement to or an interest in the performance of the promise.[27]

In German and in Dutch law, the logical conclusion drawn from this is that, in order to protect the interest that the promisee has in the performance of the promise, the law should enable him to enforce this performance. In other words,

[23] With regard to the hierarchy of remedies, see ch 5, p 123; ch 7, pp 200 ff.
[24] See below, p 11.
[25] H Unberath, *Die Vertragsverletzung* (Tübingen, Mohr Siebeck, 2007) 217 ff.
[26] Compare AS Hartkamp, *Asser IV(I) Verbintenissenrecht. De verbintenis in het algemeen*, 12th edn (Deventer, Kluwer, 2004) [14]; Hijma, *Asser V(I) Bijzondere Overeenkomsten* (n 13 above) [373].
[27] Some authors even put these rights on par with rights of ownership. See further ch 3, p 48.

a natural link is made between the promisee's subjective right to performance, his entitlement to enforce the right (*ius agendi*), and the procedural instrument generally used to achieve this.[28] This is in line with Kant's view of the principle of corrective justice, which promulgates that any disregard of a party's subjective entitlement to performance creates an imbalance between the parties, which the law must correct.[29] In this view, the means of enforcement does not change the content of the original, subjective right of the promisee but merely seeks to ensure its performance. It is the responsibility of the state to provide the best possible means to secure this right and, while there may be different means of doing so, the principle of corrective justice prescribes that the protection offered must in any case not give less to the promisee than the interest embodied by his subjective right to performance.[30] The actual performance of the promise, giving the promisee that which he contracted for, by definition offers the best protection of this interest.[31]

From this perspective, performance-oriented remedies are regarded as primary remedies for breach, ranking in hierarchy above substitutory remedies such as damages, which may compensate the promisee to a certain extent but which will not give him the exact performance that he contracted for. Nevertheless, both German and Dutch law recognise that this rule cannot be absolute—in order to do justice to the interests both of the promisee and of the promisor, it is necessary to put in place certain limitations on the availability of performance-oriented remedies. Therefore, the codes provide, for example, that specific performance will not be ordered where performance has become impossible, and that repair or replacement of defective goods may not be ordered where it is disproportionate on the seller.[32] Limitations may thus be placed on the principle that performance-oriented remedies are of general availability to the promisee. Justifications for these limitations may be found in economic theory, for example in considerations related to the proportionality and efficiency of the remedies. These justifications will be further explored in chapter three.

In sum, the main focus in these systems remains on the performance interest of the promisee. Apart from the case of impossibility,[33] the limitations recognised in relation to performance-oriented remedies in general only operate where there are alternative ways to compensate the promisee. For example, replacement of defective goods may be regarded as disproportionate if the defect is minor and if it can be remedied easily through repair; or, in a different situation, if substitute goods cannot be obtained by the seller but the buyer is able to obtain them elsewhere, in which case damages may be a more appropriate remedy. In cases in

[28] Compare Unberath, *Die Vertragsverletzung* (n 25 above) 183, 219; Hartkamp, *Asser IV(I) Verbintenissenrecht* (n 26 above) [32]. See also ch 3, p 51.

[29] Compare Unberath, *Die Vertragsverletzung* (n 25 above) 85.

[30] See Unberath, *Die Vertragsverletzung* (n 25 above) 219.

[31] See further ch 3, pp 59 ff.

[32] §§ 275 I and II BGB; § 439 III BGB. Arts 6:74(2) and 7:21(4) BW.

[33] See further ch 4, pp 97–8.

which performance is possible, however, the starting point remains that the buyer is entitled to a performance-oriented remedy; disproportionality is the exception rather than the rule. Thus, it can be seen that in German and in Dutch law the emphasis is on the promise, which is embodied in the subjective right acquired by the promisee. The starting point for analysis of the rules on remedies in sale of goods law in these systems, therefore, may well be found in a promissory theory of contract.

A final point should be added to this—besides the justifications for the scope of remedies found in promissory theory, insights into the scope of the modern-day rules of sales law may be gained in other ways. For example, it is possible to rely on historical research of legal systems, which may show how rules developed in reaction to developments in society and how different rules may thus have come into being depending on the challenges faced by a particular jurisdiction at a particular time. Thus, tracing back the origins of liability rules for non-conformity in sale of goods case, it can be seen that Roman law rules relating to sales of specific goods have gradually been adapted as other types of sale, such as sale by description (ie sale of generic goods), became more commonly used in international trade.[34] A historical excursion may thus offer an explanation for the shape that these rules have today, and it may shed light on the origins of particular problems faced by sale of goods laws. Another way of analysing rules of contract law is by looking at them from the perspective of general legal principles found in a legal system. For example, it has been suggested that the content and scope of liability rules in Dutch contract law may be explained on the basis of principles normally found in other areas of law, such as the subsidiarity and proportionality principles found in administrative or in criminal law.[35] To what extent this proposition holds true may be debated. Controversy may occur over the extent to which principles may be extrapolated from one area of law to the other, especially in common law systems where an overlap like this would not normally be recognised.[36] In legal systems where a certain coherence of principles underlying the system as a whole may be recognised, however, this type of analysis may give some beneficial insights into the content of rules of law and the way in which they operate.

While these approaches may on occasion be referred to at different points in the book, the theoretical framework for the comparison will mainly focus on a rights-based, promissory theory of contract. Not only does this theory offer *explanations* for the scope and content of the rules found in German and Dutch sale of goods laws, it also offers insights in the *justifications* for adhering to these particular rules. In this way, the theory may help to uncover common principles

[34] Compare Zimmermann, *The New German Law of Obligations* (n 22 above) 85–7.

[35] A model of how this may be applied in Dutch law has been proposed by MM Stolp, *Ontbinding, schadevergoeding en nakoming; De remedies voor wanprestatie in het licht van de beginselen van subsidiariteit en proportionaliteit* (Kluwer, Deventer 2007).

[36] Principles may however be extended to areas which are linked; for example, s 62(2) of the SGA provides explicitly that general contract principles, except in so far as they are inconsistent with the Act, also apply to sale of goods. Compare *Benjamin's Sale of Goods* (n 13) [1-007].

underlying the rules, which may shed light on the possibilities for harmonisation of sales law in Europe.

2. The Common Law Tradition: English Law

An analysis based on a promissory theory of contract, it is suggested, also enables a comparison with the other main legal tradition in Europe, the common law. A theory that may usefully be adopted in this context is the rights-based, promissory theory of contract developed by Fried.[37] Like the theories underlying the remedial schemes in German and Dutch contract law, this theory starts from the premise that promises create obligations that are binding upon the parties and that give the promisee an interest in the performance of the promise. This so-called 'performance interest', in Fried's theory, deserves full protection through legally enforceable remedies.

Of course, one may wonder how this theory fits with the rules of English contract law as they stand today—the limited availability of specific performance may suggest that the system's recognition and protection of the performance interest is less than whole-hearted. It may be questioned whether the damages remedy, which, in contrast to specific performance, is of general availability, is equally well suited to compensate the promisee to the full extent of his contractual interest, in particular where the value of the interest is hard to assess.[38] However, while theories may be cited in support of a more reluctant approach to the protection of the performance interest, it is thought that none of these offers sufficiently convincing arguments to be favoured over Fried's theory of the bindingness of promises.

On a sliding scale, a contract theory may recognise one of four different levels of protection of the contractual interests of the promisee[39]: protection of the performance interest, of the 'expectation interest', or of the 'reliance interest'; or finally, it may be thought that no particular protection for any of these interests is offered by the contract itself and that it is merely a tool that the promisee may use in order to obtain a remedy. The current debate in English law focuses mainly on the first two levels; the latter two, whilst having had eminent support in the literature, do not appear to reflect the stance nowadays taken towards the protection of contractual interests. The reliance interest finds some protection in the current law, but has not become the main benchmark against which to assess contract damages, as advocated by Fuller and Perdue in a well-known 1936 article.[40] Their view was that damages should be assessed on the basis of

[37] C Fried, *Contract as Promise* (Cambridge MA, Harvard University Press, 1981).

[38] See ch 4, pp 88–9.

[39] A possible fifth category, the restitution interest, will not be explored here. Its relevance to the theory related to the binding nature of promises appears limited, since restitution may be an issue in non-contractual as well as in contractual contexts.

[40] LL Fuller and WR Perdue, Jr, 'The Reliance Interest in Contract Damages' (1936) 46 *Yale Law Journal* 52 and 373.

losses suffered in reliance on the contract, rather than on the basis of the interest in the performance of the contract. After all, the argument ran, why should a claimant be compensated for something he never had?[41] The reality of contract law is, however, that courts are prepared to acknowledge that the promisee obtains something from the promise—an expectation of performance, or an interest in the performance of it. Therefore, as stated by Fried, '[t]here is reliance because the promise is binding, and not the other way around'.[42]

An acceptance of the binding nature of promises also defies the fourth theory, of which Atiyah's contract theory is the prime example. According to this theory, bindingness of contract is nothing more than a procedural technique related to proof, serving to establish liability which exists independent of the contract itself. In other words, contracts are mere admissions of a liability that exists on the basis of other obligations, outside of the contract.[43] From a dogmatic perspective, it is hard to see how such a theory could be upheld. Subjective rights would become meaningless, as a contract would not by itself be able to create rights. The better view, as suggested by Smith,[44] would seem to be that promises can create rights in a way similar to property rights. The obligation so created embodies the promisee's ownership of the duty created by the promisor to perform the promise. Private individuals, thus, are able to create legally enforceable rights where none existed before.[45] Rather than as suggested by Atiyah, contractual obligations therefore give rise to subjective rights from the moment of their creation, and the promisee has an entitlement to the promise from that moment and may require the promisor to fulfill it.

The main tension that has emerged in English contract law in the last decades, then, relates to the extent to which the interests created by promises deserve protection through the courts. How far does the bindingness of contractual promises reach? Should remedies for non-performance or defective performance reflect the promisee's expectation interest, or should they reflect his performance interest? The former reflects the value of the promised performance, whereas the latter is concerned with the promisee's interest in the actual performance of the promise, which may encompass more than just economic value.[46] While there is a certain overlap in remedies reflecting both interests, at least in measure, the difference between them becomes apparent in cases where the value of the promised performance covers more than purely economic inter-

[41] LL Fuller and WR Perdue, Jr, 'The Reliance Interest in Contract Damages' (1936) 46 *Yale Law Journal* 53.

[42] Fried (n 37 above) 19.

[43] PS Atiyah, *The Rise and Fall of Freedom of Contract* (Oxford, Clarendon Press, 1979) 184 ff.

[44] L Smith, 'Understanding Specific Performance' in N Cohen and E McKendrick (eds), *Comparative Remedies for Breach of Contract* (Oxford, Hart Publishing, 2005). See also SA Smith, *Contract Theory* (Oxford, Oxford University Press, 2004) 73–4. A similar view may be taken in German law; see Unberath (n 25 above) 217.

[45] Compare SA Smith (n 44 above) 73.

[46] McKendrick (n 6 above) above; compare also E McKendrick, 'The Common Law at Work: the Saga of *Alfred McAlpine Construction Ltd v Panatown Ltd*' (2003) 3 *Oxford University Commonwealth Law Journal* 145 at 167 ff.

ests, or where it is hard to quantify. A famous example of such a case is *Ruxley Electronics and Construction Ltd v Forsyth*,[47] where the cost of cure of a defective performance—a swimming pool built six feet short of the contractually required depth—was very high, especially considering the economic loss suffered by the claimant, which the court deemed to be nil. The fact that, in these circumstances, the court was not prepared to award damages for the cost of cure indicates that English law does not have a whole-hearted commitment to the performance interest.[48] The claimant was compensated for loss suffered as a result of the breach of contract (in this case, the award was given only for loss of amenity), but did not receive damages that would enable him to obtain the performance that he contracted for. The decision is not uncontested, however,[49] and it may be that damages for breach will gradually be expanded to give greater protection to the performance interest.

The tension between the expectation interest and the performance interest in English law also becomes apparent in relation to the subject-matter of this book: performance-oriented remedies. In effect, courts will only award specific performance or related remedies (such as repair or replacement) if their aim is to protect the performance interest. These remedies, after all, go further than compensatory damages, not only by having an inherent ability to protect an interest that encompasses more than the economic loss suffered by the claimant, but also by *enforcing* the performance of the contract. They ensure that the promisee gets the actual performance that he contracted for, and thus exemplify the ultimate protection of the performance interest. A debate about widening the scope of these remedies, therefore, necessarily touches upon questions as to which interests deserve protection in English law. The widening of the availability of specific performance in cases of commercial uniqueness,[50] or the introduction of new remedies aimed at performance in consumer sales law,[51] therefore, need to be regarded in the light of the overall discussion about protection of the performance interest.

Fried's theory of the bindingness of promises appears an appropriate basis for further exploration of the question to what extent the performance interest deserves protection through performance-oriented remedies in English law, though the theory itself may not be able to give an answer to that question. It does not clarify in what way the performance interest should be protected, eg whether this should be through performance-oriented remedies or whether an award of damages might suffice. Nevertheless, as a basis for exploring the nature of contractual interests and the extent to which the law should offer protection of those, it appears not only to fit with, and to offer explanations

[47] *Ruxley Electronics and Construction Ltd v Forsyth* [1996] AC 344 (HL).
[48] McKendrick (n 6 above) 1017.
[49] Compare B Coote, 'Contract Damages, *Ruxley* and the Performance Interest' (1997) 56 *Cambridge Law Journal* 537 at 566–7; McKendrick (n 6 above) 1028.
[50] See ch 4, pp 84 ff.
[51] See ch 5.

for, the current state of English contract law,[52] but also to lay bare principles underlying the rules of contract that may provide solutions for problems that the current law faces. One such problem is to determine what scope performance-oriented remedies should have in English law.

Principles of English law thus unearthed may then, through comparison with the German and Dutch approaches to performance-oriented remedies, yield some answers as to the way in which harmonisation of European sales laws in this area may develop. An additional argument for referring to Fried's theory in this context, it is submitted, is its relative independence from the more temporal, social elements of contract law. While Atiyah's theory, for example, appears to be greatly influenced by sociological developments with regard to the role of contract in modern, Western societies, Fried takes a more neutral position which—though linked to societal values[53]—starts from a broader, moral premise about the nature of promises. As such, it is not defined by sociological parameters to the same extent that Atiyah's theory is—the bindingness of promises is regarded as a fundamental principle that lies at the roots of contract law at any time in any given (Western) society. It is not, however, dependent upon the view taken in that society on other values that the law seeks to reflect, for example in relation to where it strikes the balance between autonomy and solidarity between contracting partners.[54] Though such values have a role to play in the shaping of rules of contract law, and also in specific contracts such as sale of goods transactions, Fried's view appears to reflect a standpoint more commonly adopted in case law and legal scholarship that regards the bindingness of promises as following from the moral principle *pacta sunt servanda*. As a timeless and widely-adhered-to principle, it reflects a common basis of contract law in many European systems, regardless of the shifting sociological make-up of these countries. Therefore, at least as a basis for legislative harmonisation, the principle provides a good starting point. This is so despite the fact that sociological factors may of course impact on the implementation and practical usage of new rules. While this is likely to influence the degree to which harmonisation may practically be deemed successful, problems of uniform implementation and enforcement of legal rules can be observed in any legal system, even with regard to internal rules.[55]

[52] Compare SA Smith, *Contract Theory* (n 44 above) 103.

[53] Fried, *Contract as Promise* (n 37 above) 17; compare also SA Smith, *Contract Theory* (n 44 above) 71.

[54] Compare PS Atiyah, *An Introduction to the Law of Contract*, 5th edn (Oxford, Oxford University Press, 1995) 15.

[55] For further discussion of factors that may influence the successfulness of harmonisation, see ch 2, pp 21 ff.

III. OUTLINE OF THE PROJECT

The underlying issues of contract theory will be further explored in chapter three. Further background relating to the process of harmonisation of contract law in Europe, and the role of sales law, will be given in chapter two.

Having determined the extent to which harmonisation is feasible and desirable, and having identified the theoretical underpinnings of contract law that may be of help in determining the appropriate scope of performance-oriented remedies, these two chapters lay the basis for the detailed discussion of the different performance-oriented remedies in chapters four to seven. The remainder of the thesis is concerned with the functioning of these remedies in European jurisdictions. The main question running through these chapters is to what extent existing rules reflect the principles set out in chapter three—is it possible to identify common underlying principles that may enable future harmonisation of European sales laws, or at least the rules related to performance-oriented remedies? On the basis of the findings made in these chapters, the final chapter seeks to formulate some guidelines for future projects on harmonisation of sale of goods laws.

2

Harmonisation of European Sale of Goods Laws

I. INTRODUCTION

WHEN PROFESSOR ERNST RABEL first proposed the creation of a uniform sales regime in 1928,[1] he could hardly have foreseen the impact that this proposition would have on the development of the law relating to contracts for the international sale of goods. Since then, considerable efforts have been made to unify sales law, culminating in the adoption of the UN Convention on Contracts for the International Sale of Goods (CISG) in 1980.[2] The Convention contains rules on the formation of contracts, as well as on the main obligations of the seller and buyer, and also lays down a remedial scheme for both parties. It has proved a success in the world of international trade, gaining ratifications from—so far—70 countries worldwide.

European sale of goods law appears to be even more ambitious. As part of the European Union's project to further harmonise the laws of the Member States, the aim is to (gradually) develop a set of uniform rules that applies regardless of where goods are purchased within the EU. The envisaged scheme for sale of goods would apply to all types of sales, whether of a commercial nature or involving consumers.[3] Moreover, the regime would apply not just to cross-border sales but also to domestic transactions.[4] The substantive scope of application of a European sales law, therefore, is intended to be much wider than that of CISG.

The discussion of remedies in sale of goods law takes place against the background of such developments towards harmonisation of European sales and, at a wider level, contract law. In order to put the discussion in context, this chapter provides an overview of the harmonisation process of European contract law to date and the place of sales law within it. First, a general overview will be given

[1] P Schlechtriem and I Schwenzer (eds), *Commentary on the United Nations Convention on the International Sale of Goods*, 2nd English edn (Oxford, OUP, 2005) 1.

[2] UN Convention on Contracts for the International Sale of Goods (adopted 11 April 1980, entered into force 1 January 1988) 1489 UNTS 3 (CISG).

[3] See further below, pp 34 ff.

[4] Below, pp 36 ff.

of the justifications for harmonisation of contract law in Europe. With the process well underway, sceptics still find enough grounds to doubt the desirability of efforts to approximate the laws of the Member States in this area. The discussion in this chapter will take up some of the key points of the debate relating to economic benefits of harmonisation and consumer confidence, and will argue that these provide good justifications for harmonising contract law in Europe. The second part of the overview then focuses on the role of sales law in the harmonisation process. It will be argued that sale of goods law, because of the relatively dense level of harmonisation already achieved, lends itself to taking a primary position in the further process of approximating the contract laws of the Member States. Thus, instruments such as CISG, as well as European Directives relating to sale of goods law, could lay at the basis of further, perhaps even more general rules aimed at harmonisation.

A further question addressed in this chapter relates to the geographical scope of instruments aimed at harmonisation. From a viewpoint of uniformity, the ideal situation would be for both cross-border and domestic sales to fall within the ambit of a uniform set of rules. Initially, however, harmonisation efforts mostly focused on international sales, leaving domestic transactions to be governed by national laws. It will be argued that, in the light of the ongoing process of European integration, the time has come to revise this standpoint and gradually to start including domestic transactions in the harmonisation programme. A shift in this direction may already be gleaned from the responses to the European Commission's Green Paper on the review of the consumer acquis, with the majority of the respondents favouring a horizontal instrument applying to domestic as well as to cross-border transactions.[5]

II. CONTRACTS, SALES CONTRACTS AND HARMONISATION

The Green Paper on the review of the consumer acquis highlights the importance of the contract of sale as the 'most common and broad consumer contract'.[6] It is not surprising, therefore, that a number of the eight Directives under review in this project have a bearing on sale of goods law, directly or indirectly. For example, the Doorstep Selling Directive, the Unfair Terms Directive, the Distance Selling Directive and the Consumer Sales Directive all lay down rules that are of relevance to consumer sales contracts.[7] Given the apparent promi-

[5] Green Paper on the Review of the Consumer Acquis COM(2006) 744 final (8 February 2007) 3.

[6] *Ibid*, 8.

[7] Council Directive (EEC) 85/577 to protect the consumer in respect of contracts negotiated away from business premises [1985] OJ L372/31; Council Directive (EEC) 93/13 on unfair terms in consumer contracts [1993] OJ L95/29; Directive (EC) 97/7 of the European Parliament and of the Council on the protection of consumers in respect of distance contracts [1997] OJ L144/19; Directive (EC) 99/44 of the European Parliament and of the Council on certain aspects of the sale of consumer goods and associated guarantees [1999] OJ L171/12. Other Directives included in the review are Council Directive (EEC) 90/314 on package travel, package holidays and package tours [1990]

nence of sales contracts in the context of consumer contracts, it is thought appropriate, therefore, to include rules regulating sales contracts in the general regimes for revision of the consumer acquis that are currently being developed.[8] In this, the Green Paper follows suit with a string of documents on harmonisation that have been released by the European Commission in recent years, emphasising that sale of goods law forms a key part of the review of current legislation and of other projects aimed at harmonisation, further to be discussed below. In this respect, a number of reasons may be put forward to justify the leading role of sales law, as opposed to other areas of contract law. Mainly, it seems that the presence of a significant number of harmonising Directives, in combination with the examples set by uniform sets of rules such as CISG and the PECL, facilitates the development of instruments for the approximation of sales of goods laws in Europe.[9]

The current developments in the harmonisation process, however, were preceded by an intense debate about the desirability and feasibility of unifying European contract law. In order to put in context the comparative research on remedies in sale of goods law, further explored in the subsequent chapters, it is important to go back to some of the earlier stages of the discussion and to revisit the main questions of why and how: *why* harmonisation? And, if it is desirable to approximate domestic laws, *how* to go about achieving this?

1. Sales Law and European Contract Law

The questions of desirability and feasibility of harmonisation of sales law in Europe are inextricably linked with the wider discourse on European contract law, a relatively young field of research with its origins reaching back only about 30 years. The 'founding father' of the field, Danish professor Ole Lando, recognised the need for and the possibility of the convergence of the contract laws of the Member States as early as 1976.[10] However, not many shared his vision at that time, and it was not until several years later, in 1982, that Lando succeeded in setting up the Commission on European Contract Law (CECL), a working group including many renowned legal scholars from across Europe. In 2000, after 17 years and 22 meetings,[11] the Commission published the first two parts

OJ L158/59; Directive (EC) 94/47 of the European Parliament and of the Council on the protection of purchasers in respect of certain aspects of contracts relating to the purchase of a right to use immovable properties on a timeshare basis [1994] OJ L280/83; Directive (EC) 98/6 of the European Parliament and of the Council on consumer protection in the indication of the prices of products offered to consumers [1998] OJ L80/27; Directive (EC) 98/27 of the European Parliament and of the Council on injunctions for the protection of consumers' interests [1998] OJ L166/51.

[8] Green Paper on the Review of the Consumer Acquis (n 5 above). See further below, p 29.

[9] See below, pp 26 ff.

[10] O Lando, 'My life as a lawyer' [2002] *Zeitschrift für Europäisches Privatrecht* 508 at 519.

[11] *Ibid*, 520.

of the PECL, followed by the publication of part three in 2003.[12] The Principles are representative of the common legal principles shared by the Member States, and they can be seen as the first major step towards codification of European contract law.

Legal scholars were amongst the first actively to consider the convergence of contract law in Europe, and have been involved in the discussion ever since. Apart from the CECL, several study groups have emerged, seeking to investigate the possibility of drafting a European Civil Code (ECC) or at least the possibilities for harmonising the laws of the Member States.[13] The debate keeps pace with related developments within the framework of the European Communities (EC). Amongst the institutions of the EC, it was the Parliament that took the lead and in two resolutions, one in the late '80s, the other in the mid-'90s, called for work to be started on the possibility of drawing up a common European Code of Private Law.[14] This appeal was repeated in the Parliament's resolution of 16 March 2000.[15] As a reaction to this resolution the European Commission has published three consultation papers—first the Communication on European Contract Law,[16] then an Action Plan[17] containing the Commission's conclusions based on the responses to the Communication, and following this a third document which gives feedback on the Action Plan and seeks to map the way forward for European contract law.[18] As a result of these consultations, more recent developments have seen a joining of forces of the European institutions and the existing research groups. Since May 2005, several research groups—universities, institutions, and other organisations and researchers—have been joined in a Network of Excellence, called CoPECL. The abbreviation stands for Common Principles of European Contract Law and refers to the set

[12] O Lando and H Beale (eds), *Principles of European Contract Law. Part I and II* (The Hague, Kluwer Law International, 2000); O Lando and others (eds), *Principles of European Contract Law. Part III* (The Hague, Kluwer Law International, 2003).

[13] The main ones are the Trento Common Core of European Private Law Project, the Study Group on a European Civil Code (the Von Bar Group) and the Acquis Group. For more information, see www.jus.unitn.it/dsg/common-core/home.html; www.sgecc.net; www.acquis-group.org. The Utrecht Team of the Von Bar Group deals with certain long-term contracts, sales and services; see E Hondius, V Heutger and C Jeloschek, *Principles of European Law. Vol 5. Sales Contracts* (Munich, Sellier, 2007). Compare also AS Hartkamp and others (eds), *Towards a European Civil Code*, 3rd revised edn (The Hague, Kluwer Law International, 2004).

[14] European Parliament Resolution on action to bring into line the private law of the Member States [1989] OJ C158/400; European Parliament Resolution on the harmonization of certain sectors of the private law of the Member States [1994] OJ C205/518.

[15] European Parliament Resolution on the Commission's annual legislative programme for 2000 [2000] OJ C377/323.

[16] Communication from the Commission to the Council and the European Parliament on European Contract Law COM(2001) 398 final (11 July 2001) ('Communication on European Contract Law').

[17] Communication from the Commission to the European Parliament and the Council, 'A more coherent European contract law—an action plan' COM(2003) 68 final (12 February 2003) ('Action Plan').

[18] Communication from the Commission to the European Parliament and the Council, 'European Contract Law and the revision of the *acquis*: the way forward' COM(2004) 651 final (11 October 2004) ('The Way Forward').

of principles to be completed under the Common Frame of Reference (CFR) scheme proposed in the Commission's Action Plan and its 2004 'The Way Forward' Communication. A first draft was completed at the end of 2007 and a final draft is expected by the end of 2008.[19]

Thus, both academics and the institutions of the EU have become involved in the debate on European contract law. It has become clear, however, that the initial fervour has diminished, and that in its place loom reservations regarding the necessity and possible form of a codification of contract law. While at the outset comparative lawyers envisaged a unification of European contract law that would form the basis for a European Civil Code, a more cautious approach now seems to be favoured. Still, there are strong arguments in favour of harmonisation, or possibly unification of contract law, that hold ground even in the light of the recognition that such developments may not come about in the near future. Further, although the convergence of general contract law is developing at a slower pace, it is thought that sales law might be in a further stage of development and thus more ready for the introduction of rules aimed at harmonisation.

a) Harmonisation of Contract Law in Europe

Harmonisation of laws cannot be seen separately from the economic, political and social circumstances of the countries involved.[20] It is these factors that determine whether any kind of harmonisation or uniformity of laws is desirable, as well as whether it is feasible. Only if economic interests so require—and if there is a sufficient level of political will to back up the process—will harmonisation be deemed desirable. As to feasibility, neighbouring countries often have similar economic, political and social backgrounds, which means that fewer differences have to be overcome and that the harmonisation process will therefore be easier. It is for this reason that it is often thought that regional harmonisation has more chances of being successful than international harmonisation on a global level.[21]

Within the context of the European Union, the concept of regional harmonisation takes on particular significance. Though economic, political and social differences still exist, the level of unity reached between the Member States is incredibly high. Whereas the European Community started out as a co-operation between a small number of European states aiming to improve

[19] Study Group on a European Civil Code/Research Group on EC Private Law (Acquis Group) (eds), *Principles, Definitions and Model Rules of European Private Law. Draft Common Frame of Reference (DCFR). Interim Outline Edition* (Munich, Sellier, 2008). For further details, see www.copecl.org. Also, below p 27.

[20] This is true not only for harmonisation of public laws but also of harmonisation in the private law sphere. For a discussion of the political dimension of the European private law debate, see (2002) 10 *European Review of Private Law*, issue 1. Also U Mattei, 'Hard Code Now!' (2002) 2 *Global Jurist Frontiers* 1.

[21] For example, E Hondius, *Consumer Guarantees: Towards a European Sale of Goods Act* (Centro di Studi e Ricerche di Diritto Comparato e Straniero, Roma 1996) 7.

economic relations between them, the goals soon became loftier, and the competence of the European institutions nowadays reaches far beyond mere economic issues, including co-operation in the field of international justice and foreign policy. Harmonisation of private law seems a favourable next step to take in order to further the unity between the Member States. However, the desirability and feasibility of such harmonisation are not uncontested.

(i) European Contract Law in a Wider Perspective—Economic and Political Issues It has been said that codification, historically, has only followed when an advanced level of economic and political integration had been reached—and that the European Union in this respect still has a long way to go.[22] Little doubt exists as to the truth of the latter part of this statement. Events in recent years have confirmed that political unity can hardly be said to have been achieved, leaving Europe divided over many issues, such as the war on Iraq and the creation of a European Constitution. On an economic level, also, tensions persist, mainly with regard to the common European currency, where, by ever delaying its accession to the Euro, Britain asserts its ambiguous attitude towards Europe. However, even if political clashes may form an obstacle to European unity right now, making the codification of private law practically unthinkable, ongoing developments in the economic sphere do ask for positive action to be taken by the European institutions in the form of some kind of harmonisation of the private laws of the Member States.

What has to be recognised is that the EU is first and foremost an economic union. Economic integration has been the main objective from the beginning, and to this day, trade has proved to be a major factor in the European context. From the start, the driving forces behind harmonisation of laws have been the objectives to facilitate trade between the Member States and to contribute to the completion of the internal market.[23] Differences in national laws may form obstacles to the achievement of these objectives. The responses to the Commission's consultation, for example, show that legal disparities cause trouble, hindering the functioning of the internal market. Businesses especially, are confronted with problems arising out of the divergence of mandatory rules protecting consumers in domestic laws.[24] Due to this, they are faced with higher transaction costs, for example because they have to obtain legal advice in the country where the consumer has its residence and to which the goods are being dispatched.[25] Harmonisation would take away these differences and would therefore make a valuable contribution to the process of European integration.

Nevertheless, one needs to be aware that market integration is not a goal in itself—the savings achieved as a result of harmonisation would need to be set off

[22] BS Markesinis, 'Why a code is not the best way to advance the cause of European legal unity' (1997) 5 *European Review of Private Law* 519 at 519.

[23] Treaty establishing the European Community (consolidated text) (EC Treaty) arts 94–95.

[24] European Commission, Action Plan (n 17 above) 14.

[25] Compare U Mattei, 'A Transaction Costs Approach to the European Code' (1997) 5 *European Review of Private Law* 537 at 538.

against the benefits of diversity.[26] It has been questioned whether economic arguments in favour of harmonisation of contract law based on the benefits of economies of scale and inherent transaction costs savings, or on the idea of curing inefficient state laws, would in effect result in an optimal regime.[27] A natural process of spontaneous harmonisation occurring as a result of competitive processes between national legislators might respond to economic needs more efficiently than an imposed uniform regime would. Therefore, forced harmonisation would not be desirable at this point in time. However, while it may be true that in certain areas, such as civil procedure,[28] the current regimes are far apart and may therefore benefit from a more gradual, natural development towards convergence, other areas of contract or sales law may benefit from a more pro-active approach. Responses to the Green Paper on the review of the consumer acquis support this notion, with the majority of stakeholders favouring full, targeted harmonisation in relation to those issues that raise substantial barriers to trade for business and/or deter consumers from entering into cross-border transactions.[29] For example, it is suggested that the rules relating to the consumer's right of withdrawal may well benefit from active harmonisation, as it might simplify procedures, reduce costs and increase transparency and consumer confidence.[30]

Over all, the issue thus seems to be not so much whether the EU Member States are too far apart, on an economic or political level, to make the convergence of private law desirable and feasible. Rather, the question is at what speed and to what extent such harmonisation or unification should take place. Apart from political and economic aspects, the divergence of legal systems in the EU is a determinative factor in this respect.

(ii) Legal Debate In the early stages of the discussion on codification of European private law,[31] a firm stand against the development of a European

[26] R Van den Bergh, 'Forced Harmonisation of Contract Law in Europe: Not to be Continued' in S Grundmann and J Stuyck (eds), *An Academic Green Paper on European Contract Law* (The Hague, Kluwer Law International, 2002) 249 at 258.

[27] *Ibid*, 263–5.

[28] Compare M Kuneva, 'Healthy markets need effective redress' (Conference on Collective Redress, 2007), available at http://ec.europa.eu/commission_barroso/kuneva/speeches/speech_10112007_en.pdf.

[29] DG Health and Consumer Protection, 'Preparatory Work for the Impact Assessment on the Review of the Consumer Acquis' (6 November 2007), available at http://ec.europa.eu/consumers/rights/detailed_analysis_en.pdf, pp 7, 10. Report on the Outcome of the Public Consultation on the Green Paper on the Review of the Consumer Acquis (9 October 2007), available at http://ec.europa.eu/consumers/cons_int/safe_shop/acquis/acquis_working_doc.pdf, p 3. Compare also S Vogenauer and S Weatherill, 'The European Community's Competence to Pursue the Harmonisation of Contract Law—an Empirical Contribution to the Debate' in S Vogenauer and S Weatherill (eds), *The Harmonisation of European Contract Law* (Oxford, Hart Publishing, 2006) 105 at 130–32.

[30] *Ibid*, 9.

[31] Within the scope of this thesis, I can only touch upon the most prominent aspects of the debate. For a full discussion see P Legrand, 'Against a European Civil Code' (1997) 60 *Modern Law Review* 44; A Chamboredon, 'The Debate on a European Civil Code: For an "Open Texture"' in M Van Hoecke and F Ost (eds), *The Harmonisation of European Private Law* (Oxford, Hart Publishing,

Civil Code was taken by Professor Pierre Legrand.[32] His—extreme—position has been criticised by many authors, but, although Legrand's arguments seem excessively negative, his attack on the ECC has opened up the debate on European contract law, which appeared rather one-sided as well as overly optimistic at the outset. The shortcomings of some rather naïve or rash approaches have been exposed, and over all, the discussion has led to a more cautious and thoughtful approach.[33] Legrand's main proposition was that the different legal traditions existing in Europe, being the common law and the civil law, are too far apart to be reconciled in a uniform Civil Code. The differences between the two, according to Legrand, are so deeply entrenched that we are not merely talking about different rules or methodology, but even of different *mentalities* (or *mentalités*) towards law.[34] It will, therefore, never be possible to create a truly uniform law such as a European Civil Code.

However, the clash between common law and civil law systems, though unavoidable, does not in practice seem to have such a devastating effect as Legrand suggests. The ultimate example proving that there is a possibility for symbiosis between the two traditions, of course, is given by so-called mixed legal systems. The legal systems of Scotland, South-Africa, Quebec and Louisiana, to name but a few, have in common that they find their origins in a clash between common law and civil law traditions and that they have managed successfully to integrate the two influences in their legal culture. What these systems show is that where legal norms clash, it is possible to rely on competition between legal rules in order to select the best solutions for a particular legal system.[35] Regardless of the different *mentalités* spoken of by Legrand, it may thus be very well possible for solutions originating in different legal traditions to coexist side by side in a mixed system. A precondition to achieve this result, however, must be that in the formation of the mixed system there are strong supporters of the civil law as well as the common law approach. Only if all available rules are defended with equal rigour will competition mechanisms be able to come up with the solutions that are best on grounds other than legal culture and that may, for example, be defended on grounds of economic efficiency.[36] The current debate on European private law, with stakeholder representation in a number of different forums, appears to provide this necessary

2000) 63; W van Gerven, 'Codifying European private law? Yes, if . . .!' (2002) 27 *European Law Review* 156; M Van Hoecke, 'The harmonisation of private law in Europe: some misunderstandings' in M Van Hoecke and F Ost (eds), *The Harmonisation of European Private Law* (Oxford, Hart Publishing, 2000) 1; Mattei, 'Hard Code Now!' (n 20 above) 1.

[32] Legrand, 'Against a European Civil Code' (n 31 above).

[33] Van Hoecke, 'The harmonisation of private law in Europe: some misunderstandings' (n 31 above) 2.

[34] Legrand, 'Against a European Civil Code' (n 31 above) 45.

[35] Compare J Smits, 'A European Private Law as a Mixed Legal System' (1998) 5 *Maastricht Journal of European and Comparative Law* 328 at 336–7.

[36] J Smits, *The Making of European Private Law. Towards a Ius Commune Europaeum as a Mixed Legal System* (Antwerp, Intersentia, 2002) 148.

background.[37] Apart from this active process of harmonisation, moreover, other factors may contribute to the creation of a mixed legal system of European contract law.

First, it can be seen that common law and civil law systems are in practice no longer as far apart as they once were—the systems are converging. Where common law systems once were the ultimate examples of judge-made law, and civilian systems were rooted in codifications of law, contrary trends have long been recognised.[38] Statute law has gained prominence in the common law world, whereas civil law systems have seen a movement towards development of law through case law. The sources of law have moved in opposite directions in the different systems: the common law tradition used to be exclusively based on case law and is now mainly based on case law and partly based on legislation; civilian systems used to be exclusively based on legislation and are nowadays mainly based on legislation and partly on case law.[39] Of course, the traditions spring from different approaches, and these can still be seen in the systems as they exist today, but the divide is no longer so broad as to entirely rule out the coming together of the two systems in codification or harmonisation.

Furthermore, though differences in legal culture cannot be set aside without serious consideration, they do not stand in the way of a convergence between systems, and *have* not done so til now. Legal cultures have—informally—influenced one another already on points of substantive law; for example, common law concepts such as the lease, franchising and the trust have become more and more common in civil law countries.[40] Moreover, it should be kept in mind that, since harmonisation, at least initially, is limited to the core parts of private law, cultural differences are unlikely to be so big as to cause insurmountable difficulties.[41]

It can thus be seen that, despite it being widely accepted that it is too early for codification,[42] this should not automatically lead to the conclusion that harmonisation of the private laws of the Member States is out of the question. The European framework has only been in place for a little over five decades, and in this relatively short period of time huge progress has already been made towards European integration. As part of this bigger scheme, the private laws of the Member States also are likely to grow closer together. Nevertheless, as with many grand-scale reviews of legislation, such developments take time.[43] A

[37] See p 20.

[38] T Koopmans, 'Towards a European Civil Code?' (1997) 5 *European Review of Private Law* 541 at 544–5; Van Hoecke 'The harmonisation of private law in Europe: some misunderstandings' (n 31 above) 15–17.

[39] Chamboredon, 'The Debate on a European Civil Code: For an "Open Texture"' (n 31 above) 70.

[40] Koopmans, 'Towards a European Civil Code?' (n 38 above) 544.

[41] Van Gerven, 'Codifying European private law? Yes, if . . .!' (n 31 above) 162.

[42] This is reflected in the wording used today: 'harmonisation' and 'convergence' have become the commonly used terms, as opposed to 'unification' or 'codification'; Van Hoecke, 'The harmonisation of private law in Europe: some misunderstandings' (n 31 above) 2–3.

[43] Compare the re-codification of Dutch civil law, which took 43 years; Markesinis, 'Why a code is not the best way to advance the cause of European legal unity' (n 22 above) 519.

certain amount of patience is needed, therefore, by those involved in the project of harmonisation of European private law.

b) Should Sales Law Lead the Way?

Still, short-term objectives may focus on a more rapid process of harmonisation in specific areas. The Green Paper on the review of the consumer acquis confirms that the fact that European contract law is not converging as quickly as was first envisaged should not stand in the way of the creation of harmonising rules in areas where these are needed and for which such harmonisation would be a feasible objective in the short term.[44] The harmonisation of European contract law has until now been characterised by a sector-specific approach, and inevitably, some areas have seen faster developments than others. Sales law, for example, is one of the areas in which some degree of convergence of national laws has been achieved, partly through EC Directives in the field of consumer law, partly by external influences such as CISG. In comparison to other areas of contract law, this area seems to have made more progress and it is submitted therefore that it may be a starting point for further harmonisation of contract law. Apart from the Green Paper, indications in support of this proposition can also be found in the Commission's Action Plan and in the focus points of the current harmonisation programme set out in The Way Forward.

In its Action Plan, the starting point adopted by the Commission states that there is no need to abandon the current sector-specific approach. However, the consultation process has identified a number of problems that require some sort of solution, either by regulatory or by non-regulatory measures. The difficulties encountered include problems resulting from the divergence of national mandatory contract law provisions; the divergence of rules on the inclusion and application of standard contract terms; the divergence of national rules on contract law on the one hand and rules on transfer of property and securities concerning movable goods on the other hand; and, in the field of consumer protection, the pertaining diversity in national regimes due to the principle of minimum harmonisation on which most measures are based.[45] Of these, the problems relating to consumer sales law are most likely the easiest to solve, for a certain level of harmonisation has already been reached in this field through EC Directives.[46] With regard to the others, virtually no harmonising legislation is as yet in place, making them much harder to tackle. Seeing that the Commission has chosen to focus, in the first instance, on the improvement of the quality of the EC acquis in the area of contract law, that is, to areas that are already, at least partially,

[44] Report on the Outcome of the Public Consultation on the Green Paper on the Review of the Consumer Acquis (n 29 above) 3–4.
[45] European Commission, Action Plan (n 17 above) 10–14.
[46] See pp 28 ff.

covered by EC legislation,[47] consumer legislation is high on the agenda for improvement.[48]

The measures suggested by the Commission, nevertheless, aim for a broader approach, going beyond a sector-specific approach in order to provide a stronger framework for general contract law in Europe. One element of this is the creation of a Common Frame of Reference, establishing common principles and terminology in the area of European contract law. In addition to this, the Commission's investigations show an increasing trend in favour of the adoption of non-sector-specific measures such as an optional instrument, for which the CFR may serve as a basis.[49] Though these measures, in principle, are aimed at broader areas of contract law, some emphasis is placed on sales law. For instance, the importance of CISG to the harmonisation process is explicitly acknowledged at several points in the Action Plan. The Common Frame of Reference should 'deal essentially with contract law, above all the relevant cross-border types of contract such as contracts of sale and service contracts', and, in relation to this, 'the existing EC *acquis* and relevant binding international instruments, above all the UN Convention on the International Sale of Goods (CISG), should be analysed.'[50]

With regard to an optional instrument, which would provide parties to a contract with a modern body of rules particularly adapted to cross-border contracts in the internal market,[51] the Commission invites comments as to its relation to CISG. The optional instrument could either be comprehensive, meaning that—amongst other things—it would cover cross-border contracts of sale between businesses, and thereby include the area covered by CISG, or it could exclude this area and leave it to the application of the Convention.[52]

These recurring references to CISG, in addition to the existing body of consumer-related legislation, fortify the case for focusing on sales law as one of the key areas in the current harmonisation process. It seems that harmonisation efforts are very much focused on areas in which existing legislation is in

[47] European Commission, Action Plan (n 17 above) 15, 21; European Commission, The Way Forward (n 18 above) 2–4; Report on the Outcome of the Public Consultation on the Green Paper on the Review of the Consumer Acquis (n 29 above) 3.

[48] Notice also the Communication from the Commission to the European Parliament, the Council, the Economic and Social Committee and the Committee of the Regions, 'Consumer Policy Strategy 2002–2006' [2002] OJ C137/2, and the Council Resolution on consumer policy strategy 2002–2006 [2003] OJ C11/1.

[49] European Commission, Action Plan (n 17 above) 16, 24; European Commission, The Way Forward (n 18 above) 8; Report on the Outcome of the Public Consultation on the Green Paper on the Review of the Consumer Acquis (n 29 above) 3.

[50] European Commission, Action Plan (n 17 above) 17; see also European Commission, The Way Forward (n 18 above) 11.

[51] European Commission, Action Plan (n 17 above) 23.

[52] European Commission, Action Plan (n 17 above) 24. A comprehensive approach may be preferable; see JM Smits, 'De toekomst van het Europees privaatrecht: Gemeenschappelijk Referentiekader, optionele code en implementatie van richtlijnen' in AS Hartkamp, CH Sieburgh and LAD Keus, *De invloed van het Europese recht op het Nederlandse privaatrecht*, Serie Onderneming en Recht, deel 42-I (Deventer, Kluwer, 2007) 281 at 292. Also below, pp 31 ff.

place,[53] such as sales law, making for a more readily achievable goal since previous instruments have already smoothed out the main differences between national laws. Thus, one traveller may venture ahead on the road to a uniform European contract law—harmonised rules of sales law may pave the way for further harmonisation of contract law.

2. European Sales Law—The Road Ahead

The road towards further harmonisation of European sales law, however, remains to a large extent uncharted. Several harmonising instruments are already in place—European Directives on consumer sales law have been mentioned, and on a global level there is CISG to regulate international commercial contracts for the sale of goods. Furthermore, the PECL provide a set of rules for the general law of contract in Europe. However, it remains unclear if, and in which way, a uniform regime such as the CFR or an optional instrument will incorporate these. A closer examination of the various instruments relevant to sale of goods law may give some insight into their potential to further the harmonisation process.

a) Harmonisation of Consumer Sales Law

Consumer-related legislation has made a rapid ascent since the entry into force of the Single European Act in 1987, which instigated initiatives in the field of consumer protection within the framework of the EC's internal market strategy.[54] The Treaty of Maastricht has given a specific legal basis to the Community policy in favour of consumer protection by the insertion of Article 153 into the EC Treaty.[55] Parallel to these developments, in the period from 1985 to 1999, no fewer than seven Directives have emerged,[56] of which the Consumer Sales

[53] Improvement of the Community *acquis* through the creation of a CFR is the primary measure suggested by the Commission in its Action Plan (n 17 above) and in The Way Forward (n 18 above).

[54] Single European Act [1987] OJ L169/1. See J Calais-Auloy, 'Un code européen de la consommation?' in F Osman (ed), *Vers un code européen de la consommation. Codification, unification et harmonisation du droit des États-membres de l'Union européenne/Towards a European Consumer Code. Codification, unification and harmonisation of European Union Member States law* (Bruylant, Bruxelles 1998) 399 at 404; L Landy, 'Le consommateur européen: une notion éclatée' in Filali Osman (ed), *Vers un code européen de la consommation. Codification, unification et harmonisation du droit des États-membres de l'Union européenne/Towards a European Consumer Code. Codification, unification and harmonisation of European Union Member States law* (Bruylant, Bruxelles 1998) 57 at 57–8; Stephen Weatherill, *EC Consumer Law and Policy*, 2nd edn (Cheltenham, Edward Elgar, 2005) 8.

[55] Treaty on European Union (Maastricht Treaty) Title XI. Calais-Auloy, 'Un code européen de la consommation?' (n 54 above) 404.

[56] Doorstep Selling Directive (n 7 above); Council Directive (EEC) 87/102 for the approximation of the laws, regulations and administrative provisions of the Member States concerning consumer credit [1987] OJ L42/48 (as modified by Directive 90/88 (EEC) [1990] OJ L61/14 and Directive 98/7 (EEC) [1998] OJ L101/17); Package Travel Directive (n 7 above); Unfair Terms Directive (n 7 above); Timeshare Directive (n 7 above); Distance Selling Directive (n 7 above); Consumer Sales Directive (n 7 above).

Directive is the most relevant to the harmonisation of the substantive law relating to the sale of goods in Europe. Its objectives are to ensure consumer protection and to strengthen consumer confidence in cross-border shopping—and thus improve the functioning of the internal market—by laying down a common set of minimum rules valid no matter where the goods are purchased.[57] These rules include provisions on conformity of goods, on the rights of the consumer in case of non-conformity, and on guarantees.[58]

The emergence of this body of consumer-related legislation has not gone unnoticed. The Consumer Sales Directive has been the topic of many academic writings, giving a new impulse to the debate on European contract law.[59] Moreover, even before the European Commission published its Communications and Action Plan on European Contract Law, consumer protection had been the subject of a similar consultation based on a Green Paper prepared by the Commission.[60] A second Green Paper was published in 2002,[61] which in various respects is complementary to the Commission's Communication.[62]

The review of the consumer acquis currently taking place can be seen as the logical follow-up to these developments.[63] The increased prominence of consumer law both in legislation and in works of legal scholarship has almost naturally made it one of the key areas on which harmonisation efforts should focus. Since most consumer-related provisions in national laws first appeared only shortly before the Brussels legislator took an interest in the matter and imposed harmonising rules by way of Directives,[64] the laws of the Member States have not had a chance to diverge very much. Moreover, through instruments of minimum harmonisation, the Directives have achieved a respectable level of convergence of the laws of the EU Member States with regard to cross-border and domestic sales. As a result, consumer legislation in the Member States is probably close enough to make further harmonisation a feasible option.[65] The Consumer Sales Directive will play an important role in the

[57] Consumer Sales Directive art 1(1) and recitals 1–5; Communication on European Contract Law, Annex I, 19.

[58] Consumer Sales Directive arts 2, 3 and 6.

[59] The Directive has been deemed 'a milestone in the European consumer and private law'; see D Staudenmayer, 'The Directive on the Sale of Consumer Goods and Associated Guarantees—a Milestone in the European Consumer and Private Law' (2000) 8 *European Review of Private Law* 547; also (2001) 9 *European Review of Private Law*, issues 2 & 3.

[60] Green Paper on guarantees for consumer goods and after-sales services COM(1993) 509 final (15 November 1993).

[61] Green Paper on European Union Consumer Protection COM(2001) 531 final (2 October 2001); Commission follow-up Communication to the Green Paper on EU Consumer Protection COM(2002) 289 (11 June 2002).

[62] Van Gerven, 'Codifying European private law? Yes, if . . .!' (n 31 above) 156, n 1.

[63] Green Paper on the Review of the Consumer Acquis (n 5 above).

[64] Compare Landy, 'Le consommateur européen: une notion éclatée' (n 54 above) 60.

[65] Calais-Auloy, 'Un code européen de la consommation?' (n 54 above) 409. On the harmonising effect of Directives, see also A Johnston and H Unberath, 'Law at, to or from the Centre? The European Court of Justice and the Harmonization of Private Law in the European Union' in Fabrizio Cafaggi, *The Institutional Framework of European Private Law* (Oxford, OUP, 2006) 149.

process, being concerned with some of the major aspects of sales law, such as non-conformity of goods and the remedies available to the buyer in case of non-conformity.[66] The interest shown by the academic world in this Directive makes clear that it is indeed a major step forward in the process of harmonisation, and that it could well be the starting point for further harmonisation in the area of sales law. A first step in this direction, as said earlier, may be made in the development of a horizontal instrument, as suggested by the Green Paper on the review of the consumer acquis. Since the contract of sale is the most common consumer contract, a horizontal instrument regulating consumer law may well include a separate part relating to sale of goods, for which the Directive may lay the basis.[67]

b) CISG and European Sales Law

In relation to contracts for the sale of goods that do not qualify as consumer sales, harmonising rules have also been developed. The major example is of course CISG. The Convention, which entered into force in 1988, is probably the first uniform international sales law to have achieved a respectable level of success in practice. Its predecessors, the Uniform Law for the International Sale of Goods (ULIS) and the Uniform Law on the Formation of Contracts for the International Sale of Goods (ULF),[68] never acquired a significant number of ratifications.[69] The Conventions were thus not very successful, though they did have some practical impact in the courts of Germany, the Benelux countries and Italy, and they have sometimes been used for the development of domestic sale of goods laws.[70] Furthermore, with the examples of these Conventions in mind, the drafters of CISG managed to create a uniform sales law that, though unfortunately containing more 'vague' rules and compromises than its predecessors,[71] has proved to be acceptable to the majority of the global community. The Convention has now been ratified by 70 countries worldwide, including the majority of the EU Member States. The exceptions are Portugal, Ireland, Malta, and, most notably, the United Kingdom.[72]

[66] Hondius has suggested that the Directive may be a first building block for a European Sale of Goods Act; Hondius, *Consumer Guarantees: Towards a European Sale of Goods Act* (n 21 above) 20.

[67] Green Paper on the Review of the Consumer Acquis (n 5 above) 8. See above, p 18.

[68] Uniform Law for the International Sale of Goods (adopted 1 July 1964, entered into force 18 August 1972) (ULIS); Uniform Law on the Formation of Contracts for the International Sale of Goods (adopted 1 July 1964, entered into force 18 August 1972) (ULF).

[69] The Conventions were ratified by only nine states: Belgium, the Federal Republic of Germany, Gambia, Israel, Italy, Luxembourg, the Netherlands and the United Kingdom. MC Bianca and MJ Bonell (eds), *Commentary on the International Sales Law. The 1980 Vienna Sales Convention* (Milan, Giuffrè, 1987) 4.

[70] Schlechtriem and Schwenzer, *Commentary on the UN Convention on the International Sale of Goods* (n 1 above) 1–2.

[71] *Ibid*, 4.

[72] For an up-to-date overview of the status of CISG, consult the United Nations Commission on International Trade Law (UNCITRAL) website, www.uncitral.org.

The role of CISG in the harmonisation process in Europe, however, has not become clear yet. The European Commission will analyse the Convention in relation to the creation of a CFR,[73] and CISG will likely be of relevance to the possible adoption of an optional instrument,[74] but no mention is made in the Commission's Action Plan of the possibility of creating a uniform European sales law similar to CISG and the relationship of the Convention thereto. It has been suggested that, instead of creating a new uniform sales law for Europe, the better solution would be to encourage those Member States that have not yet ratified or acceded to the Convention to do so.[75] However, while this approach would save time and effort and, more importantly, would have the benefit of keeping European sales law in line with existing global schemes, it is submitted that this is not the preferable road to take. True, CISG may be as good as it gets for international sales of goods on an international, worldwide level. However, in the European context, the completion of the common market may ask for more extensive measures than those offered by the Convention, which may be criticised on certain important points. European instruments aimed at harmonisation of sales law may be able to overcome, to a certain extent, some of these objections.

The main drawbacks of CISG relate to its limited scope, both with regard to the subject-matter covered and in relation to its geographical application. To begin with the latter, CISG applies to contracts for the international sale of goods and does not, therefore, include domestic sales. It can be argued that a uniform European sales law should apply equally to cross-border and domestic sales, for in that case no difficulties of delimitation can arise, and, furthermore, this solution seems to be commanded by a European spirit.[76] However, seeing that CISG applies to *international* commercial sales of goods, its appropriateness in respect of domestic sales has been questioned.[77] Nevertheless, though drafted with international sales in mind, the text of the Convention may not be wholly unsuitable for application to domestic sales. It has been argued that, in comparison to certain national laws, the main solutions of CISG seem to be superior and better suited not only to transnational, but to domestic sales as well.[78] The merit of this statement in the European context will have to be tested against current solutions in the national laws of the EU Member States. There are indications, however, that support may indeed be found in national systems for the extension of CISG's provisions to domestic sales. First, some national

[73] European Commission, Action Plan (n 17 above) 17.

[74] European Commission, Action Plan (n 17 above) 23–4.

[75] U Drobnig, 'Scope and General Rules of a European Civil Code' (1997) 5 *European Review of Private Law* 489 at 489.

[76] *Ibid*, 492. See pp 36 ff.

[77] For example, F Reynolds, 'A Note of Caution' in P Birks (ed), *The Frontiers of Liability* (Oxford, OUP, 1994) 18 at 27.

[78] P Schlechtriem, 'Some Observations on the United Nations Convention on Contracts for the International Sale of Goods' in P Birks (ed), *The Frontiers of Liability* (Oxford, OUP, 1994) 29 at 45, making a comparison with German law.

sales laws derive from the same source as the UN Convention, or have been influenced by its provisions. The new Dutch Civil Code for example, has been strongly influenced by CISG and its predecessor, ULIS.[79] Likewise, CISG has left its marks on the re-codifications of sales law in the Scandinavian countries, and it has influenced reforms of the German law of obligations.[80] The second indication in support of the application of CISG to domestic sales is based on the PECL and the Unidroit Principles.[81] A comparison with these instruments shows that the main solutions of CISG are consistent with what some leading scholars regarded as the common core solutions for issues of contract law,[82] which of course also find their origin in national laws.

Furthermore, CISG can be criticised for its restricted scope in relation to the subject-matter covered. Consumer sales have been excluded, as well as contracts for the supply of services.[83] Moreover, the Convention is not concerned with the validity of the contract or the effect which the contract may have on issues of property, and it does not apply to the liability of the seller for death or personal injury caused by the goods to any person.[84] A uniform European sales law, likewise, may not cover all possible areas related to sales law—most notably, harmonisation in relation to the property aspects of sales law has in the past proved to be extremely difficult—but there seems room for a more comprehensive approach than the one taken by CISG. Consumer sales especially should fall within its ambit.

Thus, there seems to be a case for seeking to harmonise European sales law, rather than simply promoting ratification or accession to CISG by all EU Member States. Such efforts could go further than CISG by, for example, including domestic and consumer sales in its scope. Though CISG, therefore, can be a building block for a harmonised European sales regime in addition to the Directives in the field of consumer sales, a final point remains—its relation to the PECL.

c) PECL or CISG as a Basis for Harmonisation of European Sales Law?

The PECL, being a first attempt at the harmonisation of European contract law, may prove fertile ground for the further harmonisation sales law in Europe. They contain a set of rules that is thought to be representative of the common principles found in the contract laws of the European Member States, thus providing a general background for a uniform regime containing specific rules of

[79] J Hijma, *Asser V(I) Bijzondere overeenkomsten. Koop en ruil*, 6th edn (Deventer, WEJ Tjeenk Willink, 2001) 22; Schlechtriem, 'Some Observations on the UN Convention on Contracts for the International Sale of Goods' (n 78 above) [36].

[80] *Ibid.*

[81] Unidroit Principles of International Commercial Contracts (PICC).

[82] Schlechtriem, 'Some Observations on the UN Convention on Contracts for the International Sale of Goods' (n 78 above) 45.

[83] CISG arts 2 and 3.

[84] CISG arts 4 and 5.

sales law. The rules found in the PECL may, however, differ from CISG or the consumer protection Directives in some respects, for example in relation to the remedial scheme. This divergence, notably, may cause friction in relation to CISG. The Convention's sphere of application, in contrast to the PECL, encompasses sales transactions throughout the world. The inconvenience of having two substantially different sets of rules concerning international sales in place—one an intra-European regime based on the PECL, the other CISG, applicable to transactions between parties based in EU Member States and trading partners outside Europe—would be considerable. One should not lose sight of Europe's place in the global market—while the EU may benefit from having a strong internal market, the creation of a 'fortress Europe' should be avoided. Therefore, it would be wise to at least keep CISG in mind when drafting a uniform European sales law. This does, however, bring up the question of what the relationship between CISG and the PECL should be in the drafting process. In cases of conflict between the two texts, one has to provide the default rule. The question is, which one should prevail?

It is hard to lay down a strict rule that says that either CISG or the PECL should provide the general default rule for a uniform sales law for Europe. Arguments can be made in favour of either. The PECL may be preferred on the ground that, although the approach has so far been sector-specific—that is, the focus has been on separate areas of law, such as the law related to the sale of goods, to services, or to property issues—there is a wider aim to the harmonisation programme that focuses on the area of contract law as a whole. The interconnection between the different parts of such a scheme should therefore be kept in mind, even when only concentrating on the harmonisation of one particular field of law.[85] The PECL may be helpful in this respect for, according to the Commentary,

> [u]ltimately the Member States of the European Union may wish to harmonise their contract law. The Principles can serve as a model on which harmonisation work may be based.[86]

Since sale of goods law is a subspecies of contract law, it could be argued that the Principles may be used as a foundation for harmonising sales law as well.[87] The Utrecht Team of the Von Bar Group relies on this course and in its draft Principles of European Sales Law (PESL) explicitly refer to the PECL as the wider framework in which to fit the sales principles.[88]

[85] Koopmans, 'Towards a European Civil Code?' (n 38 above) 543; Markesinis, 'Why a code is not the best way to advance the cause of European legal unity' (n 22 above) 520. Compare also the European Commission Action Plan (n 17 above) 6, 14.

[86] Lando and Beale, *Principles of European Contract Law* (n 12 above) xxiv.

[87] Neither the European Commission's Action Plan (n 17 above) nor The Way Forward (n 18 above), however, refers to the PECL. This does not necessarily mean that the PECL will not be taken into account in the creation of a CFR. However, the role of the PECL in respect to the CFR as envisaged by the Commission remains unclear.

[88] PESL art 1:201.

Nevertheless, there is a downside to relying on the PECL, which is that they are non-binding. CISG, on the other hand, is a binding instrument, ie it applies to all contracts that fall within its ambit unless the parties have expressly excluded its application. As such, it has stronger authority than a set of rules like the Principles, which will only apply if the parties have made stipulations to this effect. Since the PECL have not got this binding force, it is doubtful how much value actually is attached to the solutions laid down in the instrument. Some of the drafters may have been willing to agree to certain compromises on the basis that at least the rules would not be binding on parties unless provision to this effect was made.

Thus, while the PECL may have a closer link to European legislation and may for that reason be preferred as a general model for harmonisation, it is thought that their persuasive value may be open to question. On this ground, it is thought that where CISG offers a better solution for a particular issue than the PECL, harmonising legislation may adopt the rule of CISG as the default rule. The same should be permitted for other rules of a binding nature, such as rules of national laws. In other words, efforts at harmonisation of sales law should not blindly focus on their compatibility with the PECL, but instead they should critically assess the appropriateness of the solution found in the Principles and be willing to adopt solutions found in other instruments if they appear more persuasive.

3. Conclusion

The drafting of a uniform European sales law should be high on the agenda in the debate on European contract law. Europe is in need of a harmonising measure that brings closer together the sales laws of the Member States and, in that way, solves the problems encountered by parties involved in cross-border transactions and reduces transaction costs. Though it is too early to harmonise the general law of contract, sales law may take a leading role and thus provide the basis for further harmonisation of European contract law. The chances of success are favourable, for the basis for harmonisation of sales law in Europe has already been laid—the PECL, CISG and the Consumer Sales Directive may be the first building blocks on which to build a European sales regime.

III. THE BOUNDARIES OF EUROPEAN SALES LAW

What should be the scope of such an instrument? The 'sale of goods' is a generic term referring to a category that is far from homogenous. Some sales are of a commercial nature, whereas others involve consumers; contracting parties may be based in different states, thus adding an international element to the contract of sale, whereas other transactions are purely domestic. This diversity can complicate the development of uniform rules for sale of goods law.

Defining and categorising the different sale types may help to identify the elements that are to be taken into account in the harmonisation of European sales law. To begin with, one of the defining factors in the delimitation of the sales categories is the status of the contracting parties. Depending on the professional quality of the seller and the buyer, four different types of sale can be distinguished:[89]

1. a sale in which neither of the parties acts in the course of a business (a purely private sale);
2. a sale in which both parties act in the course of a business (a purely commercial sale);
3. a sale in which one of the parties acts in the course of a business while the other one does not—this intermediate form can be subdivided into:

    a. a sale in which the seller acts in the course of a business but the buyer does not (a consumer sale);

    b. a sale in which the buyer acts in the course of a business but the seller does not (eg the sale of an estate to an antique dealer).

This is merely a rough classification,[90] but it makes clear that sales can be of a very different nature depending on the status of the parties involved.

Nevertheless, the professional status of the parties is only one factor on which to base a classification of sale types. In the process of drafting a uniform sales law for Europe, another important element to be taken into account is the distinction between cross-border[91] and domestic sales. All identified sale types can, in theory, occur in an international as well as a national context. True, in contrast with the other sale types, private sales used to rarely occur outside the domestic sphere. However, recent developments, such as the expansive growth of the internet and the emergence of online markets such as eBay, may encourage the buyers and sellers involved in these sales also to engage in cross-border transactions on a more regular basis. Thus, the distinction between cross-border and domestic sales is of importance in respect of all sale types, and the question arises whether a uniform sales law for Europe should include both domestic and cross-border transactions in its scope. A quick glance at existing regimes shows that the answer to this question is not without ambiguity. To date, only consumer sales have been subject to uniform rules applying to domestic and cross-border transactions alike. In the field of commercial sales, on the other hand, domestic transactions have long been the sole territory of national laws—which have not been the subject of any European or international harmonising measures—whereas the majority of cross-border sales in Europe are governed by a

[89] Hijma, *Asser V(I) Bijzondere overeenkomsten* (n 79 above) [95].

[90] Notably, the phrase 'in the course of a business' has been subject to different approaches in national legal systems, thus affecting the delimitation of the sales categories.

[91] The term is used in relation to the parties to the contract; if they reside or have their places of business in different countries, the sale is a cross-border or international sale. Whether the goods in fact cross any borders or not is irrelevant. Compare also CISG art 1(1).

uniform set of rules, laid down in CISG. With regard to the remaining category, private sales, there has so far hardly been a need for international harmonisation, due to their rare occurrence outside national boundaries. In the light of these differences between the sale types, the question remains how further efforts at harmonisation of European sales law should deal with the distinction between cross-border and domestic sales.

1. 'One is More than Two'

In principle, the most favourable option would be for uniform rules of European sales law to include both international and domestic sales in their ambit. A number of arguments can be put forward in support of this view. The main argument is concerned with the disadvantages flowing from the concurrent existence of two separate regimes in the Member States, ie one for international sales, and one for domestic sales. This argument is essentially the same for all sale types, although there may be a difference in emphasis depending on whether it is applied to commercial sales, consumer sales, or private sales. For example, with regard to consumer sales the notion of consumer protection plays a key part. This being said, although the broad approach may, as a matter of principle, be the most favourable solution, whether it is justifiable on practical grounds is another question altogether—one that has to be answered on the basis of the current state of European contract law. I will deal with each of these issues in turn.

a) Issues of Delimitation

The first argument in support of a comprehensive regime of European sales law, ie the introduction of a regime applying both to international and to domestic transactions, is that, this way, no issues of delimitation would arise.[92] If the other road were chosen, that is, to have in place two separate regimes, one dealing with international transactions, the other with domestic contracts, it would have to be decided where the line should be drawn between the two. This can be a complicated task, for many transactions have some international aspects and it is not necessarily obvious which criteria should be used to determine the applicability of either of the regimes.

For example, article 1 of CISG suffers from ambiguities in its application. Even if it may be argued that 'international' relates to contracts where the parties have their residence in different countries, it is uncertain whether this observation will lead to the application of international rules. Conflict of law rules may come into play in determining whether the Convention applies or whether a contract is governed by national law. Article 1(1)(b) provides that the

[92] U Drobnig 'Scope and General Rules of a European Civil Code' (1997) 5 *European Review of Private Law* 489, 491.

Convention applies to contracts of sale of goods between parties whose places of business are in different states 'when the rules of private international law lead to the application of the law of a Contracting State'. While Contracting States are allowed to make reservations with regard to this provision,[93] there is some controversy as to whether such a reservation will in fact prevent the application of CISG to contracts between parties which are not both based in Contracting States. One of the main issues yet unresolved in judicial practice and academic literature is whether a forum state that has not made such a reservation is allowed to apply article 1(1)(b) in cases in which the Contracting State to whose law the rules of private international law of the forum state lead has made a reservation. The general opinion seems to be in favour of the application of article 1(1)(b) by the forum state in such a case, since to hold otherwise would infringe upon the sovereignty of that state by having another state set the limits to its conflict of laws rules.[94] Other views have been brought forward, however, referring to the interests of parties in the reservation state, as well as to the relation to other reservations permitted by the Convention.[95] Though perhaps less convincing than the arguments pleading in favour of the application of article 1(1)(b), these contentions show that there is room for debate, and that, therefore, the provision has failed to set out a conclusive delimitation of when international, as opposed to domestic, rules will apply.

A European sales regime, ideally, would want to avoid such difficulties. Commercial parties in particular, due to the important interests at stake in most commercial dealings, have an interest in certainty as to the applicable law. Consumers, from the viewpoint of what is called 'consumer confidence',[96] would also benefit from a degree of certainty. Even if experience with international conventions on uniform private law has shown that delimitation difficulties can be overcome to some degree,[97] with these interests in mind, it is submitted that a uniform sales regime for Europe would do well to apply to cross-border and domestic sales alike.[98]

b) A Transaction Costs Approach

Strong arguments in favour of a broad approach—ie to extend the scope of a uniform sales regime both to cross-border and to domestic sales—may further

93 CISG art 95.

94 Compare F Ferrari, 'Specific Topics of CISG in the Light of Judicial Application and Scholarly Writing' (1995) 15 *Journal of Law and Commerce* 1 at 46–7. Also, M Bridge, *The International Sale of Goods. Law and Practice* (Oxford, OUP, 1999) 66–7, fn 172. Of different opinion, Schlechtriem and Schwenzer, *Commentary on the UN Convention on the International Sale of Goods* (n 1 above) 37.

95 JH Honnold, *Uniform Law for International Sales under the 1980 United Nations Convention*, 3rd edn (The Hague, Kluwer Law International, 1999) 44.

96 See pp 39 ff.

97 Drobnig, 'Scope and General Rules of a European Civil Code' (n 75 above) 491.

98 Though valid in principle, the argument is not as strong with regard to sales involving private sellers due to their, as yet, infrequent occurrence outside the domestic sphere.

be gleaned from economic theory. It uses the notion of transaction costs, which are, generally speaking all those costs which preclude or reduce the possibility of smooth market transactions,[99] to show that a broad approach would be the most advantageous option for all parties involved in sales transactions in Europe.

In relation to sales transactions, the costs involved are mostly information costs, such as the costs of hiring specialised practitioners to give legal advice and litigation assistance.[100] These costs do not only flow from the differences in national legal systems, as a result of which parties involved in cross-border sales transactions need the assistance of local legal specialists,[101] but also, it is submitted, from differences in international and domestic sales law. Nowadays, most parties involved in domestic sales are also involved in international sales. They will need to obtain separate legal advice in relation to these, which raises transaction costs. A uniform regime applicable to both types of sales would, however, reduce these costs, for there would be no need to hire experts on both national and international, or European, law—the applicable law would be the same in either case. Therefore, the uniform sales regime would be the only set of rules to be mastered by legal practitioners in the field.[102]

Furthermore, transaction costs do not only arise in relation to substantive legal issues—the delimitation problem, evolving around the question which regime will govern a specific transaction, also needs to be considered in this respect. Considerable costs can flow from the uncertainty that the concurrent existence of separate regimes for cross-border and domestic transactions can create. Legal advice has to be gained in order to determine which set of rules should be adhered to, and long-drawn-out judicial procedures may follow to determine the applicable law once a dispute has arisen. If a uniform European sales regime were to apply to cross-border and domestic sales alike, the occurrence of such complications would belong to the past, at least as far as internal European transactions are concerned.

With regard to international sales transactions in which trading partners outside Europe take part, it is recognised, a different regime would still be in place and delimitation issues would therefore not entirely be eliminated. The borders would merely be shifted—whereas traditionally the divide has been between domestic sales and international sales, the new regime would distinguish between, on the one hand internal European transactions, encompassing domestic and cross-border sales, and on the other hand international sales on a

[99] Mattei, 'A Transaction Costs Approach to the European Code' (n 25 above) 537. Compare R Cooter and T Ulen, *Law and Economics*, 3rd edn (Reading MA, Addison-Wesley, 2000) 87–8.

[100] Mattei, 'A Transaction Costs Approach to the European Code' (n 25 above) 538; D Staudenmayer, 'The Commission Communication on European Contract Law and the Future Prospects' (2002) 51 *International Comparative Law Quarterly* 673 at 676.

[101] *Ibid.*

[102] Compare E McKendrick, 'Harmonisation of European Contract Law: The State We Are In' in S Vogenauer and S Weatherill (eds), *The Harmonisation of European Contract Law* (Oxford, Hart Publishing, 2006) 5 at 15.

global level. Nevertheless, the introduction of an all-inclusive European sales regime would still be worthwhile. Numerous sales contracts are concluded by parties based in different EU Member States every day. A significant reduction of transaction costs might thus be achieved by liberating the internal European market for the sale of goods from delimitation issues in relation to domestic and cross-border sales.

Having said this, at this point in time the transaction costs approach provides the strongest argument in relation to commercial sales. With regard to consumer sales or private sales, the argument carries less weight, since the costs made in those areas are almost negligible compared to commercial sales. Most consumers, and private sellers likewise, will be involved in cross-border sales far more rarely than they are in domestic sale transactions, and the instances in which legal advice or assistance is required are, for most of them, equally rare. Neither the companies dealing with consumers nor the consumers themselves, nor private sellers, will thus benefit greatly from a cut in the cost of legal advice. This might change, however, as cross-border consumer sales become more frequent.

c) Consumer Protection and Consumer Confidence

When consumer sales are concerned, another argument has gained prominence in recent years—the Community policy in favour of consumer protection. On the reasoning that consumers are usually the weaker party in sales contracts, it is thought that they deserve some kind of protection in order to compensate for their lack of bargaining power. In general, such protection takes the form of a measure of minimum harmonisation, usually a Directive, bringing together the national laws of the Member States, whilst allowing individual states to adopt stricter rules than those imposed by the Directive. Since the consumer's bargaining power is no less weak in a domestic context than it is internationally, the objective of these Directives is to constitute a minimum level of consumer protection in respect of *all* consumer sales in the European Union. Therefore, they apply to cross-border and domestic sales alike.

These considerations come shining through in the most recent EC Directive in the field of consumer law, the Consumer Sales Directive, of which the first recital refers to the Community's obligation to contribute to the achievement of a high level of consumer protection by the measures it adopts pursuant to article 95 of the EC Treaty.[103] The Directive consequently includes both cross-border and purely domestic sales in its scope.[104]

[103] Consumer Sales Directive, recital 1. The choice of art 95 as a legal basis rather than art 153 may be criticised. However, the issue is outside the scope of this paper and will not be further discussed here.

[104] Staudenmayer, 'The Directive on the Sale of Consumer Goods and Associated Guarantees' (n 59 above) 548.

There may, however, be another argument on which to base the Consumer Sales Directive's broad scope. Apart from seeking to attain a high level of consumer protection, the Directive aims to contribute to the completion of the internal market. More specifically, it states that

> the creation of a common set of minimum rules of consumer law, valid no matter where goods are purchased within the Community, will strengthen consumer confidence and enable consumers to make the most of the internal market.[105]

The argument thus hinges on the notion of consumer confidence: if consumers feel confident about their legal rights and remedies as against the seller or manufacturer of the goods, they will be more inclined to get involved in cross-border sales transactions, thus encouraging the free movement of goods and contributing to the completion of the internal market. Though not directly aimed at domestic sales, the pursuit of this goal may nevertheless have an impact on the inclusion of purely national sales in the scope of a uniform sales regime.[106] For, although consumers may gain confidence from the knowledge that there is a uniform international sales regime in place offering them protection in relation to cross-border sales, what good will this be if they do not know its contents? It is generally assumed that consumers are reasonably well informed about their rights under national laws,[107] but the same cannot be said with regard to international or European law. If the rules for cross-border sales differ from national standards, this will harm consumer confidence rather than strengthen it. There may, for example, be different limitation periods for the consumer to invoke a remedy, and uncertainty about these may prevent him from entering into a cross-border transaction.[108] Problems like these can be avoided by creating a uniform sales regime that applies to cross-border and domestic sales alike.[109]

2. Harmonisation—An Assessment of the Current Position

It can be seen that a broad approach towards the geographical scope of a uniform European sales law, in principle, is defendable. From a practical point of view, however, the position is more dubious, and it remains to be seen whether this approach would do justice to the various sale types.

[105] Consumer Sales Directive, recital 5.

[106] Of contrary opinion, J Smits, 'Naar een nieuw Europees consumentenkooprecht: Over de Europese richtlijn verkoop van en garanties voor consumentengoederen in het Nederlandse recht' [2000] *Nederlands Juristenblad* 1825 at 1827.

[107] *Ibid*, 1826.

[108] A problem that the Directive does not solve, *ibid*, 1830.

[109] Though, of course, the Consumer Sales Directive is not all-comprehensive in scope, and therefore there may still remain practical obstacles, such as problems of enforcement, disencouraging consumers from entering into cross-border sales. T Krummel and R D'Sa, 'Sale of consumer goods and associated guarantees: a minimalist approach to harmonised European Union consumer protection' (2001) 26 *European Law Review* 312 at 312–13.

The main argument in favour of harmonisation rests on the assumption that a certain level of integration has to be reached to enable the replacement of national laws by a uniform regime.[110] Only if domestic sales in several countries share similar characteristics will such a uniform regime be able to do justice to the interests of the parties involved. Thus, the level of economic, political and legal integration within the European Union will decide whether harmonisation is a feasible objective. It is submitted, however, that at this point in time the required level of integration has not yet been achieved, and that it is therefore doubtful whether a uniform European sales law would do justice to the interests of parties involved in purely domestic sales, whether commercial, consumer or private sales. However, these objections seem only temporary and do not, in principle, affect the question of the extension of the scope to domestic sales. A number of arguments may serve to illustrate the point.

To begin with, it should be noted that already there are signs that in Europe the resistance to the subjection of domestic contracts to anything other than national laws is diminishing. For example, there are developments towards recognition of a stronger legal nature of the PECL. There have been proposals to widen the scope of article 3 of the Rome Convention[111]—which is to be converted into a European Regulation—so as to include sets of rules such as the PECL or the PICC.[112] This would enable parties to choose any of those instruments as the governing law of their contract, whereas up to now article 3 limited any potential choice of law to the law of a country.[113] These proposals indicate that there appears to be a greater willingness to recognise the PECL as a *law* which contracting parties may choose to govern their contract, which could be regarded as an indication that the level of integration is apparently deemed great enough for the European legislature to gradually give the Principles a more significant role to play. While the latest developments appear to have back-pedalled on the original proposal, acknowledging only the possibility for parties to incorporate by reference into their contract a non-state body of law or an international convention,[114] the possibility of recognition of the PECL as an alternative system of rules besides national laws may remain on the agenda. The suggestion of introducing an optional instrument,[115] which parties would be able to choose as an alternative to the domestic laws of the Member States, presupposes the possibility that a set of non-binding rules may be

[110] 'Replacement' is used here in a sense that encompasses both mandatory and non-mandatory rules. See also above, p 34.

[111] Rome Convention on the Law Applicable to Contractual Obligations (consolidated version) [1998] OJ C27/34.

[112] Proposal for a Regulation of the European Parliament and the Council on the law applicable to contractual obligations (Rome I) (presented by the Commission) COM(2005) 650 final (15 December 2005) 5.

[113] PM North and JJ Fawcett, *Cheshire and North's Private International Law*, 13th edn (London, Butterworths, 1999) 559–60.

[114] Council of the European Union, Interinstitutional File 2005/0261 (COD) (3 December 2007), available at http://register.consilium.europa.eu/pdf/en/07/st15/st15832.en07.pdf, [15].

[115] Above, p 27.

adopted as the governing law of a contract. Since the PECL may well have a significant influence on the substance of such an instrument, they may after all, through the backdoor, be raised to the standard of law under the Rome I Regulation.

Furthermore, the PECL were drafted with the aim that they could be invoked to govern domestic contracts as well as international transactions.[116] This broad geographical scope may indicate a tendency towards allowing the application of uniform rules to domestic sales contracts. In comparison to other uniform regimes, such as CISG, which applies exclusively to international sales of goods,[117] the PECL certainly take a huge step in that direction. At first sight, this difference could be explained by the PECL's manifestly non-binding character. The Principles will only apply if the parties choose to incorporate their provisions into the contract. Thus, the application of the PECL to a domestic transaction wholly depends on the will of the parties, and thus does not infringe upon their freedom of contract. In contrast, CISG, in principle, automatically applies to any international sale of goods. Closer examination shows, however, that the rules of the Convention are not sacred as far as the parties are concerned; they can opt out of almost all of these provisions.[118] Here as well, the parties' freedom of contract is paramount. The binding or non-binding nature of the rules, therefore, is not the distinguishing factor. A more compelling reason for the difference in scope between the two instruments can be found in the range of countries they seek to cover: CISG is a global convention, whereas the PECL are only aimed at the Member States of the European Union.[119] The level of integration is easily greater in a regional context than it is on a worldwide level, and harmonisation of laws will thus be a more readily achievable goal.[120] This reasoning applies equally to total unification, where the aim is not merely to bring legal regimes closer together, but actually to introduce a uniform regime for both international and domestic transactions that entirely replaces national laws.[121] Likewise, this effort can only succeed if the countries concerned have reached a sufficient level of economic, political and legal integration. Although in the European context the level of integration needed to enable unification of laws may not have been reached yet, at least it is within closer reach than it is on a global level. The PECL, in this light, can be seen as a first step towards harmonisation, and at a later date possibly even unification, of contract law within the EU.

Finally, the ongoing process of harmonisation may affect the expectations of the parties as to which rules will apply by default, ie if not otherwise stipulated in the contract. At the moment, parties may not expect their contract to be

[116] Lando and Beale, *Principles of European Contract Law* (n 12 above) xxv.

[117] CISG art 1(1), discussed above, pp 36–37. For a discussion of the relation between CISG and national laws, see pp 31–32.

[118] CISG art 6.

[119] PECL art 1:101(1).

[120] See p 21.

[121] Compare Bianca and Bonell, *Commentary on the International Sales Law* (n 69 above) 8.

governed by anything other than the national law of the country in which their dealings take place. If the contract contains no international elements, and the status of the parties does not bring international aspects to the transaction, they are justified in drawing this conclusion. In the light of the principle of freedom of contract, it would seem unjustifiably harsh to subject them to a regime with whose contents they are unfamiliar, and which they did not choose as the governing law of their contract in the first place. The result of the inclusion of domestic sales in the scope of a uniform European sales regime, however, might be just that. Although, at this point in time, there therefore does not seem to be a basis for extending the scope of the uniform law beyond cross-border sales, further developments in the field of European contract law may change this point of view, and the argument based on the parties' expectations may turn in favour of a broad approach. For, the more European legislation pervades national laws, the more parties should be aware of the possible impact of it on their contracts. Further 'Europeanisation' may thus influence the parties' expectations as to the law applicable to their contract, and the inclusion of domestic sales in the scope of a uniform sales regime may on this ground be justified.

Finally, the argument that there is no ground for inclusion of domestic sales within the scope of a uniform sales regime, because it is not possible in the first place to eradicate completely the need to refer to national laws, appears to be of a temporary nature only. It is true that a uniform European sales regime will likely not be all-encompassing: for example, it may not deal with difficult questions such as the passing of property under a sales contract.[122] In those instances where a dispute arises as to aspects of the contract that are not governed by the uniform sales law, reference will have to be made to national laws after all. Though this may be unavoidable as long as other areas of European private law have not reached the same level of harmonisation as sales law, the argument does not *in principle* undercut the case for a wide geographical scope. The more areas of European private law are harmonised, the less need there will be to fall back on national laws. Only in the short term, therefore, will this argument be of any value.

3. Conclusion

A number of arguments support the development towards greater harmonisation of the laws of the Member States: the avoidance of delimitation issues, the reduction of transaction costs, and the strengthening of consumer confidence. However, further harmonisation, or later even unification, will only be possible if a sufficient level of economic, political and legal integration has been reached within Europe. Thus far, this has not been achieved. Nevertheless, the factors preventing a uniform regime from applying to domestic sales, arguably, are of a temporary nature only, and do not in principle stand in the way of harmonisation.

[122] See p 32.

Having established then, that harmonisation of sales law is a key point on the European agenda, the next question is how this will take shape in relation to the area that this thesis looks at: performance-oriented remedies. Comparative law is thought to be the most appropriate tool for determining the way forward for harmonisation.[123] Moreover, it may provide a tool for a critical assessment of solutions found in domestic sales regimes. In order to set the framework for the comparison between the relevant national and international rules, the following chapter will examine contract theories and see how they may help to identify underlying principles that determine the availability and scope of these remedies.

[123] See ch 1, p 2.

3

The Nature and Scope of Performance-Oriented Remedies

I. INTRODUCTION

OLIVER WENDELL HOLMES once famously stated: 'The duty to keep a contract at common law means a prediction that you must pay damages if you do not keep it,—and nothing else'.[1] If taken literally, this statement implies that contractual duties are not in themselves binding and that it is possible for parties to 'buy' themselves out of a contract should they so desire. While it could be argued that such an interpretation fails to take account of the context in which the statement was made,[2] the fact is that Justice Holmes's words have been used by many to justify the limited availability of specific performance in common law systems. Economic theorists in particular have accepted it as an undeniable truth that explains and supports the hegemony of damages over specific performance in those systems.[3]

Contrast this with the attitude taken towards specific performance in civil law systems. There, the promisee's entitlement to performance is regarded as a right following naturally and directly from the contract, and enforcement of the promisor's obligation is therefore readily granted if requested.[4] Damages may also be available, but as an alternative to performance, rather than as a primary remedy.

At first sight, it may be hard to find any common ground in what are, in essence, diametrically opposed views. However, on closer view, it can be seen that the primary role attributed to damages in common law systems is not at all self-evident. In fact, the nature of contractual obligations is not essentially different in common law and civil law systems—both establish relationships between parties that are aimed at the performance of certain promises made by

[1] Justice Oliver Wendell Holmes, 'The Path of the Law' (1897) 10 *Harvard Law Review* 457 at 462.

[2] A convincing case is made by Lionel Smith, who argues that Holmes's statement should not be read as a claim about the law of contract but rather as a claim about the nature of law. See L Smith, 'Understanding Specific Performance' in N Cohen and E McKendrick (eds), *Comparative Remedies for Breach of Contract* (Oxford, Hart Publishing, 2005) 221, 222.

[3] Compare G Jones and W Goodhart, *Specific Performance*, 2nd edn (London, Butterworths, 1996) 2–5. See further below, p 62.

[4] Barring certain exceptions, such as impossibility or disproportionality. See further below pp 69 ff and ch 4, pp 96 ff.

the parties. This 'performance interest', ordinarily, forms the basis for the formation of the contract between the parties. A party enters into a contract because he is interested in getting that which the other party has to offer and because he places a higher value on the other party's performance than on the cost and trouble he will incur to obtain it.[5] The fact that civil law systems in general have a greater commitment to specific performance suggests that principles of contract law as such do not necessarily put forward damages as the primary remedy for breach of contract. Is there any good reason then for the common law to maintain that damages offer adequate protection of this interest and that performance-oriented remedies should be of more limited availability? Or does contract theory open the way to a different solution?

A comparison of the theoretical underpinnings of the rules on performance-oriented remedies in, on the one hand, the English common law system and, on the other hand, Dutch and German law as examples of civil law systems may serve two purposes. First, it may provide an answer to the question just asked, in other words a reappraisal of the scope of performance-oriented remedies in a common law system. Naturally, the comparison will also work the other way and, by highlighting the arguments in favour of the more restricted approach to such remedies found in common law systems, may provide a basis for critical assessment of the scope of the remedies in civil law systems. The results of this balancing of different attitudes towards performance-oriented remedies in common law and civil law systems may then serve a second purpose. It may form the basis for determining a common ground, or a finding of common principles, which may provide a guide for harmonisation of the remedial schemes of European sale of goods laws.

Two levels of comparison present themselves. The common ground will first of all be sought in the nature of the promise to perform. As set out briefly in chapter one,[6] contract theory in German, Dutch and English law supports the notion that contractual obligations are, in essence, binding upon the parties that created them and that a party should therefore not be entitled to set them aside purely on the basis of efficiency considerations. This approach finds its basis in Kantian theory for civil law systems, while for the common law it finds its origins in Fried's rights-based theory of contract law, which explains the binding nature of promises as arising out of the act of promise-making itself, and thus as having a moral basis, rather than having a basis in efficiency considerations.[7] This notion, and the extent to which it supports the protection of the performance interest through performance-oriented remedies, will be explored in the first half of this chapter.

[5] D Friedmann, 'The Performance Interest in Contract Damages' (1995) 111 *Law Quarterly Review* 628 at 629.

[6] See pp 7 ff.

[7] I Kant, *Metaphysische Anfangsgründe der Rechtslehre* (Königsberg, Nicolovius, 1798) 97 ff; C Fried, *Contract as Promise* (Cambridge MA, Harvard University Press, 1981) 10–11.

The second strand of the argument focuses on the scope of performance-oriented remedies and their relation to other remedies, such as damages. It is important that remedies are awarded that are 'appropriate',[8] ie that achieve the result that best protects the interests of the parties and which reflects the bargain that they initially made. The rights-based theory adopted here, it shall be argued, falls short of providing justifications for limits set to performance remedies in this respect. In this context, economic considerations come back into view—the possibilities for a party to insist upon performance are unlikely to be absolute, for if that were so, there would be a risk that one party would be unduly favoured over the other. Efficiency arguments, to some extent, can offer a solution and determine where the boundaries should be set to the performance-oriented remedies.

Whilst the balance between the different interests may be struck in slightly different places depending on whether the sale is made in the consumer or in the commercial context, the arguments in principle are thought to be similar. Therefore, no explicit distinction will be made in this chapter between the two types of sale transactions.

II. THE NATURE OF PERFORMANCE-ORIENTED REMEDIES

A promise, in ordinary life, is regarded by most people as an act which creates an obligation on the party who makes it, and which is binding at least on moral (if not also on legal) grounds.[9] Law being a social institution, this notion of promise-making finds reflection also in legal norms and it can be found at the heart of the majority of modern day contract laws in European countries—or so it seems. For, while legal systems may recognise that contracts can be created out of promises that parties make one to the other, it is harder to find consensus on the question whether a party may hold the other party to his promise and, if so, which interests find legal protection and in what manner. Contract law may, for example, procure a right for the promisee to enforce performance, it may provide for compensation instead of performance, or it may provide for reliance damages. Civilian systems, archetypically, show greater commitment to specific performance and related remedies, whereas common law systems tend to favour damages.

Notwithstanding the different attitudes adopted towards remedies, at their basis civil law and common law systems appear to have more in common than appears at first glance. The starting point lies in the recognition, shared by both systems, that subjective rights lie at the heart of contract law and that it is the law's objective to uphold them.

[8] A term taken from English specific performance cases, where it is gaining ground as a substitute standard to the adequacy of damages test. See further ch 4, pp 82 ff.

[9] Compare Fried, *Contract as Promise* (n 7 above) 1.

1. The Binding Nature of Contractual Obligations

A cursory glance at the contract theories underlying German and Dutch law, as well as English law, brings to the fore two principles that regulate the bindingness of promises: the principle of *pacta sunt servanda*, which states that contracts are binding upon the parties; and the principle of *neminem laede* or harm principle, which basically states 'do no-one harm'.[10] While the different legal systems each give a slightly different slant to the way that these principles interact, they all support the bindingness of contractual obligations and may therefore, it is submitted, at least in principle provide a basis for comparison and possible harmonisation of the remedial schemes in the sales laws of these systems.

The leading principle pervading the sales laws under consideration is that of *pacta sunt servanda*: parties are bound by their contractual obligations, and therefore bound to give the other party the performance that he contracted for, or at least the value of it. The principle may be defended on different grounds. With regard to English contract law, it is commonly regarded as a moral obligation, which finds its basis in the trust that the other party puts in receiving the promised performance.[11] In the theories underlying German and Dutch law, greater emphasis is put on the nature of the subjective right created by the promise, rather than its origin, in analogy with property rights. It is said that the act of promising not only takes away part of the freedom or autonomy of the promisor—he is now bound by the promise to arrange and deliver the promised performance—but also that this part of the promisor's autonomy then comes to belong to the promisee. In other words, the promise creates in the promisee a right of ownership to the performance.[12]

The civilian view has merit, and may be preferred over the common law solution because it provides a much stronger justification to hold that promises are binding. As rightly pointed out by Smith,[13] Fried's suggestion that promises in common law are binding on the ground of a societal convention that regards them as binding is unconvincing, for it does not justify how in the first place new rights can be created where none existed before. Fried's view relies on the assumption that to invoke this convention, but then to disregard it, amounts to a wrong existing in the breach of a duty that the law may legitimately enforce. However, Smith counters, while a convention may reflect the beliefs and expectations of a social majority, that is hardly adequate justification to give a legal

[10] Compare H Unberath, *Die Vertragsverletzung* (Tübingen, Mohr Siebeck, 2007) 185; D Kimel, *From Promise to Contract. Towards a Liberal Theory of Contract* (Oxford, Hart Publishing, 2003) 16, 22.

[11] Fried, *Contract as Promise* (n 7 above) 17. Compare also Kimel, *From Promise to Contract.* (n 10 above) 22 ff, 30. Kimel makes a distinction between the levels of trust required with regard to promises on the one hand, and contracts on the other hand. For a more detailed discussion, see Kimel at 57–60.

[12] Unberath, *Die Vertragsverletzung* (n 10 above) 183, 217.

[13] SA Smith, *Contract Theory* (Oxford, Oxford University Press, 2004) 71.

sanction to that convention.[14] Therefore, the theory fails to provide a basis on which to hold promises binding in the first place. This omission may be repaired by finding an alternative justification, such as the one found in German or Dutch contract theory.[15] The principle of *pacta sunt servanda* may thus be upheld in common law and civil law systems alike.

Greater care must be taken with regard to the second principle, *neminem laede* or the harm principle, for it appears to fulfill a different function in civilian theory than it does in common law theory. German and Dutch theory regard the principle as preceding that of *pacta sunt servanda*. To illustrate this, three levels for the existence of legal entitlements (or, in the context of contract law, the bindingness of promises) may be distinguished: first, there is the creation of subjective rights through promise-making; secondly, it needs to be determined whether the rights created at the first level fulfill the requirements for enforceability as legal actions (*Rechtsakte* in German, *rechtshandeling* in Dutch); finally, the third level is concerned with the enforcement of rights, so created, by the state.[16] The principle of *neminem laede*, which states that no harm should be done to another, may be invoked at the first two levels—for it serves to protect the entitlements so created, since harm would be done if their bindingness were not observed. In this sense, the principle of *pacta sunt servanda* is merely a specific principle derived from the general principle of *neminem laede*.[17]

The harm principle in common law contract theory has a different connotation. While it may also be applied at the first two levels in order to defend the creation of rights where none existed before,[18] its main relevance is at the third level, where it looks at the protection or enforcement of entitlements by the state.[19] The harm principle in this sense, first formulated by John Stuart Mill, holds that it is illegitimate for the state to interfere with an individual's liberty unless that individual has harmed, or is about to harm, another individual.[20] Thus, in contract law it appears that courts may only interfere if the non-performance or defective performance of a party's obligation is regarded as causing harm to the other party.

The two approaches are not incompatible, however. The harm principle in common law contract theory merely has a wider function than Kant's notion of *neminem laede* and extends to the third level, that of enforcement. The question that remains then is: What does 'harm' mean in this context? A convincing argument is made by Kimel, who argues that the harm principle is a forward-looking

[14] *Ibid.*

[15] Smith adopts a view similar to Unberath's on the bindingness of promises through an analogy with property rights (*ibid*, 73–4).

[16] Unberath, *Die Vertragsverletzung* (n 10 above) 183; AS Hartkamp, *Asser IV(I) Verbintenissenrecht. De verbintenis in het algemeen*, 12th edn (Deventer, Kluwer, 2004) [32].

[17] Unberath, *Die Vertragsverletzung* (n 10 above) 185.

[18] Compare SA Smith, *Contract Theory* (n 13) 74 ff.

[19] SA Smith, *Contract Theory* (n 13 above) 69. Also Unberath, *Die Vertragsverletzung* (n 10 above) 183.

[20] SA Smith, *Contract Theory* (n 13 above) 69. Compare also J Raz, *The Morality of Freedom* (Oxford, Clarendon Press, 1986) 400–401.

concept and that it can therefore take account of the parties' interest in performance from the time of creation of the obligation. In his words,

> if the benefits of the bargain are something to which parties to contract are entitled—part and parcel of seeing them as the subject of the parties' core rights—then at least inasmuch as these benefits are of a discernible value for a party, denying them to this party is harming it. The fact that the innocent party had not yet had, prior to the breach or indeed prior to the formation of the contract, the very benefits (profit, etc) that it was denied through the breach (as opposed to, say, the money it lost through reasonable expenditure in reliance) simply does not matter.[21]

Thus, even if the innocent party has not yet received the benefits of the bargain contracted for, this does not mean that no harm has been suffered. What matters is that the innocent party had been promised something which, as a consequence of a failure in performance by the other party, it is now deprived of receiving. The harm principle, to this extent, lends support to the view that the performance interest deserves protection, and so is similar to the civil law approach. Kimel's argument, in this respect, goes further than Raz's. According to Raz, the harm principle merely lends support to protection of the reliance interest.[22] The wider view adopted by Kimel, and also found in civil law systems,[23] appears the more persuasive one, since it recognises that harm may take more forms than actual losses suffered and that it may extend to the loss of the *promise* of performance. Thus, parties may acquire an interest in performance on the basis of a promise made, regardless of costs incurred and losses actually suffered in reliance on that promise.

The binding nature of contractual obligations may thus be considered regulated by two contractual principles, which, though in somewhat different ways, are at the basis of the contract and sale of goods laws of all three legal systems under consideration. Whether the performance interest is best protected through the general availability of performance-oriented remedies, however, remains open to question.

2. The Nature of Performance: Rights or Remedies?

This brings us to the second, and more interesting, strand of the argument. Does contract theory support the protection of the performance interest through actual enforcement of contractual obligations? The simple answer to the question would appear to be 'no'. The Kantian theory adopted for civil law systems, as well as Fried's rights-based theory of contract in the common law, both regard 'rights' as essentially negative in nature. The main focus of the theories

21 Kimel, *From Promise to Contract* (n 10 above) 106.

22 Compare J Raz, 'Book Review: Promises in Morality and Law' (1982) 95 *Harvard Law Review* 916 at 934.

23 Unberath, *Die Vertragsverletzung* (n 10 above) 189; see also H Stoll, 'Abschied von der Lehre von der positiven Vertragsverletzung' (1932) 136 *ACP* 257 at 287 ff.

is on the protection of individual rights, that is, '[r]ights-based theories regard contractual obligations as obligations not to infringe individual rights, and regard contract law as giving legal force to such obligations'.[24]

It follows that neither of the theories necessarily lends support to positive entitlements to performance—rather, they primarily rely on negative duties not to infringe individual rights. Thus, a duty not to infringe individual rights may be owed by one party to the other, or on a larger scale by the state to contracting parties. These duties are aimed at protecting the interests of individual parties, but they do not guarantee that a party receives actual performance of a contractual obligation. If the performance interest can be protected by other means, for example by awarding a monetary remedy, there is no clear reason to prefer performance over this other remedy.

On what basis, then, may rules of contract law enable protection of the performance interest through remedies aimed at performance, such as specific performance in English law or equivalents of it in civilian systems? First, a distinction must be made between the substantive remedies and their enforcement through the courts. The term 'remedies' is not consistently used in the literature and may, depending on the context, refer to either category. Thus, while many authors use the term to refer to a legal response to a wrong, for example a breach of contract, reflecting substantive rights for the aggrieved party to obtain the performance that he contracted for or a (monetary) equivalent of it,[25] it is also possible to use the term in a narrower sense and to refer only to the means of enforcement of substantive, contractual rights, which will normally take the form of a court order of some sort.[26] The latter connotation of remedies corresponds with the third level of the existence of legal entitlements defined by Unberath, the enforcement level.[27] While the study of remedies in this narrow sense is useful and may yield some valuable insights into the functioning of remedies, in particular with regard to the interaction between substantive rights and rules of enforcement, the question of protection of the performance interest demands that focus is put on the substantive rights of the contracting parties. Before deciding on the appropriate ways of enforcement, after all, it first has to be determined what the substance is of the rules of which enforcement is sought.[28]

[24] SA Smith, *Contract Theory* (n 13 above) 140. Compare Unberath, *Die Vertragsverletzung* (n 10 above) 186; Kant, *Metaphysische Anfangsgründe der Rechtslehre* (n 7 above) 101.

[25] The majority of textbooks related to contract in general or remedies in particular uses the term in this sense. See, for example, A Burrows, *Remedies for Torts and Breach of Contract*, 3rd edn (Oxford, Oxford University Press, 2004); GH Treitel, *Remedies for Breach of Contract. A Comparative Account* (Oxford, Clarendon Press, 1988); H Beale, *Remedies for Breach of Contract* (London, Sweet & Maxwell, 1980). Compare for Germany and The Netherlands: F Faust in HG Bamberger and H Roth, *Kommentar zum Bürgerlichen Gesetzbuch* (München, Beck, 2007) § 439 [5], which speaks of 'Rechtsbehelfe'; MM Stolp, *Ontbinding, schadevergoeding en nakoming; De remedies voor wanprestatie in het licht van de beginselen van subsidiariteit en proportionaliteit* (Deventer, Kluwer, 2007).

[26] In this sense, R Zakrzewski, *Remedies Reclassified* (Oxford, Oxford University Press, 2005).

[27] Unberath, *Die Vertragsverletzung* (n 10 above) 186; see above, p 49.

[28] Compare Unberath, *Die Vertragsverletzung* (n 10 above) 187.

The use of the term 'substantive rights', however, denotes another problem that needs to be addressed in order to obtain a full picture of the scope of performance-oriented remedies in sales law. For, while it may be true that a remedy, in the sense of a response to a wrong, gives rise to the creation of new, substantive rights, it is not clear how these relate to the pre-existing rights of the parties embodied in the contract. It may be that the term 'rights' is inappropriate in this context, since it does not refer to rights that flow directly from the contract. Instead, as responses to wrongs, remedies only come into being upon a breach of contract. Moreover, in every legal system the courts have some discretion, be it wider or narrower, to decide which remedy to award—in this sense, remedies are more flexible than the rights flowing directly from the contract. Such rights, on the other hand, exist from the time of formation of the contract onwards and their content, for example that of the promised performance, is determined by the provisions of the contract.[29]

Why does this matter? Because it is directly linked to the search for justifications for the general availability of performance-oriented remedies as a means to protect the performance interest in sales contracts. Problematic is the fact that, in the same way that rights-based theories do not promote actual performance of contractual obligations, they also do not impose specific duties on the courts with regard to remedies.[30] Remedies, by their nature, a response to the non-performance of a party, and thus to the infringement of a party's rights. Therefore, they appear to fall outside the scope of rights-based theories, which recognise a negative duty not to infringe but which do not oblige the courts to *prevent* the infringement of individual rights. It is thus necessary to supplement rights-based theory with other justifications for the form and scope of remedies.

As a preliminary point, therefore, what needs to be determined is whether the performance-oriented remedies here considered are remedies in their true sense, called into being as a response to a wrong, or whether they are rights flowing from the contract. The justifications for general availability of the remedies depend on their classification either as rights or as remedies in this narrow sense.

a) Basic Notion: 'Performance-Oriented Remedies'

Broadly speaking, there are two groups of performance-oriented remedies: on the one hand, specific performance and cure; and on the other hand, repair and replacement. Some contract lawyers would say that the latter are a sub-category of the former. This point, however, may be left for now and will be returned to in a later chapter.[31] Looking at the broader classification of rights and remedies,

[29] This division between rights and remedies finds its origin in Blackstone's *Commentaries*; compare P Birks, 'Rights, Wrongs and Remedies' (2000) 20 *Oxford Journal of Legal Studies* 1 at 5.
[30] Compare SA Smith, *Contract Theory* (n 13 above) 144.
[31] See ch 5, p 120.

it will be argued that specific performance and cure fit best into the rights category, whereas repair and replacement should be regarded as remedies.[32]

First, some clarification of the rights and remedies terminology should be given. As a common denominator, the term used throughout this chapter to refer to specific performance, repair, replacement and cure is 'performance-oriented remedies'. This obscures the fact that the remedies concerned are not all of the same nature and that some, in particular specific performance and cure, may more accurately be called rights, since they follow directly from the contract. As a common denominator, however, the term 'performance-oriented remedies' appears appropriate, if used in the proper context. The term will be used only in two narrowly defined meanings: on a general level, to refer to those legal mechanisms that ensure actual performance of the contract, whether at the request of the buyer or at the insistence of the seller (ie mechanisms that 'remedy' the performance); and, on a more specific level, to refer to the entitlement of the buyer to request repair or replacement of defective goods (ie mechanisms that not only 'remedy' the performance, but that 'remedy' the breach committed against, or the failure in performance suffered by the buyer).

One reason to use a general term like this is a practical one. The term 'remedy' is used by the majority of legal scholars,[33] and to divert from it for the benefit of alternative terms such as 'remedial rights',[34] it is feared, may lead to unnecessary confusion. A *Westlaw* internet search for 'remedies' is likely to bring up most of the relevant literature on the topic, whereas a search for 'remedial rights' or equivalent terms may not spawn very many results.

On a substantive level, an argument for grouping the remedies in this overarching category is that they share a common objective—they are aimed at achieving performance by the seller of his obligation to deliver goods that are in conformity with the contract.[35] Moreover, this aim finds its practical realisation in similar circumstances, namely the remedies are invoked in situations where performance for one reason or another has not come about. Remedies in this sense may be regarded as responses to failure in performance, as well as, in a more narrow way, as responses to breach. Thus, if a remedy is defined as a 'right born of a wrong',[36] and if failure to perform a contract is regarded as a wrong,[37] it follows that responses to non-performance or defective performance should be called remedies.

[32] See below, pp 56 ff.

[33] Examples are Treitel, *Remedies for Breach of Contract. A Comparative Account* (n 25 above); Burrows, *Remedies for Torts and Breach of Contract* (n 25 above).

[34] Suggested by Birks, 'Rights, Wrongs and Remedies' (n 29 above) 5–6, 12.

[35] Damages fall outside this notion for, while they may enable the buyer to obtain substitute goods, performance will not generally be effected by the original seller (who has shown himself unwilling to perform).

[36] This coincides with the second meaning of the word distinguished by Birks, 'Rights, Wrongs and Remedies' (n 29 above) at 12.

[37] Further, pp 72–3 below.

What should be noted is that failure in performance is a wider concept than breach of contract—it includes also situations in which a failure cannot be regarded as a(n) (anticipatory) breach, for example, because performance has not become claimable and the seller is willing to make another attempt at it. Thus, while a defective performance may relate to a condition in English law (eg the implied terms relating to conformity found in section 14 of the Sale of Goods Act (SGA)), it is thought that it will not always amount to a repudiatory breach, in particular if it occurred before the contractual time for performance. Similarly, in Dutch or German law, while it may be sufficient to put the seller in default (*verzuim* or *Verzug*) where it occurs after the stipulated time for performance, a failure in performance before that time will generally not qualify as a breach for which the buyer becomes entitled to terminate.[38] Since the notion of repudiatory breach seems closely linked to the English law notion of breach of condition, a concept foreign to civilian systems, reference to 'failure in performance' rather than to 'breach' seems preferable. In the following chapters, therefore, the distinction made will not be between 'breach' and 'repudiatory breach', but between 'failure in performance' and 'breach that gives rise to termination'. For reasons of convenience, the term 'breach' will still be used to refer to the latter—narrower—type of failure in performance. Breach then refers to failures in performance that may give rise to termination or to other remedies to which the buyer becomes entitled.

In any case, it follows that non-delivery of goods or delivery of non-conforming goods, depending on the circumstances, may call into life a range of different remedies: damages, termination, specific performance, cure, repair, replacement. The latter four share similar aims and origins and may therefore be grouped into a category named performance-oriented remedies. An alternative term to define them could be 'performance remedies'. However, it is thought that the meaning of this term is unclear and that it may lead to confusion. Two possible meanings spring to mind. First, where the word 'performance' refers to the initial defective performance of the seller, the term indicates that the remedies are a *response* to a breach of contract. They remedy the (defective) performance. However, it does not signify what shape this response will take. Secondly, it may be thought that the term refers to a remedy that takes the *form* of performance. The word is thus interpreted as emphasising the nature of the remedy. However, if used in this second sense, it is unclear whether 'performance' implies that the only performance that will qualify as a proper remedy is one equal to the seller's initial obligation under the contract, or whether a different but equivalent performance may suffice. Only the latter interpretation would include repair or replacement.

For the sake of clarity, therefore, 'performance-oriented remedies' would appear the better term. It signifies that the remedies are aimed at achieving performance and are not merely a response to a defective performance.

[38] See pp 154 ff.

Furthermore, the term is wide enough to include all four remedies—specific performance, cure, repair and replacement. The fact that these are 'oriented' at performance implies that the performance sought does not have to be directly stipulated for in the contract. Thus, repair may fall within this category, even if it is only derived from the contract and not directly contracted for.

b) 'Discretionary Remedialism'

The notion of remedies is also seen at the second level, where the distinction is made between specific performance and cure as rights on the one hand, and repair and replacement as remedies on the other hand. Here, the term is used in a narrower, more specific sense rather than as an overarching concept. In this respect, a final observation on the terminology needs to be made before moving on to the actual classification of the performance-oriented remedies.

As observed by Birks, the term 'remedy' may have many possible meanings and may therefore lead to confusion in legal scholarship.[39] In his classification, there are at least five different meanings, if not more, some of which overlap with the notion of 'rights'. Nevertheless, while it may be true that different meanings can be ascribed to the term, as set out above, it appears that 'remedy' is the most accurate word to use in relation to responses to failure of performance in sales cases, as long as it is clearly defined and used in the proper context.

Concerns voiced by Birks that use of the term 'remedy' carries with it the danger of awarding too much discretion to the courts may be countered. According to Birks,

> some excellent lawyers, with the highest and most humane motives, are now building a new model of the law in which the dominant taxonomy is a taxonomy of remedies, to be applied in the court's discretion in an instance-specific manner according to criteria of appropriateness.[40]

He calls this 'discretionary remedialism'—a remedy in this sense is not available as of right, but the court has a discretion as to which remedy to award, to be exercised on the basis of appropriateness. However, while appropriateness is gaining ground as a test used by the courts to decide whether or not to award a remedy, it is thought that it is unlikely to turn into the 'nightmare' that Birks feared it might become.

First, the courts do not seem to have such a large measure of discretion as may appear. It is submitted that the courts' test of appropriateness of the remedy is only marginal. It is up to the parties to decide which remedy they prefer, either by making express provision in the contract or by choosing a remedy once a failure in performance has occurred, and the court will only divert from this choice where it is thought to be disproportionate on the other party.[41] The establishing

[39] Birks, 'Rights, Wrongs and Remedies' (n 29 above) 7.
[40] *Ibid*, 22–3.
[41] A point also recognised by Birks; *ibid*, 24.

of liability, thus, does not give free rein to the court to decide which remedy to award. The term 'discretionary remedialism', in this light, appears to distract from the true objective of the test—it being a factor that may limit rather than determine the availability of remedies.

Secondly, the courts' discretion in the application of the appropriateness test would also seem to be limited. As the Consumer Sales Directive lays down guidelines for determining when repair or replacement are disproportionate,[42] so do pre-existing laws contain restrictions on the availability of performance-oriented remedies. Even if an appropriateness test is adhered to, it will therefore only operate within narrow confines.

As long as the discretion of the courts remains limited, Birks's warning about the 'rightlessness' of remedies may not give real cause for concern. If it is clear in which circumstances a remedy will normally be awarded, there is little reason to fear that the courts will divert from this and make judgments about the appropriateness of remedies that should better be left to the parties. As Birks concedes, courts seem to be aware of the dangers related to a widening of the scope of their discretion,[43] and they are unlikely to make swift moves in this direction themselves. Moreover, statute law may not leave them room to widen the scope of the appropriateness test. If European instruments, such as the Consumer Sales Directive, are to set the norm for the future, they may contain guidelines that restrict the courts' discretion.[44] Therefore, the fear that use of the term 'remedies' may encourage the courts to interfere unnecessarily in the dealings between the parties would seem unfounded.

c) Sub-Division into Rights and Remedies

With these observations in mind, an attempt can now be made to classify the performance-oriented remedies into categories of rights and remedies. It is thought that a sub-division can be made into two groups: on the one hand, specific performance and cure; and, on the other hand, repair and replacement. Whereas the latter are essentially remedies as defined above, the other two have an overlap with the rights category.

The crux to regarding specific performance as a right rather than a remedy lies in its relation to the parties' obligations under the contract; in this case the delivery obligation of the seller. Unlike with remedies, the entitlement to specific performance exists independent of the occurrence of breach. Of course the buyer may be able to claim specific performance also in cases where a breach does occur—though it appears of more limited availability in common law than

[42] Directive (EC) 99/44 of the European Parliament and of the Council on certain aspects of the sale of consumer goods and associated guarantees [1999] OJ L171/12 (Consumer Sales Directive).

[43] Birks, 'Rights, Wrongs and Remedies' (n 29 above) 24.

[44] Though, unfortunately, there is some room for interpretation as to what the scope is of the guidelines laid down in the Consumer Sales Directive. However, any uncertainties are likely to be smoothed out with time. See further ch 5, pp 132 ff.

in civil law systems.[45] However, it is not limited to these situations and it is therefore not merely a 'response to a wrong'. This is generally recognised in civil law systems, which allow a claim for specific performance even before the due date for performance. Though the practical usefulness of this may be limited (the court would merely confirm that a party is entitled to the performance that the other party should render before the due date),[46] it shows that specific performance is a right which is available by virtue of the contractual obligations undertaken by the parties, and independent of the occurrence of breach.

Though the position to be taken with regard to cure is somewhat less straightforward, it is submitted that a similar argument can be made in this respect. While the right to cure would not seem to derive directly from the contract—unless a stipulation to this effect has been made—it could be argued that it is a right that is 'latent' or 'dormant' until it becomes effective upon a failure in performance by the seller. The right to cure seeks to limit the losses or expenses that the seller may suffer in providing a remedy to the buyer for his defective performance. Thus, it is technically not a remedy—at least not of the seller—for it does not seek to make up for a performance that *he* was entitled to under the contract. Rather, systems that recognise cure reflect that the seller has a (limited) right to be protected against disproportionate losses. It is related to the seller's duty to perform under the initial contract between him and the buyer. With the limitation that it should not do injustice to the position of the buyer, the seller should be allowed to perform this duty where he is able to do so, even after he has initially failed to perform satisfactorily. However, the seller's right to cure is not a right that can be invoked from the time of formation of the contract. It is embedded within the seller's duty to deliver conforming goods but it does not become exercisable until the seller has defaulted. Thus, since the seller may only have recourse to the right to cure if performance has failed, it could be called a latent or dormant right.

The basis of this right, however, appears different for cure before the due delivery date than for cure after that date. The right to cure before the due delivery date, arguably, finds its basis in the contractual relationship between the parties. After all, before the contractual time for performance has arrived, the seller's obligation to deliver conforming goods is not claimable by the buyer.[47] In other words, an action brought by the buyer to demand the seller's performance before this date must fail, since the seller still has time to perform. The buyer may not unilaterally bring forward the date for performance. It follows that, until the time for performance expires, the seller has a right to perform on which he may rely as long as his initial failure in performance does not prevent him from giving the buyer the performance that he contracted for.

[45] See p 81.
[46] J Hijma, *Asser V(I) Bijzondere Overeenkomsten. Koop en Ruil*, 6th edn (Deventer, WEJ Tjeenk Willink, 2001) [373].
[47] See in more detail p 154 ff.

In order to establish a right to cure after the due delivery date recourse needs to be had to policy arguments. Once this date has passed, the seller's time for performance has expired and he may therefore no longer rely on his pre-delivery date right to cure. The performance has become claimable and a failure by the seller satisfactorily to perform may entitle the buyer to a remedy, such as termination. Policy reasons, however, may suggest that cure could result in more beneficial results for both parties than an immediate termination of the contract. On this basis, a right to cure could be adopted for sale of goods contracts. If this view is accepted, it is submitted that the right to cure should be regarded as a term implied by law—that is, it is a term that is 'consistently implied into all contracts of a particular type because of the nature of the contract, rather than the supposed intentions of the parties'.[48] In sale of goods contracts, the policy of minimising economic losses may thus form the basis for this implied term.

The situation is different for repair and replacement, however. To begin with, they need to be distinguished from cure. While the seller's right to cure may take the *form* of repair or replacement, it finds its basis in the protection of the interests of the seller. Repair and replacement, as entitlements of the buyer, fulfill a different function. They are a response to the seller's defective performance and they come into being only where this failure in performance qualifies as a breach. In other words, they are not available to the buyer where the seller's performance has not become claimable (for example, because the time for performance has not yet arrived). As a result, their application is generally limited to cases where the time for performance has expired. In exceptional circumstances, they may become available to the buyer at an earlier time. For example, this may happen where there is an anticipatory breach, ie where it is clear that the seller is not going to render a satisfactory performance by the due delivery date.[49] In these circumstances, however, repair and replacement still are responses to breach, and therefore remedies rather than rights.

In this light, it is submitted that repair and replacement are essentially remedies and not rights. What is more, while civilian systems may include them in a wider notion of specific performance, their nature suggests that they do not naturally fit into this category. They do not derive directly from the contract unless it expressly so provides, for the seller's obligation to deliver conforming goods would not normally extend to a second delivery of goods after an initial failure in performance. Instead, the right to demand repair or replacement of defective goods is thought to come into being only at a secondary stage, upon breach of contract. Unlike the rights discussed, a failure in performance not qualifying as a breach would not naturally suffice to allow the buyer to demand the remedy

[48] E Peden, 'Policy Concerns Behind Implication of Terms in Law' (2001) 117 *Law Quarterly Review* 459.

[49] This is the case when, before performance is due, a party either renounces the contract or disables himself from performing it. *Universal Cargo Carriers Corp v Citati* [1957] 2 QB 401 (QBD) 438; compare E Peel (ed), *Treitel on the Law of Contract*, 12th edn (London, Sweet & Maxwell, 2007) [17-073] ff. For Dutch law, see art 6:80 *Burgerlijk Wetboek* (BW), and for German law § 323 IV *Bürgerliches Gesetzbuch* (BGB).

of repair or replacement. Unless breach occurs, the parties are bound and restricted by the terms of their contract and they are unable to invoke secondary rights.

Nevertheless, there is something to be said for the fiction adopted in civilian systems to include repair and replacement in the notions of specific performance. By including repair and replacement in the wider concept, it becomes easier to find justifications for extending the scope of specific performance to non-conformity cases. Principles that apply to situations of non-delivery, where English law to a certain extent recognises rights to specific performance, may thus be extended to situations where the defect in performance lies in the non-conformity of the goods. To the extent that repair and replacement are regarded as equivalents of specific performance that may give the buyer exactly the performance that he contracted for, this approach may thus be in line with a development towards greater recognition of the performance interest.[50]

3. The Performance Interest Protected through Performance-Oriented Remedies

The classification of rights and remedies proposed, now makes it possible to formulate justifications for the scope of the different performance-oriented remedies. First, if specific performance and cure are rights, rather than remedies, it follows that they should be of general availability. They follow directly from the contract and, therefore, should be regarded as 'obligations not to infringe individual rights', to which contract law gives legal force.[51] Cure, for example, could be seen as part of the buyer's obligation not to infringe the seller's right to perform. Specific performance, on the other hand, could be seen as part of the seller's obligation not to infringe the buyer's entitlement to performance. Thus, they are not merely a *response* to an infringement of individual rights but they reflect the duty itself not to infringe individual rights.

At the same time, it is thought that the theory may be extended to include repair and replacement, so as to provide a justification for making these remedies generally available. According to Smith, there are two ways in which a legal system may give force to a concern for rights-based contractual obligations: first, by directly enforcing contractual obligations; and secondly, by attaching consequences to the breach of such obligations.[52] These justifications thus cover, on the one hand, performance-oriented remedies such as repair and replacement, and, on the other hand, other types of remedies, such as damages. Essentially, the former are justified 'when, and because, the defendant has shown herself unwilling to perform her legal obligations'.[53] In this situation, the

[50] See p 120.
[51] Above, p 49.
[52] SA Smith, *Contract Theory* (n 13 above) 144–6.
[53] *Ibid*, 145.

courts are allowed to interfere simply to prevent a wrong from happening or continuing to happen. In the second situation, an interference with the parties' dealings through an award of damages may be justified on the basis of justice, eg to correct a wrong that has already happened. Thus, damages may compensate a party for losses suffered as a result of wrongful actions of the other party.

The general availability of repair and replacement may be defended on the basis of the first justification. They prevent the infringement of individual rights, for they ensure that the contract is performed. Thus, they prevent the infringement of the rights of the buyer by giving him the performance that he contracted for, and nothing less.[54] They also may protect the interests of the seller by providing a cost-effective alternative to termination and damages.

However, more is necessary to support the notion that the four performance-oriented remedies should be generally available, in the way that monetary remedies are. If one adopts the view that a promissory obligation entitles the promisee to receive the full value of the promised performance, as Fried does,[55] and as is also supported by Kantian theory,[56] this is a first step towards recognition of a general right to performance. This approach advocates the need for an assessment of the appropriate remedy on the basis of the entitlement of the promisee, rather than on a different basis (eg reliance). More specifically, it advocates the choice of a remedy that best protects the performance interest of the party, ie the interest that a party has in actual performance of the contract.

The second step is to determine whether performance-oriented remedies can compete with other remedies, such as damages—in other words, whether there are justifications for their availability alongside or even in priority to such remedies, rather than as a secondary option. One way of doing this, in accordance with a theory defended by Kimel,[57] is to accept performance-oriented remedies as the instruments that best protect the performance interest of the buyer and to hold that they should therefore be the standard remedy. This approach seems more plausible than a theory advocated by Craswell, which states that all remedies are 'equally compatible' with the notion of individual autonomy.[58] In this view, a promise makes non-optional a course of conduct that would otherwise be optional, and the protection of interests so created (ie the value of the promise) may be secured by each of the remedies. It may be too simple to state the argument like this—after all, if a promise is binding, it creates an entitlement in the promisee. Some remedies are likely to protect such an entitlement better than others. For example, expectation damages may provide stronger protection of this entitlement than reliance damages, for their award does not depend

[54] Compare ch 5, pp 117 ff.

[55] Fried, *Contract as Promise* (n 7 above) 21.

[56] Kant, *Metaphysische Anfangsgründe der Rechtslehre* (n 7 above) 101; see Unberath, *Die Vertragsverletzung* (n 10 above) 188–9.

[57] Kimel, *From Promise to Contract* (n 10 above) 89 ff.

[58] R Craswell, 'Contract Law, Default Rules, and the Philosophy of Promising' (1989) 88 *Michigan Law Review* 489; compare Kimel, *From Promise to Contract* (n 10 above) 93.

on the contingency of expenditure made in reliance on the promise.[59] Similarly, performance-oriented remedies may offer greater protection of the promisee's interests than damages. On this basis, there is at least one strong argument in favour of the general availability of performance-oriented remedies: they give a party exactly the performance that he bargained for, instead of damages, which can merely be an approximation of the loss suffered as a result of a defective performance. Thus, they offer better protection of the performance interest than damages do and they should therefore be available at the option of the buyer.

If the buyer so prefers, he should of course be free to opt for damages even if that remedy does not offer the same protection as a performance-oriented remedy does.[60] Nevertheless, that does not diminish the argument that, even if not the standard or primary remedy, performance-oriented remedies should be available alongside other remedies. Two further arguments may be put forward in support of the general availability of the remedies: the under-compensation argument and the intentions of the parties.

a) The Under-Compensation Argument

By making an order for specific performance, courts avoid a common deficiency relating to awards of damages, namely that they can be under-compensatory.[61] Especially in relation to consumer sales, a monetary remedy is not always the answer to the buyer's complaint if the goods are defective. English law has recognised a concept of 'consumer surplus', which refers to the extra, non-monetary value that consumers may attach to their purchases on top of the economic value of the goods. This may, for example, relate to sentimental value—inherent to the purchase of pets, or even cars—or it may relate to higher expectations as to the quality of the goods than commonly encountered in commercial transactions. In such cases, specific performance will often be a more appropriate remedy than damages because it protects the buyer's interest not only in the monetary value of performance but also in this 'surplus'. Civilian systems, with their general right to specific performance, do protect these interests, but English law until now has been hesitant.[62] Of course, one may say that these interests can also be protected by invoking the assistance of a third party, the costs of which could be covered by an award of damages. However, the extent to which this would actually lead to similar results may be limited. For example, where there have been multiple dealings between the buyer and the

[59] Compare Kimel, *From Promise to Contract* (n 10 above) 93.

[60] See further ch 4, p 110.

[61] Compare A Schwartz, 'The Case for Specific Performance' (1979) 89 *Yale Law Journal* 271 at 274 ff.

[62] To what extent damages protect, and should protect, more than just the economic value of a performance is unclear in English law. Compare the discussion of *Panatown* in E McKendrick, *Contract Law: Text, Cases and Materials*, 2nd edn (Oxford, Oxford University Press, 2005) 1029 ff. Also, E McKendrick, 'The Common Law at Work: the Saga of *Alfred McAlpine Construction Ltd v Panatown Ltd*' (2003) 3 *Oxford University Commonwealth Law Journal* 145 at 167 ff.

seller for a prolonged period of time, the parties may have established a certain level of mutual reliance that cannot easily be substituted by a third party's performance. This may be especially significant where specialist knowledge is required for making repairs to the goods, eg with complicated machinery or technical equipment.

Damages can be under-compensatory not only in consumer sales but in commercial sales as well, though this is likely to occur more rarely. The interests at stake are of an economic nature and there is little room for an equivalent of the 'consumer surplus'—though situations may be conceived in which the relations of the parties go further than mere economic dealings.[63] From an economic perspective, nevertheless, damages may also occasionally be under-compensatory, for example, in cases of a purchase of machinery to be used in the buyer's business.[64] A general right to specific performance would ensure that the appropriate remedy is available to the buyer in such situations.

A counter-argument that should be mentioned here, however, relates to the doctrine of mitigation: in English law, the buyer has a duty to mitigate and can therefore not recover damages for losses that he ought to have avoided;[65] a duty which is of no relevance in cases in which specific performance is ordered. An order for performance may be made even where the buyer has not mitigated his loss—and so it may be said that there is a risk that by granting the remedy a buyer will be *over*-compensated.

The value of this argument, nevertheless, may be questioned, for it is relative to the general attitude that English law takes towards the protection of the performance interest. In a system that does not give full recognition to the buyer's interest in receiving the performance which he contracted for—whether through specific performance or in the form of a monetary award—it is not surprising to see that inroads are made on the buyer's entitlement to receive full compensation for this interest. The doctrine of mitigation finds its origin in considerations of economic efficiency and reasonableness—it is aimed at reducing unnecessary expenditure and also takes account of benefits that the aggrieved party may derive from the breach. On this basis, it is a general rule that in cases of non-delivery or delivery of defective goods a buyer is obliged to go out into the market in order to try and secure a cover purchase.[66] In commercial cases, this will usually be a cost-effective solution both for the buyer and for the seller. Moreover, where the buyer manages to make a profit out of the use or resale of goods, it may be thought reasonable to deduct this from his claim for damages. This way, it is ensured that the buyer will not be over-compensated.

In the light of the view that the performance interest in sale of goods cases should be paramount and that, therefore, performance-oriented remedies should be generally available, however, the argument that these remedies may

[63] For example if the parties have been dealing with each other over the course of several years.
[64] Eg *Bronx Engineering*, see ch 4, p 88.
[65] Peel (ed), *Treitel on the Law of Contract* (n 49 above) [20-097].
[66] *Ibid*, [20-099].

over-compensate appears less appealing. In this view, if the buyer has a general entitlement to performance, remedies ought to ensure full protection of this interest. Therefore, the remedies are not considered to over-compensate, but merely to compensate. Against this background, it seems logical not to impose a duty of mitigation on the buyer, which may limit a claim for damages on his part. Damages, after all, are meant to give a reflection of the performance interest and should therefore offer protection of this interest—as far as possible—to a similar extent as actual performance would. The provisions of Dutch sales law confirm this view: not only does the buyer have a general entitlement to a performance-oriented remedy, but there are few limitations to this right and those that exist apply equally to a claim for damages in lieu of performance. The good faith or disproportionality restriction on performance-oriented remedies is mirrored for damages in article 6:109(1) *BW*, which provides that a court may reduce an award of damages where, in the circumstances of the case, full compensation would have unacceptable consequences.[67] The possibility of mitigation, like the restrictions to performance-oriented remedies, is of limited application in practice and courts will make restrictive use of their discretion.[68]

All of this is not to say that a duty to mitigate may not be adopted in systems that adhere to the general availability of performance-oriented remedies. German law, for example, stipulates in § 254 II *BGB* that an award of damages may be reduced in cases where the aggrieved party has failed to avert or mitigate the loss. While this provision, according to § 442 in combination with § 651 *BGB*, does not apply to cases of non-conformity in sale of goods law,[69] it may be relevant in cases of non-delivery. Hence, a buyer may be obliged to procure a substitute transaction (where possible), rather than be entitled to an order for performance from the original seller. A provision of similar effect can be found in article 9:505(1) of the Principles of European Contract Law (PECL). It goes to show, then, that when it comes to damages these systems are prepared to make inroads on the right of the aggrieved party to receive full compensation. Reasons for this may be—as in English law—that mitigation is considered reasonable, or that it reduces economic waste.[70] As a result, damages may not cover the value of the performance interest of the buyer. Notably, however, this in itself may lend strength to the argument that, whilst performance-oriented remedies give full protection to the performance interest, damages do not and therefore run the risk of being under-compensatory.

[67] In Dutch: 'Indien toekenning van volledige schadevergoeding in de gegeven omstandigheden, waaronder de aard van de aansprakelijkheid, de tussen partijen bestaande rechtsverhouding en hun beider draagkracht, tot kennelijk onaanvaardbare gevolgen zou leiden, kan de rechter een wettelijke verplichting tot schadevergoeding matigen'.

[68] Hartkamp, *Asser IV(I) Verbintenissenrecht* (n 16 above) [494]. With regard to the limitations to performance-oriented remedies, see further below, pp 69 ff and ch 4, pp 95 ff.

[69] BGH, *VersR* 1981, 1179; OLG Hamm, *NJW-RR* 1990, 1054. See also C Grüneberg in Bamberger and Roth, *Kommentar zum Bürgerlichen Gesetzbuch* (n 25 above) § 254 [4].

[70] Compare H Oetker in W Krüger (ed), *Münchener Kommentar zum Bürgerlichen Gesetzbuch*, 5th edn, vol 2 (München, CH Beck, 2007) § 254, [76] ff; O Lando and H Beale (eds), *Principles of European Contract Law. Parts I and II* (The Hague, Kluwer Law International, 2000) 445.

b) The Intentions of the Parties

Another argument in favour of the general availability of specific performance and related remedies is that they can give effect to the intentions of the parties.[71] This can be understood in two senses—on the one hand, the intentions of the parties to be bound by their contractual promises, and on the other hand, the intentions of the parties with regard to the availability of particular remedies.

Some English lawyers argue that specific performance should not be made generally available because it interferes with the performing party's individual liberty[72]—if the buyer has an entitlement to specific performance, the seller can be forced to perform a physical obligation instead of paying off his obligations through an award of damages. However, a persuasive counter-argument is the fact that the seller has agreed in the first place to take upon him the obligations of which the buyer seeks specific performance by entering into the contract of sale.[73] The seller had the intent to perform and the buyer should be able to enforce this. This, of course, is the philosophy that underlies the general availability of the remedy in civilian systems, in which the sanctity of contract is paramount.[74]

Nevertheless, the parties could have different intentions with regard to the *remedies* that should be available in case of defective performance. Commercial buyers may indeed prefer damages to specific performance because they are looking for a swift remedy that enables them to continue their dealings with a minimum of economic loss. On the other hand, there may be situations in which the buyer would rather opt for specific performance because that is the more appropriate remedy, for example, because there would be a delay in obtaining substitute goods that would cause the buyer considerable (economic) hardship. Similarly, for consumer sales a general rule can be formulated, which would be that a buyer of defective goods prefers a remedy of specific performance because it protects the so-called 'consumer surplus', but this as well is merely a general rule. The problem with these propositions is that there is very little empirical evidence to support them. Therefore, it is difficult to use this argument either in favour of or against the argument that the present common law solution is congruent with the intentions of the contracting parties and hence reduces the costs of negotiating contracts,[75] as suggested by some authors.[76] Likewise, it is difficult to use the intentions of the parties as an argument to support the civilian solution.

[71] Generally on the intentions of the parties with regard to specific performance, McKendrick, *Contract Law: Text, Cases and Materials* (n 62 above) 1161–2; SA Smith, 'Performance, Punishment and the Nature of Contractual Obligation' (1997) 60 *Modern Law Review* 360; AT Kronman, 'Specific Performance' (1978) 45 *University of Chicago Law Review* 351 at 365 ff; Schwartz, 'The Case for Specific Performance' (n 61 above) 277.

[72] See Burrows, *Remedies for Torts and Breach of Contract* (n 25 above) 473.

[73] Compare McKendrick, *Contract Law: Text, Cases and Materials* (n 62 above) 1161.

[74] Compare p 48.

[75] McKendrick, *Contract Law: Text, Cases and Materials* (n 62 above) 1161–2.

[76] Kronman, 'Specific Performance' (n 71 above) 369.

There may be some scope, nevertheless, for the courts to take into account the intentions of the parties with regard to the availability of remedies in deciding whether or not to grant the remedy of specific performance.[77] This may either be because the parties have included express provisions on remedies within their contract, or because the intentions of the parties follow implicitly from the terms of the contract.[78] The latter situation occurred, for example, in the Dutch *Multi Vastgoed* case, in which the court was persuaded to grant specific performance (in Dutch law: *nakoming*)[79] partly on the basis that a number of guarantees were included in the contract and that the alternative remedy offered by the constructor, ie repair of the defect, was insufficient in the light of these guarantees.[80] A similar conclusion may be drawn for English law, where the courts may also consider the intentions of the parties to be of relevance. Nevertheless, the decision whether or not to order specific performance lies in the discretion of the court and the parties cannot, by the terms of their contract, confine the role of the court to that of a 'rubber stamp'.[81] Still, while it is right that the courts should not be bound by the stipulations of the parties, it can be argued that they should treat them with considerable respect, particularly where the parties are of equal bargaining power, and only refuse to give effect to it where there are strong countervailing policy considerations.[82]

It follows from the arguments based on under-compensation of damages and on the intentions of the parties that there is a basis for the general availability of performance-oriented remedies alongside damages and other remedies. This position, even in the context of English law where damages are regarded as a primary remedy, is reflected also in an analysis made by Charlie Webb of the substance of the performance interest and the extent to which expectation damages protect it.[83] Webb's argument hinges on the recognition of two distinct contractual interests: receiving performance, and being compensated for losses caused by non-performance. The protection of these interests does not always coincide—eg it is possible for a defendant to breach his contract without causing any loss to the claimant. Therefore, damages may be sought for either of these distinct interests. However, it is doubtful whether, currently, compensatory damages in English law are capable of sufficiently protecting the

[77] Of course, in civil law systems, the availability of specific performance does not depend on the discretion of the court, as it does in England. However, the intentions of the parties will hardly be scrutinised except in cases that are brought before the court or are made subject of some other form of proceedings, such as arbitration.

[78] Note, however, that there are limitations on the exclusion of certain remedies in consumer contracts; compare art 7:6 *BW* and the Unfair Contract Terms Act 1977 ss 6(2)(a) and 13(1)(b).

[79] See ch 4, p 91.

[80] *Multi Vastgoed BV/Onroerend Goed Maatschappij Nethou BV*, HR 5 januari 2001, *NJ* 2001, 79 (Hof at [13]), see ch 4 p 101.

[81] *Quadrant Visual Communications Ltd v Hutchison Telephone UK Ltd* [1993] BCLC 442 (CA) 451; McKendrick, *Contract Law: Text, Cases and Materials* (n 62 above) 1162.

[82] *Ibid.*

[83] C Webb, 'Performance and Compensation: An Analysis of Contract Damages and Contractual Obligation' (2006) 26 *Oxford Journal of Legal Studies* 41.

performance interest. First, a possible objection that may be made is that an award of damages cannot, in any case, reflect the performance interest, since it changes the nature of the obligations that the parties have undertaken towards each other (ie it gives a monetary award instead of performance). Secondly, even if this objection can be overcome,[84] it is doubtful whether damages can protect the performance interest to the extent that performance-oriented remedies can. Problems inherent to damages would remain, such as the difficulty of assessing the measure of damages or the fact that the doctrine of mitigation (if it applies) may cause damages to be under-compensatory.[85]

Thus, the conclusion must be that, if damages are prioritised, as is currently the case in English law, there is no commitment to protecting the performance interest of the promisee, or at best it is less than whole-hearted.[86] In the words of Webb,

> [i]f we wish to continue the current prioritization of compensatory claims, an explanation is needed as to why the claimant is barred from enforcing his right to performance. It would be more honest to admit that, in such cases, the claimant acquired no such right upon contract formation.[87]

This conclusion, which denies the promisee any right to performance, is flagrantly at odds with the basic principles of Fried's (or indeed any) rights-based theory. Thus, an even stronger case can be made to say that damages are unable to protect the performance interest, and that therefore performance-oriented remedies are the better remedies.

With the protection of the performance interest as the primary concern, therefore, there is a strong basis in rights-based theories to make performance-oriented remedies generally available, besides or even primary to expectation damages.

III. THE SCOPE OF PERFORMANCE-ORIENTED REMEDIES

Nevertheless, the law of contract also takes its shape from other policies and it may, for example, be influenced by considerations of economic efficiency. Such arguments are likely to be highly relevant in the European context, keeping in mind the EU's focus on economic cooperation. Economic policy underlies a range of public law measures relating to the functioning of the internal market, for example in relation to the abolition of internal barriers to trade, and it can also be seen to have an influence on measures that seek to regulate the private laws of the Member States. A primary example is the Consumer Sales Directive,

[84] Webb suggests two ways in which this may be done, see *ibid*, 58–61.

[85] *Ibid*, 66–8. See further pp 61 ff.

[86] Compare also McKendrick, *Contract Law: Text, Cases and Materials* (n 62 above) 1017.

[87] Webb, 'Performance and Compensation: An Analysis of Contract Damages and Contractual Obligation' (n 83 above) 71.

which, although presented as a measure of consumer protection, has as one of its main objectives to improve the functioning of the internal market.[88]

In relation to performance-oriented remedies in sales law, it is submitted that efficiency arguments may be called upon to define the boundaries of these remedies. Thus, the buyer's right to specific performance or a related remedy may be limited on grounds of efficiency. At the same time, efficiency arguments may provide an additional justification for the seller's right to cure. It is submitted that where arguments based on the protection of the performance interest are insufficient, for example, because the buyer is willing to accept a remedy in damages, efficiency reasons may still support a right to cure for the seller.

Apart from limiting factors related to efficiency, there is also a moral side to the argument. It will be argued that performance-oriented remedies may to a certain extent be limited by considerations of a moral nature. In particular, the fact that it is the seller who performed unsatisfactorily may to some extent influence the scope of his right to cure.

1. Utilitarianism v Rights-Based Theory

The use of efficiency arguments does not necessarily clash with the rights-based justifications for generally available performance-oriented remedies set out in the previous half of this chapter. As stated by Burrows,[89]

> [t]he common law is best regarded as a coherent system of principle, reflecting a complex mix of 'moral rights' reasoning, modified and tempered by the desire to pursue certain long-term social policies. One important social policy is efficiency.

The same may be said of civil law systems, which are also shaped by a mixture of legal principles and social policies.

Burrows adds, however, that the place of efficiency 'is alongside, not as a replacement for, moral rights reasoning'.[90] This reflects the scepticism often encountered in European legal scholarship towards economic analysis of the law, at least to the extent that it is seen as a substitute for traditional contract theory. Though economic analysis may provide some valuable insights into the workings of contract law and the incentives that influence the choices that contracting parties make, its role appears to be *additional* only to traditional, rights-based theories.[91] With regard to performance-oriented remedies, this view is supported by two main criticisms of the use of economic analysis as a primary theory to justify the shape and content of contractual rules.

First, economic theory has failed to come up with a conclusive justification for the wider or narrower scope of specific performance and equivalent

[88] Directive 99/44/EC Recital 5. See also ch 7, p 201.

[89] Burrows, *Remedies for Torts and Breach of Contract* (n 25 above) 20–22.

[90] *Ibid*.

[91] Compare Unberath, *Die Vertragsverletzung* (n 10 above) 231.

remedies. Examples can be found in civilian legal scholarship of defences for the general availability of such remedies,[92] whereas economic analysis in common law systems has been invoked in support of a more limited availability of specific performance, granted only at the discretion of the court.[93] The distinction is not just between common law and civil law systems, however, for also in a common law context, economic analysis has been invoked in support of a wider approach to specific performance.[94] This lack of consensus can be attributed to a dearth of empirical evidence on the matter, in particular with regard to the workings of the market and the level of transaction costs.[95] As a result we remain in the dark as to whether efficiency is best promoted through a limited right of specific performance, or by making the remedy of general availability.

Secondly, and more fundamentally, economic theories of contract law appear to put too strong an emphasis on considerations of efficiency, whilst paying little attention to traditional views on the bindingness or moral aspects of contract. While this does not automatically lead economic theory to support 'efficient breach'[96]—ie the sanctioning of breach of contract where it would be more efficient for parties not to perform, regardless of moral notions of bindingness of contract—it may obscure some of the fundamental values that contract law seeks to protect. For example, by focusing on economic incentives, non-monetary interests that a party may have in the performance of the contract are disregarded. Also, standards of good faith or fair dealing may become subordinate to economic factors. An inherent danger of economic analysis of contract law, thus, is that it may lead to an erosion of standards of behaviour between contracting parties.

In relation to performance-oriented remedies, therefore, a balanced approach that takes account of multi-faceted considerations is preferable to a purely efficiency-based theory. It seems more realistic than an efficiency-based theory, since most actors in sale of goods law, or the wider field of contract law, do not appear to think of contract as a disposable commodity. Contracts are made with

[92] Though flexibility must be observed in order to prevent inefficient solutions where enforcement of performance would lead to additional costs; compare H-B Schäfer and C Ott, *Lehrbuch der ökonomischen Analyse des Zivilrechts*, 4th edn (Berlin, Springer, 2005) 464–7. See also G De Geest, *Economische analyse van het contracten- en quasi-contractenrecht. Een onderzoek naar de wetenschappelijke waarde van de rechtseconomie* (Antwerpen, MAKLU, 1994) 264.

[93] For example, Kronman, 'Specific Performance' (n 71 above) 351.

[94] For an example of US literature on the issue, TS Ulen, 'The Efficiency of Specific Performance: Toward a Unified Theory of Contract Remedies' (1984) 83 *Michigan Law Review* 341; Schwartz, 'The Case for Specific Performance' (n 61 above) 271.

[95] For example, it is unclear whether the current rules on specific performance are in line with the parties preferences and thus whether an expansion of the availability of the remedy would lead to an increase in transaction costs for pre-breach negotiations. Compare Schwartz, 'The Case for Specific Performance' (n 61 above) 279 ff. Also, SA Smith, *Contract Theory* (n 13 above) 405. An empirical overview of specific performance in civil law systems by Lando and Rose also does not give conclusive evidence; see H Lando and C Rose, 'The Myth of Specific Performance in Civil Law Countries', *American Law & Economics Association Annual Meetings* (paper 15, 2004) 14.

[96] Compare Schäfer and Ott (n 92 above) 464.

a view to having them performed, not with a view to breaking them.[97] Efficiency considerations may, however, be called upon to limit the scope of such remedies in cases where the enforcement of performance would not be beneficial to either or both of the contracting parties.

2. Limitations Based in Efficiency

Apart from cases in which performance has become impossible,[98] a buyer's entitlement to a performance-oriented remedy may be limited on grounds of efficiency. Both common law and civil law systems recognise this as a ground for limitation of the scope of such remedies. Efficiency considerations, in this respect, are regarded as a necessary factor to counterbalance the strong rights of the buyer and to offer protection to the interest of the seller.

Justification for this view may be based on different grounds. For example, it may be supported by considerations to do with the autonomy of the parties, as Unberath suggests.[99] In this view, the protection of the performance interest retains centre-stage, so that the starting point remains that damages may only be awarded if the buyer considers them equal to performance. Damages may, however, be preferred if the extra costs falling on the seller for providing a performance-oriented remedy are disproportionate in comparison to the buyer's interest in receiving the contractual performance. This limitation to the scope of performance-oriented remedies would lead to economically efficient results for both parties.[100] According to Unberath, legislation to this effect then is in accordance with what parties would autonomously have agreed upon. As a result, transaction costs will be kept to a minimum, since the default rules on which the contract is based do not need to be negotiated.[101]

Alternatively, the use of efficiency considerations as a limitation on the buyer's entitlement to a performance-oriented remedy may be justified by the harm principle. The principle, as set out above, supports the bindingness of promises on the basis that harm would be done if subjective rights were not upheld. Furthermore, in order to protect against such harm, it justifies the intervention of courts in the enforcement of subjective rights.[102] Now, a further step can be taken in linking the harm principle to the subjective rights of the promisor, rather than the promisee. Thus, it is arguable that performance-oriented remedies may not be enforced where this would unduly harm the interests of the promisor (ie the seller).

[97] Compare *Cehave NV v Bremer Handelsgesellschaft mbH (The Hansa Nord)* [1976] QB 44 (CA) 71: 'contracts are made to be performed and not to be avoided'. Friedmann, 'The Performance Interest in Contract Damages' (n 5 above) 629.

[98] See further ch 4, pp 97–8, 100.

[99] Unberath, *Die Vertragsverletzung* (n 10 above) 277 ff.

[100] *Ibid*, 238.

[101] *Ibid*, 278.

[102] See above, p 49.

On this basis, a justification for limiting the buyer's entitlement to a performance-oriented remedy may be found in liberal theory, to which the harm principle is central.[103] A convincing argument on the intrusiveness of remedies—to the effect that the remedy sought should cause as little harm as possible to the other party—is made by Kimel:

> My suggestion as to how the harm principle can be brought to bear on the contest between specific performance and expectation damages is simple. Though it is only from the perspective of a substantive theory of political freedom that the harm principle can be defended and given concrete content, the very fact that it is a principle of restraint reflecting concern for personal freedom renders it a rather straightforward implication of (any satisfactory interpretation of) this principle that whenever a certain harm could be effectively prevented in more than one way, the measure that must be used is the least intrusive one—the measure that, compared to its alternatives, amounts to a lesser interference with the freedom of the person against whom it is taken.[104]

In the context of performance-oriented remedies in sales law, it could be argued that the 'least intrusive' remedy is that which (i) gives effect to the performance that was contracted for, whilst (ii) not putting a disproportionate burden on the other party. On this point, the harm principle therefore leads to similar results as those reached by Unberath on the basis of the principle of party autonomy.

A final justification for restricting the scope of performance-oriented remedies on the basis of efficiency considerations may be found in the principle of good faith. As will be seen,[105] civil law systems have recognised restrictions to specific performance on the basis of this principle where the remedy would involve disproportionate expenditure on the part of the seller. A balancing of the interests of the parties, and the obligations that they have towards each other to pay heed to these interests, means that a seller acting in good faith may not be required to effect performance where costs are disproportionate. While such a general principle is not part of English law, a certain overlap may be found with the severe hardship bar to specific performance.[106] To this extent, good faith also lends support to the limitation of performance-oriented remedies on the basis of efficiency considerations.

Different justifications that may be invoked in support of efficiency-based limitations to the scope of performance-oriented remedies thus merge into one. To what extent current law reflects these standards for finding the most appropriate remedy will be further explored in chapters four and five. Suffice it for now to say that arguments of economic efficiency play an important role in sale of goods contracts, for, by the nature of these transactions, the interests of buyer and seller are likely to turn on monetary aspects of the sale rather than on

[103] Compare SA Smith, *Contract Theory* (n 13 above) 69.
[104] Kimel, *From Promise to Contract* (n 10 above) 103.
[105] Ch 4, pp 100 ff.
[106] Ch 4, pp 98, 103.

considerations that may be important in other types of contract, such as supervision of performance or interference with personal freedom.[107]

3. Limitations Based in Moral Rights Reasoning

Another shaping force of contract law is moral rights reasoning. So, it was seen that the starting point for the recognition of the binding nature of promises, and of the protection of the performance interest, is found in morality.[108] The binding nature of promises, and contracts, is derived from the operation of a principle of trust between promisor and promisee. Promises or contracts are made in the belief that the other party will stick to his word and deliver the agreed performance. Moral rights, however, may also to some extent create limitations to the parties' entitlements to invoke performance-oriented remedies, at least from the *seller's* perspective. If a failure in performance is regarded as a wrong—in other words, if a moral connotation is attached to it that makes us regard it as bad behaviour on the part of the seller—this might imply that the seller should be punished in some way, or that he should at least in some way be held accountable for breaching the trust that the buyer has put in his performance.

However, a preliminary comment needs to be made with regard to sale of goods. In German and in Dutch law, liability for defective performance is based on fault. Dogmatically, therefore, a wrongdoing of the seller lies at the root of his liability.[109] In English law, by contrast, the duties of the seller with regard to non-conformity are strict.[110] Therefore, it may be questioned to what extent the seller is *morally* wrong if his performance is defective. For example, a seller may be held liable for non-conformity even in situations where he did not know and could not have known that the goods were in some way defective. It would seem that, in these circumstances, the seller is not in breach of any moral obligation; instead, his 'wrong' is based on the fact that he simply failed in his legal obligation to provide the performance that he promised. To relate the legal wrong to moral rights reasoning, even without fault on the part of the seller, nevertheless, could be defended on the ground that 'wrong', ultimately, is a moral concept. It denotes that the seller has done something bad, something that society would generally disapprove of. The fact that the law regards a defective performance as a wrong, also, must have a basis in this. Thus, even if there is no requirement

[107] An exception may be made with regard to commodity sales, where other issues (such as certainty) may play a greater role. Further discussion of these is outside the scope of the thesis.

[108] See above, p 48.

[109] Though a reversal of the burden of proof (so that the debtor has to prove that he was *not* at fault) means that in practice liability is more or less strict. Compare BS Markesinis, H Unberath and A Johnston, *The German Law of Contract*, 2nd edn (Oxford, Hart Publishing, 2006) 445–6; Hartkamp, *Asser IV(I) Verbintenissenrecht* (n 16 above) [314]–[317].

[110] AG Guest (ed), *Benjamin's Sale of Goods*, 7th edn (London, Sweet & Maxwell, 2006) [12-017].

of fault to hold sellers liable in individual cases, there appears to be a general policy underlying the law that says that defective performance is a bad thing—a 'wrong'. Instead of a moral wrong, however, the defective performance has taken on the guise of a civil wrong, ie an action that is wrong simply because the law provides that it is. In effect, this development could be seen as a watering down of moral rights reasoning—the notion of a moral wrong is expanded to actions which would generally be regarded as bad practice on the part of the seller, even though no actual fault need be proven with regard to the seller's wrongdoing.

The question is how this applies to failure in performance or breach of contract: are they considered 'wrongs' for which the seller should in some way be punished? It may be said that 'remedy' supposes something unpleasant which needs making better, a grievance which requires relief.[111] In this sense, it would seem to respond to a wrong, or at least something that would be regarded as a civil wrong. Birks has taken the view that breach, indeed, is a wrong and he has made the following observation with regard to specific performance:

> Contract, a manifestation of consent—as opposed to breach of contract, a wrong—generates rights which English law will, under certain conditions, order to be specifically performed. Specific performance functions on the primary plane. It could, with little enough trouble, be represented as a response to the wrong of breach. But at the moment that is not the law, and only dogmatic insistence on a monopoly of wrongs could necessitate a change. It is the not-wrong of making a contract which generates the primary right realised when a court orders, and then if necessary enforces, specific performance.[112]

In other words, rights that find their basis in contractual consent, such as specific performance, are regarded as (responses to) 'not-wrongs' and do not, therefore, bring up the question of moral justification.

Nevertheless, does this mean that the opposite is also true—that breach should be regarded as a wrong? Can this be extended to failure in performance as well? And if so, should this have consequences for the breaching/non-performing party's position? It is thought that there are good reasons to support the view that failure or breach is wrong. At the same time, however, it is submitted that the fact that failure or breach may be regarded as a wrong does not necessarily wipe out the breaching/non-performing party's, ie the seller's, right to cure.

A civil wrong, according to Birks, is 'the breach of a duty owed to another at common law or in equity', including duties under statutes and under contracts.[113] Since the binding nature of contractual obligations appears to have a moral basis, as explained earlier, it would seem that the non-performance of a contractual obligation should be regarded as a wrong. In the classification

[111] Compare Birks, 'Rights, Wrongs and Remedies' (n 29 above) 25.
[112] *Ibid*, 27.
[113] *Ibid*, 31.

made earlier,[114] 'non-performance' would include breach as well as failure in performance. In other words, situations of non-delivery and situations of non-conformity would be covered.

However, the fact that the non-compliance with a legal duty is looked upon with disapproval within the legal system does not tell us to what extent this will have an effect on the remedial position of the breaching/non-performing party. According to Birks,

> [t]he label 'wrong' operates as a licence to the law to mistreat the wrongdoer. The entitlements which the law can accord to the victim of the wrong are, so to say, at large, at least until the range has been narrowed by authority, statutory or otherwise.[115]

This, indeed, would appear to be the instinctive response to a wrong committed by a party against another. Like the *talio* in Roman law, one who harms another may expect the same in retribution—'an eye for an eye, a tooth for a tooth'.

However, it was argued earlier that the basis for performance-oriented remedies should be sought in the prevention of infringement of individual rights, rather than in the correction of wrongs through compensation.[116] Thus, the main concern should be to ensure that the aggrieved party obtains the performance that he contracted for. Punishment of the wrongdoing party should be a concern of a secondary nature.

Applied to the position of the seller who performs defectively, it seems that completely to negate his right to cure would be using the 'wrong' as a 'licence to mistreat the wrongdoer'. Therefore, while the efficiency policy is regarded as insufficient for the justification of the scope and form of contract law, moral rights reasoning on its own also cannot account for the availability of remedies in contract law. It is submitted that, when balanced against the performance interest of the buyer and the economic interests of the seller, the moral argument is nothing more than a factor in the equation. Applied to cure, the argument runs as follows.

While, with regard to the remedies of the buyer, performance-oriented remedies appear to have a clear advantage over expectation damages,[117] no such preference would appear to exist in situations where the seller seeks to insist on cure. After all, in those cases the seller's preference for cure generally competes with the buyer's wish to have a remedy in damages. The fact that the buyer is willing to accept damages instead of performance suggests that a monetary award, in this situation, adequately protects the performance interest of the buyer. Nevertheless, cure would have the same result, for it would give the buyer the actual performance that he contracted for.[118] Thus, expectation

[114] Above, p 54.

[115] Birks, 'Rights, Wrongs and Remedies' (n 29 above) 33.

[116] Above, pp 59 ff.

[117] See above, p 60.

[118] That is, assuming that cure can be effected successfully. If the seller fails to cure within a reasonable time, the remedy will of course no longer be thought equal to other remedies, and the buyer will become entitled to remedies such as termination and damages; see . Until cure has proved unsuccessful, however, the argument appears to be valid.

damages and cure are equal remedies in this situation. Where this is the case, it may be thought that

> selecting a standard remedy must involve the invocation of 'some other value'—other, that is, than that (or those) which serves to justify the binding force of promises in the first place or which follows from such a justification.[119]

Since the moral criterion here discussed is related to the bindingness of promises, this is unlikely to be the 'other value' that can be invoked to select a remedy. Considerations of economic efficiency or protection of the performance interest, however, may be able to fulfill this function. For example, where the avoidance of economic waste is taken as a guideline, a strong case can be made for the availability of cure.

To what extent the moral criterion does influence the scope of cure, however, is a difficult question. Since the seller, unlike an innocent party seeking specific performance, is the wrongdoing party, it may be thought that the scope of his remedy should be more limited than the buyer's entitlement to a performance-oriented remedy. This may be reflected in the limits to cure, eg unreasonable inconvenience or unreasonable expense to the buyer may be assumed more quickly than disproportionality to the seller would be assumed in relation to specific performance. To what extent national sale of goods laws make this distinction will be discussed in a later chapter.[120]

IV. CONCLUSION

This chapter has sought to lay down a theoretical framework for performance-oriented remedies in sales law, which is intended to form the basis for the comparison between different national and international instruments following in chapters four to seven. A number of guidelines have been derived from contract theory that may help identify common underlying principles in these instruments that could be a basis for harmonisation.

Kantian theory underlying civil law rules of contract law, as well as rights-based theories underlying the common law, support the general availability of performance-oriented remedies in sales law. With the performance interest as its primary guiding principle, it justifies not only the bindingness of contractual obligations. Also, it shows that performance-oriented remedies may be best equipped to protect this interest and that they should therefore be generally available alongside other remedies that may reflect the performance interest, such as damages. It is up to the parties to make a choice between the remedies.

Furthermore, it is thought that the performance-oriented remedies—specific performance, cure, repair and replacement—should be of general availability in

[119] Craswell, 'Contract Law, Default Rules, and the Philosophy of Promising' (n 58 above); compare Kimel, *From Promise to Contract* (n 10 above) 93.

[120] See ch 7, pp 192 ff.

cases of non-delivery as well as in cases of non-conformity of goods. It is submitted that, in this respect, no distinction should be made between primary rights deriving from the contract and remedies coming into existence at a secondary stage. The fact that the delivery obligation is laid down directly in the contract, whereas the conformity obligation is not, should not in itself restrict the availability of performance-oriented remedies. This point will be explored further in a later chapter.[121]

Finally, the interests of the party against whom a remedy is sought may be protected by taking into account efficiency factors and, to a limited extent, moral arguments. Where the objective is to find the most appropriate remedy, considerations of economic efficiency may help to establish whether a remedy is disproportionate or not. Thus, a balancing exercise can be made between, on the one hand, the performance interest of the party seeking the remedy (often the buyer) and, on the other hand, the economic interests of the other party (in that case the seller). The economic interests of the seller, also, may provide a justification for awarding cure, as long as it protects the performance interest of the buyer. Since moral arguments, in this case, may suggest that the right to cure should be limited—seeing that the seller is the breaching/non-performing party—the disproportionality test may be applied in a somewhat wider sense here than in relation to the buyer. In other words, the seller may have to give way to the buyer's preferences sooner than would happen the other way around.

The following chapters will seek to determine to what extent existing rules reflect these principles and to what extent they may provide a starting point for future harmonisation. The first of the performance-oriented remedies to be considered is specific performance, which is the primary right that enables the buyer to obtain the performance that he contracted for. The two related remedies, repair and replacement, will be subject of the next chapter. Finally, chapters six and seven will examine the seller's right to cure.

[121] See ch 5, pp 120–23.

4

The Buyer's Entitlement to Specific Performance

I. INTRODUCTION

SHOULD A BUYER have the right to obtain performance from the seller if the latter does not perform satisfactorily? A comparison between common law and civil law does not lead to one inescapable answer. In fact, there is no denying that the different ideological bases of common law and civil law make themselves felt in the law on specific performance. The common law, to a large extent, chooses a pragmatic approach that takes as its guideline the achievement of the economically most beneficial results. The limited role of specific performance resulting from this fits in with the common law conception of contract as principally a means of facilitating market operations,[1] by which view damages are seen as the principal remedy for breach. The civil law, on the other hand, tends to put the emphasis on the binding nature of obligations and on this basis entertains a more liberal view of the scope of specific performance. Thus, while civilian systems show a greater commitment to specific performance, the common law view is that a promisee can only obtain specific performance at the discretion of the court—a discretion which is exercised very narrowly. Only if damages are inadequate are common law courts normally willing to award specific performance.

However, despite the different premises from which the systems begin, the underlying principles on which the rules are based appear to be more similar than this outward divergence suggests—and may thus provide a starting point for harmonisation of European sales law.[2] To some extent, similarities deriving from these principles may already be reflected in the current rules on specific performance, for example in those that limit the scope of the remedy. Nevertheless, while these similarities exist, a careful examination of the different sales laws is necessary to determine how close current systems are and which

[1] Compare J Adams and R Brownsword, 'The Ideologies of Contract Law' (1987) 7 *Legal Studies* 205 at 222. Also, A Burrows, *Remedies for Torts and Breach of Contract*, 3rd edn (Oxford, Oxford University Press, 2004) 20–22. The theory of 'efficient breach', which seeks to explain contractual relationships on the basis of economic theory, however, has not taken off in England the way it has in the United States. Compare ch 3, p 62.

[2] Compare ch 3, p 48.

rules may form the starting point for harmonisation. It has been put forward by Lord Hoffmann in *Co-operative Insurance Society Ltd v Argyll Stores (Holdings) Ltd* that

> [s]pecific performance is traditionally regarded in English law as an exceptional remedy, as opposed to the common law damages to which a successful plaintiff is entitled as of right . . . By contrast, in countries with legal systems based on civil law, such as France, Germany and Scotland, the plaintiff is prima facie entitled to specific performance. The cases in which he is confined to a claim for damages are regarded as the exceptions. In practice, however, there is less difference between common law and civilian systems than these general statements might lead one to suppose. The principles upon which English judges exercise the discretion to grant specific performance are reasonably well settled and depend upon a number of considerations, mostly of a practical nature, which are of very general application. I have made no investigation of civilian systems, but a priori I would expect that judges take much the same matters into account in deciding whether specific performance would be inappropriate in a particular case.[3]

The suggestion is, thus, that the practical application of the rules may lead to similar results, since the courts, allegedly, take into account similar considerations in deciding whether the remedy is appropriate. Nevertheless, while this seems an attractive approach to take, it is doubtful whether the matter is this straightforward—as Lord Hoffmann concedes, this is merely a general statement and no further investigation had been made of the factors taken into consideration by judges in civil law countries or, for that matter, Scotland. While the appropriateness of specific performance may, at least superficially, be judged on similar grounds in these systems as compared to English law, the problem of the different premises may not be put aside so easily. Contrasts between the English and the Scots approach to specific performance, in particular, highlight that a divergence remains, with decisions recently having come down from the Scottish courts expressly addressing, and rejecting, the restrictive application of the remedy in English law.[4] This tension is likely to be felt also in the comparison with German and Dutch law.

Against this background, this chapter will critically assess the availability of specific performance in common law and civil law systems, and will seek to formulate a framework for future harmonisation that may be applied to both types of system. Two points need addressing: (i) the general basis on which specific performance should or should not be made available to the buyer, and (ii) the more specific considerations taken into account by the courts when deciding whether or not to refuse an order for specific performance. While the latter considerations—the restrictions on specific performance—may be similar in

[3] *Co-operative Insurance Society Ltd v Argyll Stores (Holdings) Ltd* [1998] AC 1 (HL) (*Co-operative Insurance Society*) 11–12.

[4] For example in *Highland and Universal Properties Ltd v Safeway Properties Ltd* 2000 SLT 414 (IHCS). See further below, p 105.

common law and civil law systems,[5] the point is more difficult to argue in relation to the first issue. The distinctly different premises of the common law and civil law approaches appear to have a real impact in practice, making the remedy more available in the latter. Nevertheless, it will be argued that Lord Hoffmann's statement may lay bare the basis for future harmonisation, as long as two arguments are accepted.

First, it will be argued that, as a matter of general law, there are signs of convergence in the approaches to specific performance found in European systems. This chapter aims to show that civilian systems are as much influenced by notions of economic efficiency as the common law in their approach to specific performance, and that, at the same time, the common law has started to pay greater heed to the protection of the so-called 'performance interest' of the buyer, which may eventually result in a wider availability of specific performance. In order to identify these underlying policies, the first section of the chapter will seek to demonstrate a shift in English law towards a wider scope for specific performance, while the second section will focus on civilian systems and will highlight the increasing importance of efficiency influences in these systems. Thus, even though the starting points for the availability of specific performance are different—that is, it is generally available in civil law systems, whereas in common law systems it is only available at the discretion of the court—the systems are shaped by similar underlying policies. Similarities may also be discerned in the restrictions on specific performance adopted in both systems. However, as the third section of the chapter will show, the restrictions remain subsidiary to the general premise adopted for the availability of specific performance, and as such have very little influence on the wider or narrower availability of the remedy in common law and civil law systems. The final section of the chapter will therefore go back to the first level, relating to the general availability of specific performance. It is thought that the difference in the availability of specific performance is a result of a different weight accorded to the economic and performance-oriented interests. Future harmonisation of European sale of goods law, it will be argued, should balance these out in favour of a general right to specific performance, for only this will guarantee that the buyer has access to it where it would be the most appropriate remedy. In combination with the proper limitations to the availability of specific performance in appropriate situations, this would serve to protect the performance interest of the buyer to the greatest possible extent, whilst at the same time serving the goal of economic efficiency. As will be seen, it is also the approach adopted by existing uniform rules applying to sale of goods cases.

Secondly, an impulse for change has been given by the Consumer Sales Directive.[6] It has introduced two performance-oriented remedies—repair and

[5] Though the overlap is not complete and there may be individual cases in which different results are reached in otherwise similar cases, see further p 105 below.

[6] Directive (EC) 99/44 of the European Parliament and of the Council on certain aspects of the sale of consumer goods and associated guarantees [1999] OJ L171/12 (Consumer Sales Directive).

replacement—which are related to specific performance. Though the effects of the Directive have been less dramatic in England than for example in German law, the introduction of the remedies of repair and replacement has shifted the balance of the remedial scheme. It will be argued that it can be regarded as giving greater prominence to the performance interest of the buyer. The link between specific performance and these two remedies will be explored in the next chapter, which will also focus on similarities in the restrictions on the remedies.

II. THE BASIS FOR SPECIFIC PERFORMANCE IN ENGLISH SALE OF GOODS LAW

The 'performance interest' denotes the interest of a promisee in obtaining performance.[7] The protection of this interest has been said to be the general starting point for English courts in their assessment of damages for breach of contract.[8] The aim of the remedy is to put the aggrieved party in the position that he would have been in had the contract been performed according to its terms.[9] This can be done in a number of ways, one of which is to award damages for the difference in value between the performance for which a party contracted and the performance which he received. Another is the payment of damages for the cost of cure, which enables a party to obtain the performance for which he contracted.[10] The latter method is committed to enabling the claimant to obtain performance itself rather than the economic value of performance.[11] It may be questioned, however, to what extent the courts are willing to protect this interest. Recent case law shows a reluctance on the part of the judges to award damages for the cost of cure where the party seeking the remedy has no direct financial interest in the performance of the contract,[12] or is said to have no interest in actual performance of the contract.[13]

The courts' hesitance in awarding damages on the basis of cost of cure is mirrored in their restrictive attitude towards specific performance. The remedy has a long history in English law. It was first developed in the Courts of Chancery but, by the beginning of the fifteenth century, had become a useful alternative to the common law remedy of damages for breach of contract.[14] The main difference between that remedy and specific performance, however, is that the latter

[7] D Friedmann, 'The Performance Interest in Contract Damages' (1995) 111 *Law Quarterly Review* 628; see also ch 3, p 46.

[8] The classical authority for this is *Robinson v Harman* (1848) 1 Ex 850, 855. See E McKendrick, *Contract Law: Text, Cases and Materials*, 2nd edn (Oxford, Oxford University Press, 2005) 1017.

[9] Burrows, *Remedies for Torts and Breach of Contract* (n 1 above) 33.

[10] McKendrick, *Contract Law: Text, Cases and Materials* (n 8 above) 1017.

[11] *Ibid.*

[12] *Alfred McAlpine Construction Ltd v Panatown Ltd* [2000] UKHL 43, [2001] 1 AC 518 (*Panatown*).

[13] *Ruxley Electronics and Construction Ltd v Forsyth* [1996] AC 344 (HL) (*Ruxley*).

[14] G Jones and W Goodhart, *Specific Performance*, 2nd edn (London, Butterworths, 1996) 6.

has never been generally available but is only available at the discretion of the court. For the sale of goods, this is reflected in section 52(1) of the Sale of Goods Act 1979 (SGA), which provides:

> In any action for breach of contract to deliver specific or ascertained goods the court may, if it thinks fit, on the plaintiff's application, by its judgment or decree direct that the contract shall be performed specifically, without giving the defendant the option of retaining the goods on payment of damages.

To date, the courts have only made sparing use of their discretion, and the scope of specific performance in sale of goods cases has been limited. An order for specific performance will generally only be made if damages are inadequate—it is a necessary condition for the making of such an order.[15] Within the confines of this test, the main factors determining the availability of the remedy have in particular been the uniqueness of the goods and the (related) availability of substitutes in the market. Though there are many instances in which the results reached by means of this test are justifiable, the case law has shown that there are limits to the test, which may in certain circumstances lead to very harsh outcomes for buyers seeking to enforce performance.

Interestingly, section 52(1) of the SGA applies in Scots law as well, though only supplementary to, and not in derogation of, the right of specific implement.[16] The practical significance of the provision in this jurisdiction seems limited, seeing that as a general premise specific implement will be available to the promisee. A discretion for the courts to refuse the remedy was introduced in the late nineteenth century,[17] but this of course applies to the grounds for refusal of the remedy rather than to the initial question of its availability. Nevertheless, the provision highlights the possibility of cross-fertilisation between the systems. Similarities may for example be observed in the bars to specific implement developed in the Scots courts: impossibility, relative non-significance of the subject-matter of the contract combined with adequacy of damages, and the personal nature of the contract.[18] Despite this, the scope of the remedy remains wider in Scots law and one may wonder which approach is preferable.

The restrictive scope of specific performance in English contract law may be criticised on several grounds.[19] General criticisms relate to the fact that damages are often under-compensatory, or can be hard to assess. Further, it is said that specific performance gives the buyer exactly what he contracted for, whereas damages can at best provide a monetary equivalent. These arguments show that English law may have a less than satisfactory commitment not only to the

[15] Burrows, *Remedies for Torts and Breach of Contract* (n 1 above) 547; McKendrick, *Contract Law: Text, Cases and Materials* (n 8 above) 1141.

[16] Sale of Goods Act s 52(4).

[17] A Smith, 'Specific Implement' in K Reid and R Zimmermann (eds), *A History of Private Law in Scotland. Vol 2. Obligations* (Oxford, Oxford University Press, 2000) 195 at 206.

[18] Compare HL MacQueen and J Thomson, *Contract Law in Scotland* (Edinburgh, Butterworths, 2000) 221. See also below, pp 105–6.

[19] Compare A Schwartz, 'The Case for Specific Performance' (1979) 89 *Yale Law Journal* 271.

performance interest per se, ie a party's interest in *obtaining* performance, but also to that party's interest in *enforcing* performance. For there are instances in which the performance interest deserves to be protected, and where the only satisfactory way of achieving that is to enable the claimant to enforce performance of the contractual obligations by the defaulting party. In sale of goods cases, this may be because of the nature of the goods sold, but also because of circumstances that put an unreasonable burden on the buyer should he not obtain the remedy, eg in situations where the goods can be deemed 'commercially unique'. Further, consumer-buyers may attach additional value to their purchases that cannot easily be compensated for through an award of damages. This is called the 'consumer surplus'.[20]

So far, English law has only sporadically taken such criticisms to heart. The case law shows glimpses of situations in which the courts may be willing to make specific performance more generally available. That there is room for a widening of the scope of the remedy, however, is evident from the cases in which the courts have taken into account whether an order for specific performance would be the most 'appropriate' remedy.[21] Support for a widening of the scope of the remedy, furthermore, may be found in amendments made to the SGA as a result of the Sale and Supply of Goods to Consumers Regulations 2002.[22] These implement the Consumer Sales Directive in English law, and introduce new remedies for consumers in the form of repair and replacement, which are enforceable through an order for specific performance.

English law, therefore, may be beginning to show a move away from the traditional highly economics-oriented approach that ensures swift, commercially useful solutions but that at the same time may not do full justice to the performance interest. It is submitted that this is an approach that should be encouraged. A wider availability of specific performance will ensure protection of the performance interest to a greater extent than the current law does. Further, if the boundaries to the remedy are set in the right place, this should not lead to significantly less efficient results from an economic perspective. Current authorities on specific performance support this theory—an overview of the case law shows that many deficiencies that are part of the damages remedy could have been cured by an order for specific performance.

As an aside—the cases here discussed deal with situations of non-delivery rather than with the delivery of defective goods. However, it is thought that the principles in them may be transposed to situations of non-conformity to the extent that the buyer is dependent on the delivery of conforming goods. In those

[20] D Harris, A Ogus and J Phillips, 'Contract Remedies and the Consumer Surplus' (1979) 95 *Law Quarterly Review* 581.

[21] Most famously in *Beswick v Beswick* [1968] AC 58 (HL). For an overview of other cases see AS Burrows, 'Specific performance at the crossroads' [1984] *Legal Studies* 102; McKendrick, *Contract Law: Text, Cases and Materials* (n 8 above) 1141–2; ICF Spry, *Equitable Remedies*, 6th edn (Sydney, LBC Information Services, 2001) 60.

[22] Sale and Supply of Goods to Consumers Regulations 2002 (SI 2002/3045) (SSGCR 2002).

circumstances, the buyer will be equally disadvantaged where he receives goods that do not conform to what he contracted for as where he receives no goods at all. In either situation, the fact that the buyer has not received the goods that he contracted for will leave him in a disadvantaged position. There are some differences between situations of non-conformity and situations of non-delivery, but these do not affect the availability of specific performance. For example, the buyer may resort to a wider range of remedies in cases of non-conformity, eg he may seek a reduction of the price.[23] Furthermore, where goods have been delivered, the buyer may opt to accept the goods rather than reject them, which is likely to influence the measure of damages. However, where the conformity of the goods is of importance to the buyer, he is unlikely to accept unsatisfactory goods. Thus, in those cases, the situation will be similar to situations of non-delivery.

1. Unique Goods and Section 52 of the SGA

Traditionally, English courts would only use their discretion to order specific performance in cases involving 'unique' goods. The reasoning behind this was that, unlike in cases where substitute goods were available and a buyer could go out into the market to obtain these, unique goods were not easily replaceable and an award of damages would therefore not adequately compensate the buyer.[24] Thus, goods that could be ordinarily obtained in the market could not be the subject of an order for specific performance.[25] For example, in *Cohen v Roche*,[26] delivery up of a set of chairs was refused on the grounds that the chairs in question were 'ordinary Hepplewhite furniture' and 'possessed no special features at all'.[27]

The introduction of a statutory provision intending to broaden the scope of the remedy[28]—now to be found in section 52 of the SGA—at first had little effect on the practice of the courts with regard to specific performance. The section provides that a court may, if it thinks fit, order specific performance in an action for breach of a contract to deliver 'specific or ascertained goods'.[29] According to Lord Hanworth MR in *Re Wait*—for a long time the leading case on the scope of specific performance in sale of goods cases—'the section reproduces the old

[23] Compare SGA ss 51 and 53.

[24] Compare Burrows, *Remedies for Torts and Breach of Contract* (n 1 above) 459–60.

[25] *Re Wait* [1927] 633 (CA).

[26] *Cohen v Roche* [1927] 1 KB 169 (KBD) 179.

[27] Classic examples of unique goods are heirlooms, works of art, and rare antiques. Compare *Somerset v Cookson* (1735) 3 PWms 390; *Lowther v Lowther* (1806) 3 Ves 95; *Falcke v Gray* (1859) 4 Drew 651, 658; and *Pusey v Pusey* (1864) 1 Vern 273.

[28] Mercantile Law Amendment Act 1856 s 2. E Peel (ed), *Treitel on the Law of Contract*, 12th edn (London, Sweet & Maxwell, 2007) [21-023].

[29] SGA s 52(1). See p 81 above.

law in a codifying statute. It has not changed the law'.[30] Atkin LJ, in the same case, put forward the even more restrictive view that 'in contracts for the sale of goods the only remedy by way of specific performance is the statutory remedy'.[31] Developments in legislation and case law, however, have challenged the continuing applicability of these statements to modern sale of goods cases. On the one hand, a 1995 amendment of the SGA has significantly widened the scope of section 52, so that the category of 'specific' goods now includes certain categories of goods forming part of a bulk.[32] Furthermore, the courts themselves have gone some way towards awarding specific performance in a wider category of cases, even if these are outside the scope of section 52. Thus, in extraordinary circumstances, an order for specific performance can sometimes be made in relation to unascertained goods, when these are thought to be 'commercially unique'.[33]

2. Commercial Uniqueness

'Commercial uniqueness' has been recognised as a ground on which specific performance may be ordered if the circumstances of the case are such that buying substitutes would be so difficult or would cause such delay that the claimant's business would be seriously disrupted.[34] In these circumstances, damages would be an inadequate remedy for they would be

> a poor consolation if the failure of supplies forces a trader to lay off staff and disappoint his customers (whose affections may be transferred to others) and ultimately impels him towards insolvency.[35]

The concept has been applied to specific and ascertained goods, as well as occasionally to unascertained goods.[36]

Though the factors taken into account in a 'commercial uniqueness' test stem mainly from the overarching principle that inadequacy of damages justifies an

[30] *Re Wait* (n 25 above) 617. The case was decided under s 52 of the Sale of Goods Act 1893, which with some minor alterations was reproduced in the SGA 1979.

[31] *Re Wait* (n 25 above) 630. This statement is hard to reconcile with cases in which the granting of the remedy was contemplated in an action brought by the seller, rather than the buyer. Compare Jones and Goodhart, *Specific Performance* (n 14 above) 147–9.

[32] Sale of Goods (Amendment) Act 1995 s 2(d), amending s 61(1) SGA. Generally on this amendment: T Burns, 'Better Late than Never: the Reform of the Law on the Sale of Goods Forming Part of a Bulk' (1996) 59 *Modern Law Review* 260; J Ulph, 'The Sale of Goods (Amendment) Act 1995: Co-ownership and the Rogue Seller' [1996] *Lloyds Maritime and Commercial Law Quarterly* 93; R Bradgate and F White, 'Sale of Goods Forming Part of a Bulk: Proposals for Reform' [1994] *Lloyds Maritime and Commercial Law Quarterly* 315.

[33] Compare *Sky Petroleum v VIP Petroleum* [1974] 1 WLR 576 (Ch), in which the court granted an interim injunction, which leads substantially to the same result as an order for specific performance; see pp 86 ff below.

[34] Burrows, *Remedies for Torts and Breach of Contract* (n 1 above) 461–5; Burrows 'Specific performance at the crossroads' (n 21 above) 103–4. Compare Peel (ed), *Treitel on the Law of Contract* (n 28 above) [21-025].

[35] *Howard E Perry & Co Ltd v British Railways Bd* [1980] 1 WLR 1375 (Ch) 1377, 1383.

[36] See below p 86.

order for specific performance, the case law at the same time shows the courts referring to factors that may indicate a broader notion of the scope of specific performance. It may be ordered if it is the most 'appropriate' remedy in a given case.[37] The fact that the courts have so far not explicitly referred to the test as one of 'appropriateness'—engaged as they are with the notion of inadequacy of damages as a determinant for the availability of specific performance—has obscured the significance of factors other than those relating to the adequacy of damages. It has been said that the shift to an 'appropriateness' test may be no more than a change of label—in the majority of cases, one would expect a court to refuse to make an order for specific performance where damages would be an adequate remedy.[38] However, a closer observation of the reasoning of the courts in commercial uniqueness cases shows the importance of other factors besides the traditional inadequacy of damages test, and, moreover, reveals the weaknesses of the test where the court refuses to take account of wider grounds that may support an order for specific performance. It is submitted that a shift towards an 'appropriate remedy' test would serve to eradicate some of these deficiencies.

a) Value of the Goods to the Buyer

A good example of the different factors at play in commercial uniqueness cases can be found in *Behnke v Bede*.[39] The case concerned the purchase of a British ship by a German shipowner. The ship in question

> was of peculiar and practically unique value to the plaintiff. She was a cheap vessel, being old, having been built in 1892, but her engines and boilers were practically new and such as to satisfy the German regulations, and hence the plaintiff could, as a German shipowner, have her at once put on the German register.[40]

No other comparable ship was available in the market and the buyer wanted the ship for immediate use. On this basis, the court was persuaded to make an order for specific performance, for it did not think that damages would be an adequate compensation in this situation.[41]

One may wonder whether this does not merely show that the value of the goods to the buyer and the inadequacy of damages are two sides of the same coin: if the goods are of practically unique value to the buyer, then surely the availability of substitutes in the market is likely to be scarce and damages would be inadequate. The value of the goods to the buyer, from this point of view, is merely an aspect of the unique identity of the goods that makes damages an inadequate remedy. However, even if a comparable ship had been available,

[37] Compare McKendrick, *Contract Law: Text, Cases and Materials* (n 8 above) 1140.
[38] *Ibid.*
[39] *Behnke v Bede* [1927] 1 KB 649 (KBD).
[40] *Ibid*, 661.
[41] *Ibid.*

could one still not say that the purchase of this particular ship was of such value to the buyer that an order for specific performance would be the more appropriate remedy? The disadvantage of having to locate another comparable ship, which may be difficult since it has such particular characteristics, and the effort of having to bargain for that ship are factors that should not be put on the buyer simply because the seller does not live up to his promise to deliver the ship.

b) Temporary Unavailability of Substitutes

The temporary unavailability of substitutes has also been a ground on which the courts have recognised 'commercial uniqueness', though it has still mostly been linked to the well-known inadequacy of damages test. In *Sky Petroleum v VIP Petroleum*,[42] for example, an interim injunction was granted restraining the defendant sellers from withholding supplies of petroleum to the buyers. Though effectively amounting to a temporary order for specific performance for the delivery of unascertained goods, Goulding J believed that such an exception to the general rule could be justified in the light of the unusual circumstances of the case.[43] The market for petrol and motor fuel was in a state of crisis in 1973, making it impossible for a buyer to obtain alternative supplies in the market. Since the sellers were the only source of supply for the buyers' filling stations, a termination of the contract would have severe consequences, possibly forcing the buyers out of business.[44] Therefore, damages would not be an adequate remedy—an injunction was granted.[45]

Similar circumstances persuaded Sir Robert Megarry V-C to order the delivery up of certain consignments of steel in *Howard E Perry & Co Ltd v British Railways Board*.[46] The steel, belonging to the plaintiffs, was stored in two of the board's depots. A strike of steelworkers, however, prevented the plaintiffs from receiving the steel, since the defendants' road carriers refused to cross picket lines. Furthermore, the board refused to permit the plaintiffs, with their own vehicles, equipment and employees, to enter the depots and remove the steel

[42] *Sky Petroleum v VIP Petroleum* (n 33 above).

[43] *Ibid*, 578.

[44] *Ibid*.

[45] However, note that *Sky Petroleum* was a first instance decision that has yet to be followed or approved; (but see *Redler Grain Silos Ltd v BICC Ltd* [1982] 1 Lloyd's Rep 435 (CA)). Furthermore, the order of an interim injunction in respect of unascertained goods is an exception to the general rule, justified by the particular circumstances of this case. Even in respect of specific and ascertained goods, the approach of the courts towards 'commercial uniqueness' is far from settled; Burrows, *Remedies for Torts and Breach of Contract* (n 1 above) 463.

[46] *Howard E Perry & Co Ltd v British Railways Bd* [1980] 1 WLR 1375 (Ch). 'Delivery up' is comparable to specific performance, though it can only be ordered if the property in the goods has passed to the buyer; s 3 of the Torts (Interference with Goods) Act 1977. Nevertheless, the court has a discretion whether or not to make an order for delivery up, which 'rests upon a footing which fully accords with s 52 of the Sale of Goods Act, 1893'; *Cohen v Roche* (n 26 above) 181. Cf AG Guest (ed), *Benjamin's Sale of Goods*, 7th edn (London, Sweet & Maxwell, 2006) [17-098].

themselves.[47] Since the steel was not readily available on the open market, damages would not have been an adequate remedy.

However, it is thought that the non-availability of substitute goods can also lead to a situation in which specific performance could be granted, not merely on the basis of inadequacy of damages but on the ground that it is actually the appropriate remedy. A case in which wider factors were considered is the Court of Appeal decision in *Société des Industries Métallurgiques SA v The Bronx Engineering Co Ltd*,[48] though in the particular circumstances of the case the court refused to make an order for specific performance. The case concerned the sale of certain machinery by an English engineering company to a Tunisian company. After a dispute had arisen between the parties, the sellers purported to release themselves from the contract by accepting an alleged repudiation by the buyers. This would leave them at liberty to sell the machinery to a Canadian buyer at a substantially enhanced price. The buyers sought to prevent this course of action by bringing an action for specific performance, and furthermore, by seeking an injunction restraining the sellers from removing the machinery from the jurisdiction. The Court of Appeal dismissed the actions, even though this left the buyers facing a 9–12 months delay to obtain new machinery. Though sympathising with the difficult position that the buyers found themselves in, Lord Edmund Davies concluded that he saw 'nothing which removes this case from the ordinary run of cases arising out of commercial contracts where damages are claimed'.[49]

It is striking that, while the court recognised that the machinery that was the subject-matter of the contract was not 'an ordinary article of commerce',[50] it refused to make an order for specific performance. The special nature of the goods would seem to indicate that they might not easily be substituted and that they could therefore be regarded as 'commercially unique'. In comparison to, for example, *Sky Petroleum* and *Howard E Perry* did the aggrieved buyers not suffer similar losses to the buyers in those cases? Nevertheless, it appears that the reason for the court's denying specific performance in this case was that the defendants were not the only manufacturers of this type of machinery—in other words, the goods were less scarce than the oil or the steel that was in issue in the other cases. In theory, therefore, substitute goods were available in the market and on this basis damages were an adequate remedy. However, in so holding, it is thought that the court overlooked the practical aspects of the refusal of specific performance. It appears that the availability of substitutes was, due to the 9–12 months delay, more theoretical than real.

What the decision shows, therefore, is that the courts may fail to reach the appropriate result if they refuse to attach sufficient weight to wider factors than

[47] *Howard E Perry & Co Ltd v British Railways Bd* (n 35 above) 1377.

[48] *Société des Industries Métallurgiques SA v The Bronx Engineering Co Lt* [1975] 1 Lloyd's Rep 465 (CA) *(Bronx Engineering)*.

[49] *Ibid*.

[50] *Ibid*, 468.

the adequacy of damages. Even if damages *were* adequate, it may be argued that specific performance would have been a more appropriate remedy. Even though the defendants in the present case were not the only manufacturers of this type of machinery, which therefore lacked the unique quality of the ship in *Behnke*,[51] no substitute machinery was available without a 9–12 months delay. Thus, although damages would have enabled the buyers eventually to obtain new machinery, for the time being specific performance would have seemed the more appropriate remedy, as it would have avoided further economic loss on the part of the buyers, who were instead left to wrestle with the commercial difficulties and added loss and expense caused by the delay.[52]

These criticisms lend support to the proposition that an 'appropriateness' test is called for which takes into account wider considerations than the traditional test of inadequacy of damages. The focus should be not merely on the availability of substitute goods in the market but also on the practical consequences faced by the buyer in obtaining these substitutes and the economic loss suffered as a result of these. As *Bronx Engineering* shows, a too rigorous application of the adequacy of damages test will lead to decisions that are hard to defend from a commercial point of view.

c) Quantification of Damages

Finally, there is one other circumstance in which the appropriateness test may provide a safety net, catching the deficiencies of the adequacy of damages test. It has been held that where the quantification of damages is difficult, this is not a sufficient ground to conclude that damages are an inadequate remedy. In *Bronx Engineering*, for instance, the court recognised the 'considerable difficulty' the buyers might face in quantifying their damages, seeing that the machinery was to be used in a business in Tunis. Nevertheless, neither Lord Edmund Davies, nor Lord Buckley found this a sufficient ground to conclude that damages were an inadequate remedy in this case; it was the natural hazard of litigation.[53] It may be questioned, however, whether the difficulty of quantification could not have been a ground for deciding that specific performance was more appropriate.

It seems that the adequacy of damages test leaves very little scope for taking into account difficulties of quantification. Mere difficulty, as seen, was not thought to be enough—only utter *impossibility* of assessing damages might have persuaded the court to hold damages inadequate after all. This, at least, is the conclusion that can be drawn from another case, *Hart v Herwig*.[54] That case

[51] *Behnke v Bede* (n 39 above) p 71.

[52] Compare R Goode, *Commercial Law*, 3rd edn (London, LexisNexis, 2004) 363.

[53] *Bronx Engineering* (n 48 above) 468, 469. See also Jones and Goodhart, *Specific Performance* (n 14 above) 146.

[54] *Hart v Herwig* (1873) LR 8 Ch App 860 (CA) 864, 866. Compare *Fells v Read* (1796) 3 Ves 70, 71–72.

dealt with the purchase of a German ship by an English buyer. The German shipowner was ordered specifically to perform the contract, since it would be impossible for the buyer to prove in Hamburg how much the ship was worth.[55] However, it is difficult to see how the facts of *Bronx Engineering* were different in this respect. If the line between 'very difficult' and 'impossible' is indeed so thin, this might leave a buyer in a very awkward position should the court not be convinced of the utter impossibility of assessing damages. First, since the burden is on the plaintiff to prove his loss, he is seriously disadvantaged if it is 'very difficult' to do so.[56] Furthermore, mitigation efforts on his part may lead to further expense and some of his loss may be deemed speculative or too remote and hence irrecoverable.[57]

Nevertheless, the unwillingness of the courts to widen the scope of the adequacy of damages test on grounds of difficulties of quantification is understandable. As pointed out by McKendrick, the 'adequacy of damages' formula gives rise to concern on a number of grounds.[58] One concern that may apply to the quantification point is that it puts the claimant in an awkward position, for he runs a risk in arguing that the damages to which he is otherwise entitled are inadequate. If the court decides not to exercise its discretion to make a specific performance order, the claimant is left with a measure of damages which, by his own admission, is inadequate. This may be potentially damaging in the further process of assessing the measure of damages, and it would be unfair to put a claimant in the position where he has to make such a concession.

A solution, therefore, may be to adopt a test that takes into account wider factors than the adequacy of damages. Damages could still be held to be inadequate if it were impossible to assess the measure of damages with any degree of accuracy. However, in cases in which the quantification of damages is not impossible, but where it is very difficult to make a correct assessment, the court should not be restricted by the adequacy of damages test, but should be free to award a different remedy if it is more appropriate.

III. A WIDER PERSPECTIVE—SPECIFIC PERFORMANCE IN GERMAN AND DUTCH LAW

Civil law systems start from the premise that specific performance is generally available at the request of the promisee, ie the buyer. It is not merely a remedy of the buyer, it is also a *right* derived from the contract itself—it comes into life at the time of conclusion of the contract and its availability is not dependent solely upon the discretion of the court. The main concern is to enable an

[55] *Hart v Herwig* (n 54 above) 866.
[56] Jones and Goodhart, *Specific Performance* (n 14 above) 146.
[57] *Ibid.*
[58] McKendrick, *Contract Law: Text, Cases and Materials* (n 8 above) 1141.

aggrieved buyer not only to obtain performance, but also to enforce the actual performance that he contracted for by the seller with whom he contracted.

However, how 'generally available' is specific performance in civil law systems? Like the common law, civil law systems recognise restrictions on the availability of the remedy. While they appear to be of a general nature, it may be argued that they are mainly concerned with factors of an economic nature and that, in this respect, they resemble the common law. The search for an 'appropriate' remedy may start from a different premise, but ultimately it appears to rest on similar principles. This may offer a basis for harmonisation of the laws on specific performance in European sales laws.

1. General Availability of Specific Performance

The Dutch and German sale of goods laws are closely related. The Dutch Civil Code is one of the most recent re-codifications of private law in Europe,[59] and it combines elements of some of the major civilian traditions within Europe. Parts of it breathe the traditional principles derived from the French Code Civil, enacted in the Low Countries in Napoleonic times, that have stood the test of time and still find application in modern-day sales; other, newer rules find their origin in the Germanic traditions, in which the drafters of the new *Burgerlijk Wetboek* (*BW*) have found their main source of inspiration. Furthermore, Dutch and German law have both been influenced by international instruments of sales law, such as CISG[60] and the Consumer Sales Directive. The rules of sales law, therefore, are similar in outline.

A general right to enforce performance exists in German law and is called *Leistung*, or *Nacherfüllung* when it refers to the remedies of repair and replacement in the sale of goods law. The promisee's entitlement to performance is reflected in a number of provisions in the civil code, which, in accordance with its layered structure, range from the general to the specific. The general definition of a contractual entitlement can be gleaned from § 194 I of the *Bürgerliches Gesetzbuch* (*BGB*)—an *Anspruch*, according to this provision, is the right to require another either to do something or to refrain from doing something.[61] The enforceable nature of such entitlements is further defined by provisions in

[59] Title 7.1 on sale and exchange, together with Books 3, 5 and 6 of the new *Burgerlijk Wetboek* (further referred to as *BW*) came into effect on 1 January 1992.

[60] UN Convention on Contracts for the International Sale of Goods (adopted 11 April 1980, entered into force 1 January 1988) 1489 UNTS 3 (CISG). A number of national sales laws have been strongly influenced by CISG and its predecessors, eg Dutch and German sales law, as well as Scandinavian legislation; compare J Hijma, *Asser V(I) Bijzondere Overeenkomsten. Koop en Ruil*, 6th edn (Deventer, WEJ Tjeenk Willink, 2001) [23], [36]; P Schlechtriem, 'Some Observations on the United Nations Convention on Contracts for the International Sale of Goods' in P Birks (ed), *The Frontiers of Liability* (Oxford, Oxford University Press, 1994) 29 at 31.

[61] In German: 'Das Recht, von einem anderen ein Tun oder Unterlassen zu verlangen (Anspruch)'.

the general law of obligations and in the sales provisions of the *BGB*. § 241 I *BGB* provides that, by virtue of the obligation, the promisee is entitled to demand performance from the promisor.[62] For the sale of goods, this is further specified in § 433 I *BGB*, according to which (amongst other things) the seller must procure the thing for the buyer in a state that is free from defects as to quality and defects of title.[63] The provisions lay the basis for the buyer's entitlement to demand performance of the contract in cases of non-delivery. Moreover, they also provide the basis for the remedies of repair and replacement laid down in § 439 *BGB*, which, dogmatically, fall within the scope of these general provisions. While they do not have their direct origin in the contract, the aim of the remedies—to achieve performance of the contractual obligations—makes them inherently similar to the general right of the buyer to demand performance and allows them to be regarded as sub-forms of this right.[64]

Dutch sales law recognises a similar general entitlement for the buyer to insist on performance, or *nakoming* as it is called in Dutch. Based on a rule of general contract law laid down in article 3:296 *BW*, a court order for *nakoming* is available at the request of the promisee in cases where the promisor has obliged himself to give something, to do something, or to refrain from doing something. This provision forms the general basis for a buyer's claim to performance of the contract. Specific provisions relating to remedies for non-conformity in sale of goods cases can be found in article 7:17 *BW*, which sets out the conformity requirements, and article 7:21 *BW*, which lays down the buyer's entitlements to repair and replacement.

In practice, the provisions of the German and Dutch sales laws entail that a buyer will normally be able to enforce delivery in cases where the seller fails to perform, or to obtain an order for repair or replacement in cases where goods delivered turn out to be defective. The nature of the right, which finds its direct origin in the contractual obligation of the seller to perform, means that the buyer may invoke it even if no failure in performance has occurred—though in practice such situations will be rare.[65] It also means that no default notice is required,[66] which is a deviation from the standard rule of German and of Dutch law that remedies only become available once the promisor has been put into default by notice setting an additional time for performance.[67] Unlike in English law, therefore, the right is immediately accessible to the buyer and an order for

[62] In German: 'Kraft des Schuldverhältnisses ist der Gläubiger berechtigt, von dem Schuldner eine Leistung zu fordern'. Compare also § 311 I *BGB*.

[63] 'Der Verkäufer hat dem Käufer die Sache frei von Sach- und Rechtsmängeln zu verschaffen'.

[64] Compare D Reinicke and K Tiedtke, *Kaufrecht* (München, Luchterhand, 2004) [408]; P Huber, 'Der Nacherfüllungsanspruch im neuen Kaufrecht' [2002] *Neue Juristische Wochenschrift* 1004, 1005. See further ch 5, pp 120 ff.

[65] Moreover, if it turns out that the promisor is willing to perform after all, the promisee will have to bear the risk of having to pay the costs of the court proceedings. See Hijma, *Asser V(I) Bijzondere Overeenkomsten* (n 60 above) [373].

[66] *Van der Gun/Farmex*, HR 22 mei 1981, *NJ* 1982, 59.

[67] See further ch 6, p 154.

nakoming will be granted in the majority of cases in which it is sought.[68] Exceptions exist, but in practice they rarely stand in the way of a successful claim for *Leistung* or *nakoming*, or either of its sub-forms.[69]

Two further points emphasise the systems' commitment to specific performance. First, a court will not refuse a claim for performance simply on the ground that, while an obligation exists, the time for its execution has not arrived and therefore no entitlement to enforcement exists at the time the action is brought. Dutch law puts it that in these circumstances the obligation has not become *opeisbaar*—perhaps best translated as not 'claimable' or enforceable.[70] The fact that it may at that time not be enforced, however, does not preclude the court from making a conditional order, to become effective at the time that the requirements for enforcement have been fulfilled. In this, Dutch law differs from English law, where an action for specific performance may be commenced before the contractual date for performance arrives, but only in specific circumstances, such as where a party has stated an intention not to perform the contract.[71] An example of the situations in which Dutch law enables proceedings for specific performance before an obligation has become claimable may be where a claim for return of benefits to the council becomes enforceable at a later time than the receiver's acquisition of an entitlement to other, non-benefit funds. The council may in these circumstances secure its claim, and avoid expiry of its rights, through a conditional court order for specific performance.[72] While similar circumstances are unlikely to occur in sale of goods cases, the notion that performance is fundamentally binding on the parties even where the obligation to perform has not become *opeisbaar* is important in the justification of cure, further to be explored in chapter six.[73]

Secondly—similar in principle but more pronounced in German and in Dutch cases than in English case law—the availability of damages as an alternative to a performance-oriented remedy does not entail that a promisor has a choice between performance and payment of damages. In other words, a seller may not at his discretion refuse performance and buy himself out of the contract by offering damages.[74] A similar restriction applies to the buyer, who may not claim damages instead of performance before the time for performance has expired.[75] Moreover, even after the time for performance has expired, damages

[68] Compare MW Hesselink, *Contractenrecht in Perspectief* (Den Haag, Boom Juridische Uitgevers, 2004) 116.

[69] Hijma, *Asser V(I) Bijzondere Overeenkomsten* (n 60 above) [374]. See further pp 99 ff below.

[70] In German *fällig*. See further ch 6, p 154.

[71] *Hasham v Zenab* [1960] AC 316 (PC). See also Jones and Goodhart, *Specific Performance* (n 14 above) 236–7 and cases there cited.

[72] *Swaab/Gemeente Amstelveen*, HR 21 Oktober 1983, *NJ* 1984, 804.

[73] See pp 152 ff.

[74] Compare *Meegdes/Meegdes*, HR 21 December 1956, *NJ* 1957, 126; and for German law, H Unberath, *Die Vertragsverletzung* (Tübingen, Mohr Siebeck, 2007) 230. See also ch 3, p 45.

[75] AS Hartkamp, *Asser IV(I) Verbintenissenrecht. De verbintenis in het algemeen*, 12th edn (Deventer, WEJ Tjeenk Willink, 2004) [356].

are generally only available after an extra period for performance has been set and has lapsed to no avail.[76] Specific performance, therefore, has a clear prevalence over damages.

In light of this, it appears that the quotation from Lord Hoffmann's speech in *Cooperative Insurance Society*[77] cannot be applied without reservation. The statement that 'judges take much the same matters into account [in common law and civil law systems] in deciding whether specific performance would be inappropriate in a particular case' needs qualification. It may be true as far as it applies to restrictions on, or bars to specific performance, but it is far from settled whether it is a valid statement with regard to the basis of specific performance (ie the conditions for its availability in the first place). Whilst in English law there is a tension at the first level between the preference for damages and the grounds on which specific performance may be held to be a more appropriate remedy, no such tension is apparent in civil law systems. The appropriateness of specific performance, it seems, is a natural presupposition, in accordance with performance-oriented policies. The systems rely on the assumption that specific performance offers the best guarantee for the protection of the performance interest of the buyer.[78] This would include situations where goods are unique or 'commercially unique', but it goes further—if a buyer contracts for the purchase of goods, he is entitled to have conforming goods delivered to him by the seller, regardless of the availability of substitutes in the market.

This may seem a controversial premise to start from, especially from the point of view of a common law lawyer. However, it may be of relatively little significance in practice. After all, commercial buyers are often looking for a swift solution in order to limit the losses flowing from a delivery of non-conforming goods. If substitute goods are available in the market, they might opt for a remedy in damages because it can be obtained quickly and does not require the further cooperation of the other party, thus leaving the buyer free to sell off the—for his purposes—defective goods and make a cover sale in its place.

At the same time, the general availability of specific performance at the request of the buyer guarantees that where it would be an appropriate remedy, the buyer has immediate access to it without being dependent upon the discretion of the court. In consumer cases—where conformity of goods may be of greater weight than in commercial cases—or in other cases where the buyer has a legitimate interest in enforcing the seller's performance, restrictions on the availability of the remedy would seem to create unnecessary hurdles for the buyer to obtain the most appropriate remedy.

Nevertheless, the general availability of specific performance in civil law systems should not be taken as an indication that economic considerations are of less importance in those systems than in the common law. They are taken into

[76] Further, ch 6, p 169.
[77] Above, p 78.
[78] See ch 3, p 61.

account—but at a secondary level. Even if the buyer may have a general entitlement to specific performance, there may be circumstances in which he will not be able to invoke it. Restrictions, as will be seen, are mostly of an economic nature.

2. Limits to Specific Performance—The Other Side of the 'Appropriateness' Test

In exceptional circumstances, Dutch and German courts may deny the buyer an order for *nakoming* or *Leistung*. There are three general grounds on which the remedy may be unavailable: impossibility, disproportionality, and good faith.[79] The latter categories overlap to some extent. A reflection of this may, for example, be seen in the Dutch case *Multi Vastgoed/Nethou*,[80] where it was held that the buyer's entitlement to *nakoming* may be limited on grounds of 'reasonableness and equity'. The decision shows that the elements to be taken into account in determining whether the buyer may reasonably exercise his choice for *nakoming* are concerned with the proportionality of the remedy in relation to the interests of the seller, in particular (but not limited to) those of an economic nature. Two cases of similar effect can be found in German law, as a result of which a restriction based on disproportionality and good faith has been laid down in the new § 275 II *BGB*.[81]

In a sense, these restrictions give civil law systems the appearance of being a mirror image of the common law approach. The starting premise is that specific performance is available, and these bars may limit its availability—whereas in English law, the starting premise is that specific performance is unavailable, unless certain circumstances justify it. The comparison is lopsided, however. After all, while the tension between performance-oriented and economic policies in English law becomes apparent at the first level (ie, the general availability of the remedy), in civil law systems the tension is pushed back to the secondary stage, where it has already been decided that specific performance is generally available at the buyer's request.

Coming back to Lord Hoffmann's comparison of specific performance in common law and civil law systems, it seems that another qualification needs to be made. To the extent that the statement refers to matters taken into account in deciding whether specific performance would be an inappropriate remedy, it may be true that there is a similarity between both systems. English courts may, for example, take account of factors such as disproportionality, and some elements may resemble factors taken into account under the heading of good faith

[79] Arts 6:74(2), 6:265(2) and 7:21(4) *BW*; §§ 275 and 439 III *BGB*.

[80] *Multi Vastgoed BV/Onroerend Goed Maatschappij Nethou BV*, HR 5 Januari 2001, *NJ* 2001, 79.

[81] BGH, *BGHZ* 62, 388 and BGH, *NJW* 1988, 799; both are discussed in BS Markesinis, H Unberath and A Johnston, *The German Law of Contract*, 2nd edn (Oxford, Hart Publishing, 2006) 414. See further below, pp 100–101.

in civil law systems. However, what needs to be realised is that these restrictions, in English law, apply to a notion of specific performance that is already subject to severe limitations. In civil law systems, on the other hand, they seek to restrict an otherwise general entitlement to specific performance. Therefore, while the restrictions may bear a resemblance, it is doubtful whether they have enough influence to steer the courts towards similar outcomes in cases judged in different systems.

Nevertheless, what the restrictions do show is a tendency in civil law systems to rely on economic considerations in order to limit the availability of specific performance where this is deemed appropriate. While the restrictions are general in nature, arguably they relate mainly to considerations of economic efficiency similar to those found in English law. It is submitted that this realisation may form a basis for future harmonisation of the laws on this point. Civil law systems do not blindly award specific performance if the buyer requests it, but rather they also seek to lay down a test that results in the most appropriate remedy. This test is not applied at the initial level, but only as a fall back option—a defence for the seller to rely on when performance would be impossible, disproportionate, or where it would go against good faith. Nevertheless, a balance is struck between similar considerations, and to this extent it can be said that it is merely a question of approaching the appropriateness test from a different angle. While this may result in greater availability of the remedy than currently found in English law, there is something to be said for a gradual expansion of the appropriateness test, also in that system, to provide a more general availability of specific performance and to move economic considerations to the second level. At least in sale of goods cases, this would seem an appropriate route to take.[82] The possibilities for harmonisation of the systems to this effect will be considered in the final section of the chapter—first, the limitations to specific performance need to be examined in greater detail to see to what extent they represent a common ground between the common law and civil law approaches.

IV. RESTRICTIONS ON SPECIFIC PERFORMANCE—COMMON LAW AND CIVIL LAW COMPARED

Having set out the general framework, a more detailed examination of the limits of specific performance in civil law systems will show that the availability of the remedy is restricted to a different extent than in the common law. While it may be true, as Lord Hoffmann suspected, that similar considerations are taken into account, differences tend to occur in relation to the weight that is attached to these factors. In sale of goods cases, however, there may be less difficulty in aligning the different national regimes on this point than in relation to other types of cases. For example, the fact that a specific performance order may cause

[82] How this would work out in other types of cases is another matter, which falls largely outside the scope of this thesis. For a brief discussion, see p 103 below.

'severe hardship to the defendant'[83] may be a ground on which to deny it. The formula is very wide and it is not instantly clear how it will apply in individual cases. However, while it has the potential to become an umbrella under which a wide variety of factors may be caught—whether related to personal, economic or other forms of hardship—its scope would seem more limited in sale of goods cases. The factors taken into account in this context are mainly of an economic nature, eg the costs of the remedy and the value of the goods are factors that may be taken into account in determining whether the chosen remedy is proportionate. Because of the narrower application of the restrictions in such circumstances, it may be easier to find a common ground for harmonisation in the different systems. After all, as has been argued, economic considerations underlie the law on specific performance in common law as well as civil law systems and it is here that a common policy may be found.

While the common law and civil law restrictions on specific performance in the sale of goods context to a great extent overlap, it will be seen that the approaches differ substantially in one respect—the factors are of a much more general nature in civil law systems. In this respect, the relation between severe hardship, good faith and proportionality is illuminating. The latter, taken from the Consumer Sales Directive and thus restricted in application to consumer sales, will be discussed in chapter five, on repair and replacement. Here, it will be argued that the common law bar of severe hardship could be regarded as overlapping with the civilian restriction of good faith, to the extent that each relates to economic factors in sale of goods cases. As such, they may form a basis for future harmonisation.

1. English Law Bars to Specific Performance

Specific performance is a discretionary remedy in English law, but

> this does not mean that there cannot be settled principles, founded upon practical considerations . . . which do not have to be re-examined in every case, but which the courts will apply in all but exceptional circumstances.[84]

While such a list of principles does not need to be exhaustive, and different authors may put the emphasis on different factors, the following are generally recognised as factors that may form bars to specific performance: (i) the constant supervision objection; (ii) the contract is for personal service; (iii) want of mutuality; (iv) uncertainty, ie the terms of the contract are too vague; (v) the contract is not supported by valuable consideration; (vi) the contract was unfairly obtained; (vii) impossibility; (viii) the order would cause severe hard-

[83] An illustrative case in English law is *Patel v Ali* [1984] Ch 283 (ChD). See further below, p 98.

[84] Lord Hoffmann in *Co-operative Insurance Society* (n 3 above) 16. See also *Lamare v Dixon* (1873) LR 6 HL 414 (HL) 423.

ship to the defendant; (ix) the claimant's conduct, eg where the claimant has committed a serious breach of contract or where he does not come to court 'with clean hands'; (x) the contract is sought to be enforced in part only.[85]

Not all of these factors are of equal relevance for sale of goods contracts. For example, the objection related to continued judicial supervision is unlikely to apply to sale contracts where the sale is a one-off occasion. It relates to cases where there is a 'possibility of the court having to give an indefinite series of . . . rulings in order to ensure the execution of the order'.[86] This may be a concern where the contract is for a number of deliveries, some of which still have to be executed, but it appears of little relevance to one-off purchases. The threat of contempt will be a strong incentive for a defendant to comply with the initial order, and it is therefore unlikely for further rulings to be called for.

The factors that are of specific relevance in sale of goods cases appear to be impossibility (factor (vii)) and severe hardship (factor (viii)). They emphasise the economic side of sales transactions, which in the appropriateness test here advocated forms the counterbalance to the protection of the performance interest. The other factors, by contrast, relate either to particular characteristics of the contract that are not found in typical sales contracts (eg factor (ii), relating to personal service), or more general contractual problems that apply to a wider range of contracts but that may not necessarily come up in the typical sales case (factors (iii), (iv), (v), (vi) and (x)). Finally, there are two factors of a more practical nature—the constant supervision objection (factor (i)) and the conduct of the claimant (factor (ix))—which may come up in sale cases but, again, are not specific to these type of cases. Since these more general factors are not of direct relevance to sale of goods cases, they will not be further discussed here.[87] Thus, the focus is on the sales-related factors: impossibility and hardship.

a) Impossibility

It is clear that an order for specific performance will not be made if performance is physically impossible, for there is no sense in ordering the defendant to do something that he simply cannot do.[88] But how wide is its scope? It may be thought that the concept of impossibility, in relation to specific performance, has a wider connotation than it has in relation to certain other doctrines. For example, the English doctrine of frustration holds that where the impossibility of performance goes to the root of the contract, the contract is automatically brought to an end.[89] In this case, there will be nothing left to enforce, since there is no contract. The doctrine of frustration, however, is restricted in scope and it

[85] Burrows, *Remedies for Torts and Breach of Contract* (n 1 above) 458–505; Peel (ed), *Treitel on the Law of Contract* (n 28 above) [21-028] ff.

[86] *Co-operative Insurance Society* (n 3 above) 12.

[87] For the potential impact of sales reforms on the general law of contract, see ch 2, pp 26–8.

[88] Burrows, *Remedies for Torts and Breach of Contract* (n 1 above) 497.

[89] *Hirji Mulji v Cheong Yue SS Co* [1926] AC 497 (PC (HK)).

will not lightly be assumed by the courts that impossibility justifies frustration.[90] Nevertheless, this type of impossibility would seem to have little bearing on cases in which specific performance is sought. After all, a party would not be able to obtain the remedy where the contract had come to an end on the ground of frustration. Therefore, in the context of specific performance, a different kind of impossibility must be envisaged. The concept may be given a wider scope in this context than it currently has in relation to frustration.[91]

b) Severe Hardship

Severe hardship, in English law, may be a ground to refuse specific performance in cases that do not revolve primarily around economic interests. An example is the case of *Patel v Ali*,[92] in which specific performance was refused in a contract for the sale of a house on the ground that the defendant's personal circumstances were such that she would suffer severe hardship if she were forced to move. Its scope appears rather narrow, but it is clear that the courts are willing to allow it where other doctrines cannot come to the rescue. As stated by Goulding J in *Patel v Ali*,

> [e]quitable relief may . . . be refused because of an unforeseen change of circumstances not amounting to legal frustration, just as it may on the ground of mistake insufficient to avoid a contract at law.[93]

As to economic hardship, the scope appears narrow. Specific performance will not be refused simply because the defendant is in financial difficulties.[94] Nevertheless, it can be argued that the severe hardship objection may extend to economic considerations on a more objective basis, ie independent from the particular position of the seller. For example, there are circumstances in which the court can presume that performance would become too onerous on any party, regardless of the financial position that they find themselves in. This was the case in *Co-operative Insurance Society*, where specific performance was refused—amongst other reasons—on the ground that it would force the defendants to continue trading at a loss.[95]

Thus, the severe hardship bar to specific performance could be interpreted in such a way as to enable the courts to take account of economic factors that would make performance too onerous for the promisor. Its relevance for sale of goods cases, however, is likely to be modest unless the courts are willing to

[90] E McKendrick, *Contract Law*, 6th edn (Basingstoke, Palgrave Macmillan, 2005) 308.

[91] Compare Burrows, *Remedies for Torts and Breach of Contract* (n 1 above) 498.

[92] *Patel v Ali* [1984] Ch 283 (ChD).

[93] *Ibid*, 288.

[94] *Francis v Cowcliffe* (1976) 33 P & CR 368 (ChD); Burrows, *Remedies for Torts and Breach of Contract* (n 1 above) 499.

[95] *Co-operative Insurance Society* (n 3 above) 15 and 18. Burrows criticises the decision for confusing this bar with the constant supervision objection; see Burrows, *Remedies for Torts and Breach of Contract* (n 1 above) 480–81.

adopt a more lenient approach to the appropriateness of the remedy, and are willing to attach less significance to the adequacy of damages test. If the balancing of economic interests is moved to the second level—ie, the level where the bars to specific performance are considered—the severe hardship criterion is likely to be the main factor to help the courts determine the appropriateness of specific performance in sales cases.

2. Civil Law Bars to Specific Performance

Civilian systems clearly specify fewer bars to specific performance than common law systems do. Article 3:296 of the Dutch *BW* states that the remedy will be granted unless the law, the nature of the obligation or a legal act (*rechtshandeling*[96]) prescribe that *nakoming* is unavailable. It is rare, however, for cases to come within the exceptions listed here. More common is the case of impossibility, for example where the promisor has transferred ownership of the goods to a third party and therefore has made it impossible to honour his contract with the promisee.[97] A further limitation applies to the remedies of repair and replacement, which are unavailable if they are disproportionate on the seller as specified in article 7:21(4) and (5) *BW*. Similar restrictions can be found in § 275 *BGB*, which provides bars to specific performance in case of impossibility or disproportionality.[98]

What is notable is that German law links the disproportionality restriction to the general doctrine of good faith: § 275 II *BGB* provides that the proportionality of expenditure relating to the performance must be judged in the light of the subject-matter of the obligation and the principle of good faith.[99] Arguably, the disproportionality restriction in Dutch law may be brought under a similar heading of good faith.[100] This may be problematic when it comes to harmonisation of these systems with English law. Good faith is a broad concept, and in relation to specific performance it is not instantly clear what it encompasses. It would seem a far broader notion than the severe hardship bar found in English

[96] Compare arts 3:32 *BW* ff. For a comparative perspective on the concept of *legal acts*, MW Hesselink, 'The Principles of European Contract Law: Some Choices Made by the Lando Commission' in MW Hesselink and GJP de Vries, *Principles of European Contract Law* (Deventer, Kluwer, 2001) 9 at 39–40.

[97] *Budde/Toa Moa*, HR 27 juni 1997, *NJ* 1997, 641; *Oosterhuis/Unigro*, HR 21 mei 1976, *NJ* 1977, 73. See also art 6:81 BW. Further below, p 100.

[98] A third restriction laid down in § 275 III *BGB*, concerning situations where performance requires a personal service from the promisor, is rarely relevant in sale of goods cases. Compare p 97 with regard to English law.

[99] In German: 'Der Schuldner kann die Leistung verweigern, soweit diese einen Aufwand erfordert, der unter Beachtung des Inhalts des Schuldverhältnisses und der Gebote von Treu und Glauben in einem groben Missverhältnis zu dem Leistungsinteresse des Gläubigers steht'. See also § 242 *BGB*.

[100] Compare arts 6:2(2) and 6:248(2) *BW*; Hijma, *Asser V(I) Bijzondere Overeenkomsten* (n 60 above) [390].

law. However, a possible basis for harmonisation may be gleaned from the fact that the practical application of the good faith principle to cases in which performance is sought is such that it concerns mainly interests of an economic nature. To this extent, it could be said that severe hardship and good faith overlap as bars to specific performance.

a) Impossibility

Like English courts, civilian courts will not order specific performance if it is impossible[101]—it is clear that in this situation the remedy is not appropriate. Or, as Hijma puts it in relation to Dutch law, in these circumstances the promisee lacks sufficient interest in an order for specific performance. In this respect, impossibility would seem to fall more naturally within article 3:303 *BW* than within the 'unless' clause in article 3:296 *BW*.[102]

Impossibility in this context appears to relate to physical impossibility only, and not to cases of economic hardship. In Dutch and in German law, there is some scope for relief in cases of economic hardship, for example on the basis of supervening circumstances. Courts may, in such cases, deny specific performance, or even change the contents of the contract.[103] In German law such a doctrine, now codified in § 313 *BGB*, was developed on the basis of the general principle of good faith.[104] The test differs from that of proportionality in that it focuses on the interests of the buyer rather than the seller—performance may become too onerous because of a rising market, where the interest of the buyer does not remain the same but grows symmetrically.[105] However, in the German system as well as in Dutch law the courts exercise their discretion only in exceptional cases where unforeseen events have caused an imbalance in the contract.

b) Good Faith as a Bar to Specific Performance

The doctrine of good faith may, nevertheless, leave some scope for taking account of economic hardship in a wider context. As said, §275 II *BGB* includes it as a factor that may limit the creditor's entitlement to specific performance. In practice this means that an order for *Leistung* may be refused where, having regard to the requirement of good faith and the subject-matter of the contract, it would be disproportionate to require the seller to perform. The provision finds its origin in the case law from the German Supreme Court, the

[101] Arts 3:296(1) and 6:74(2) *BW*; § 275 I *BGB*.

[102] Hijma, *Asser V(I) Bijzondere Overeenkomsten* (n 60 above) [374].

[103] Art 6:258 *BW*; § 313 *BGB*; compare the Principles of European Contract Law (PECL) art 6:111.

[104] See the case law based on § 242 *BGB* (BGH, *NJW* 1977, 2262, 2263; BGH, *NJW* 1976, 565, 566).

[105] Markesinis, Unberath and Johnston, *The German Law of Contract* (n 81 above) 413–14.

Bundesgerichtshof (*BGH*). One of the leading cases concerned the construction of an underground car park, which, by mistake, ended up covering some 20 square meters of the land of the plaintiffs.[106] The court refused the plaintiffs' request for removal of the interference on the ground that, taking account of the interests of the defendants and the expense of such a removal (in particular the costs related to rebuilding the entrance of the car park), it would be unreasonable to enforce a demand for such reconstruction. Similar considerations underlie the decision in the second leading authority.[107] In this case, land owned by the plaintiff was held in trust by the defendant who, on his own account, sold part of it to a third party. The plaintiff demanded that the defendant should hand the land over to him. The third party, however, had a stronger proprietary interest than the plaintiff and declared itself willing to renounce the right only on the condition that the defendant bought it back at thirty times the estimated value of the land. In these circumstances, referring to the principle of good faith, the court held that the defendant could not reasonably be required to buy the land back. Both cases, therefore, lay down limits to the availability of *Leistung* based on good faith, ie which take into account the reasonable interests of the party from whom performance is requested. As will be seen, in sale of goods cases the interests considered in relation to the proportionality restriction will mainly be of an economic nature, and may for example be related to the price or to the costs of repair or replacement.[108]

An analysis of Dutch law shows a similar development. In the Dutch case *Multi Vastgoed/Nethou*,[109] it was held that, whilst a creditor, in case of delivery of non-conforming goods, in principle has a choice between *nakoming* and damages, in the exercise of his choice he is bound to the requirements of 'reasonableness and equity'[110] and will have to take into account, amongst other things, the justified interests of the other party. As the case shows, such interests are likely to relate to the economic efficiency of awarding *nakoming*.

The case concerned a contract for the design and construction of a block of offices in the centre of Rotterdam called 'Rotterdam-Plaza'. Due to a deficiency in the construction, the aluminium sheets covering the outer walls of the building had corroded around the edges. Summoned before the court in an action for *nakoming*—in the form of replacement of the metal sheets—brought by the purchaser, the building contractor argued that such an order should not be made if it would be economically detrimental to him, the debtor, taking into account the fact that he had proposed a different solution to the problem that would be less

[106] BGH, *BGHZ* 62, 388. See also Markesinis, Unberath and Johnston, *The German Law of Contract* (n 81 above) 414.

[107] BGH, *NJW* 1988, 799. Also Markesinis, Unberath and Johnston, *The German Law of Contract* (n 81 above) 414.

[108] See ch 5, pp 132 ff.

[109] *Multi Vastgoed* (n 80 above).

[110] *Redelijkheid en billijkheid*, arts 6:2(2) and 6:248(2) *BW*. The terminology used in international instruments is 'good faith and fair dealing'; compare PECL, art 1:201(1).

oppressive to him.[111] The *Gerechtshof* (Court of Appeal) dismissed this defence on the ground that the requested remedy was not disproportionate for the defendant and, moreover, that the defendant was bound to effect replacement, on the basis of a number of express guarantees that he had undertaken in the contract. Whilst conceding that the requirements of good faith and fair dealing, including the justified interests of the debtor, may stand in the way of an order for *nakoming*, the Dutch Supreme Court upheld this ruling on the ground that the balancing of the parties' interests by the Court of Appeal did not demonstrate an incorrect understanding of the law.[112]

A closer examination of the factors that could have persuaded the *Gerechtshof* to make a different decision reveals that these are mainly of an economic nature. It was recognised that the costs of replacing the sheets covering the building's façade in their entirety would be substantial (approximately six million guilders). Thus, the costs of the remedy were considered to be a factor that may persuade a court not to order *nakoming*. However, in the circumstances of the case, seeing that the total contract price was 157 million guilders, it was held that the costs of replacement were not disproportionate.[113]

As will be seen in the next chapter, a similar test of proportionality was introduced by the Consumer Sales Directive with regard to repair and replacement in consumer cases.[114] It is in accordance with the general test laid down in *Multi Vastgoed*, which also focuses on factors of an economic nature. Therefore, the basis for future harmonisation may be found not only in the pre-existing bars to specific performance recognised in civil law systems but also in modifications made by the European Directive. It appears that a starting point for further harmonisation may be found in the overlap between the factors of severe hardship, good faith and proportionality.

3. Common Law and Civil Law Restrictions Compared

Nevertheless, while there may be an overlap between the restrictions on specific performance recognised in common law and civil law systems, it is clear that there is a difference in their application. English law does not rely on a general principle of good faith in order to provide a basis for the severe hardship objection. To this extent, the overlap is not complete. Moreover, even if similar factors are taken into account, it is still possible for courts to attach different weight to them. Depending on the policies followed by courts in different

[111] *Multi Vastgoed* (n 80 above) *cassatiemiddel* [1.2]. Multi Vastgoed had proposed to replace those metal sheets that were most visible, as well as to finance an adapted programme for maintenance of the outer walls; *Hof* [4c].

[112] *Multi Vastgoed* (n 80 above) *HR* [3.5]-[3.6].

[113] *Ibid*, *Hof* [13]–[14]. The defence also failed on the ground that Multi Vastgoed's proposal for repair was in conflict with express guarantees made by them in the contract.

[114] See pp 132 ff.

systems, a factor may lead to the denial of an order for specific performance in one case, but it may not in an otherwise similar case ruled on by a court in a different jurisdiction.

In order to achieve harmonisation of the systems, therefore, what is necessary is not just to ensure that similar bars to specific performance are taken into account, but also that similar weight is attached to each of the restrictions. Inevitably, the question of where to strike the balance between the different interests will be influenced by the general attitude to specific performance. If, as suggested, the trend is adopted that it should be made generally available, some of the considerations that are important now in English law will lose weight. A good illustration may be given by comparing *Co-operative Insurance Society* with similar cases in civil law systems. While not a sale of goods case, it does illustrate the different considerations that are relevant in specific performance cases and that will, to a great extent, also apply in sales cases. At the same time, a comparison between these cases will show that economic considerations are likely to gain weight in civil law systems, as a counterweight to the general availability of the remedy in cases where it is appropriate. These may slide the balance slightly in the opposite direction, ie towards greater restrictions on specific performance.

With regard to good faith, glimpses can be caught that show that there is some likelihood for it to attain greater significance in common law systems. Should this development continue, then it may be possible to bring the common law bar of severe hardship under the umbrella of the general doctrine. For the moment, however, good faith remains a problematic concept in European contract law. Nevertheless, it may be possible to rely on it in specific areas of harmonisation, such as in relation to the bars to specific performance, as long as a narrow definition of the concept is applied.

a) Weight Attached to Restrictions on Specific Performance

Co-operative Insurance Society concerned a supermarket chain which sought to shut down one of its stores because it was losing money. The supermarket being the main customer attraction in a shopping centre, its presence was of commercial benefit to the shops nearby. The lease was for 35 years and it contained express provisions delineating the type of use that should be made of the premises (ie the store was to be used as a supermarket), as well as a clause stipulating that the premises should be kept 'open for retail trade during the usual hours of business'. The owners of the mall sought to oppose the unilateral ending of the lease by the supermarket owners and made a claim for specific performance of the 'keep open' covenant. The House of Lords denied the action for specific performance on a number of grounds, including (i) that according to settled practice a specific performance order would not be made that would require a defendant to run a business; (ii) that an order to continue trading would have exposed the defendants to enormous losses; (iii) that the task of framing the order was not an easy one; (iv) that there was a risk of wasteful litigation over compliance, the so-called 'constant supervision' objection; (v) that it would be oppressive for the defendants to be compelled to run a business under the threat of proceedings for contempt, and (vi) that it was not in the public interest to require someone to carry on a business at a loss if there was a plausible alternative by which the other party could be compensated for the loss it has suffered.[115]

What weight should be attached to each of these factors? It appears that, of the elements taken into account by the House of Lords, only (i) and (ii) correspond with the severe hardship objection. To this extent, the overlap can be seen between this bar to specific performance and the good faith restriction found in civil law systems. 'Reasonableness and equity' set the limit to *nakoming* in *Amsterdamse Poort I BV/NTU Nederland BV*,[116] the factual circumstances of which show great similarity with those of *Co-operative Insurance Society*. An order requiring the defendant shop owner to re-open his store was denied on the basis that the defendant could not be compelled to continue running a business at a loss.

The other elements appear of less significance to harmonisation in this area of law, for they do not relate directly to factors of economic efficiency that could influence the restrictions on specific performance. It is thought that they lose weight if they are applied in systems other than English law. Points (iii)–(v) appear to relate to issues of English procedural law that do not share a direct similarity with civilian systems. First, framing the order would not be so problematic under civilian law, since the concept of specific performance in general is wider than it is under the common law.[117] Thus, a lesser degree of precision is needed when making the order.[118] Secondly, the possibility of the court making an order compelling a defendant to perform under the threat of payment of a *dwangsom* (comparable to the French *astreinte*) largely overcomes the 'constant supervision' objection. This mechanism forces the defendant to pay a sum of money in case of failure to fulfill the order for specific performance. It is not necessary for the parties to return to court to obtain payment every time the order is breached.[119] Thirdly, the doctrine of contempt is particular to common law systems and does not have a direct correspondent in civil law systems. Other, less Draconian means of enforcement are used there, such as the *dwangsom*.

[115] *Co-operative Insurance Society* (n 3 above). Compare McKendrick, *Contract Law: Text, Cases and Materials* (n 8 above) 1158.

[116] President van de Rechtbank Amsterdam, 6 april 2000, *KG* 2000, 98.

[117] See ch 5, p 120.

[118] Though the obligation of which performance is sought should be sufficiently determined; see P Bassenge, G Brudermüller and others (eds), *Palandt Kommentare zum Bürgerliches Gesetzbuch*, 66th edn (Munchen, Beck, 2007) § 241 BGB, [3]; OLG Köln, *RG* 85, 291; OLG Frankfurt/Main, *BGH* 55, 250. Also, Hartkamp, *Asser IV(I) Verbintenissenrecht* (n 75 above) [23].

[119] The assistance of a bailiff ('deurwaarder') can be sought in case of non-payment. If the defendant remains unwilling to pay, the possibility to return to court is open. However, in many cases it will be unnecessary for the court to get involved again.

Therefore, an order for specific performance is less likely to be unduly oppressive on a defendant. The public interest element, finally—factor (vi) from Lord Hoffmann's speech—does not enjoy general recognition in civilian systems. At most, it can be said that the interests of direct associates of the defendant may be taken into account when deciding whether or not to make the order. For example, in *Amsterdamse Poort I*, the interests of creditors and staff of the store were taken into account as a factor speaking against the making of an order that would require the business to continue running at a loss.[120]

Nevertheless, even if factors (i) and (ii) are similar to civil law restrictions, the fact remains that the civil law starts from a different premise—and it may well lead to different outcomes in similar cases. A comparison with a Scottish decision may illustrate this. The leading modern authority on specific implement, *Retail Parks Investments Ltd v Royal Bank of Scotland plc (No 2)*,[121] held that a covenant to keep retail trading premises open for a significant period of time was specifically enforceable. The decision has been followed by the Inner House of the Court of Session in *Highland and Universal Properties Ltd v Safeway Properties Ltd*,[122] in which the court explicitly refused to follow *Co-operative Insurance Society*. Lord President Rodger stated that

> [t]he mere fact that the two systems may come to different results in particular cases is not in my view a sufficient reason for saying that this court should remould our law so as to reach the same result as would be reached under English law in a particular situation.[123]

On the facts of the case, the court could not see any reason to deny the remedy of specific implement. The fact that the defendants would be compelled to trade at a loss was not, under Scots law, recognised as a ground in itself on which to deny the remedy. This case could be seen as an indication that the recognition of generally available specific performance may result in a wider recourse to the right in practice.

It is notable, moreover, that the wider recourse to specific performance, or specific implement, found in Scots law is not necessarily at odds with commercial needs. The case law shows that it is possible for economically beneficial solutions to be reached even where performance is enforced. For example, in case of 'keep open' clauses, it may be possible for the original tenant, with the landlord's consent, to assign the lease to a new tenant, which is what happened in the *Co-operative Insurance Society* case after the decision of the Court of Appeal.[124] Furthermore, it remains open to courts in civil law systems, or mixed

[120] *Amsterdamse Poort I* (n 116 above).

[121] *Retail Parks Investments Ltd v Royal Bank of Scotland plc (No 2)*1996 SLT 669 (Ex Div).

[122] *Highland and Universal Properties Ltd v Safeway Properties Ltd* 2000 SLT 414 (IHCS). Compare also *Co-operative Insurance Society Ltd v Halfords Ltd* 1998 SC 212, 229.

[123] *Highland and Universal Properties* (n 122 above) 417.

[124] *Co-operative Insurance Society* (n 3 above) 9. Compare also MacQueen and Thomson, *Contract Law in Scotland* (n 18 above) 224.

systems such as the Scottish one, to introduce restrictions on the right to specific performance if this is deemed in accordance with business reality. As stated by Lord President Rodger in *Highland and Universal Properties*,

> Keep open clauses and their enforcement have come to prominence, in Scotland at least, only in recent years. If, therefore, one could identify sufficiently compelling reasons for holding that specific implement was an inappropriate remedy for the breach of such an obligation, I see no reason in principle why a further exception to the general rule should not be recognised.[125]

Thus, the possibility is held open that restrictions may be used to this effect in cases where it is appropriate. Other—civil law—systems also acknowledge this possibility, as may be seen for example in the Dutch case *Amsterdamse Poort I*.[126]

The careful balancing made in these cases between the restrictions to specific performance and the interests of the creditor in obtaining the remedy show that civil law systems deal with the complexities of performance-oriented claims in a different way to common law systems, though similar considerations are taken into account. As in common law systems, it is recognised that sales law evolves around allocations of financial risks, and that, therefore, the scope of the remedies depends also on considerations of an economic nature. These are likely to gain in prominence as civilian systems are beginning to recognise disproportionality as a ground on which to deny specific performance. The restrictions, however, do not distract from the initial premise that specific performance should be generally available at the request of the buyer. If this is the general premise on which to build harmonising rules, then for harmonisation to be successful, a review of the restrictions on specific performance is called for in civil law as well as common law systems. While there are similarities between the systems, it is important also to determine a common view on the weight that should be attached to these limitations. It is here, where the specific (economic and moral) interests relating to the performance of the contract are balanced against the general rule, that common law and civil law systems may find a basis on which to grow closer together.

b) Good Faith as a General Restriction on Specific Performance

Whilst a notion of good faith is not entirely foreign to common law systems, its role is much more limited than in civilian systems such as the Dutch one, where the principle of good faith is a central theme against which the parties dealings with each other are tested at all stages of the contracting process, including negotiation,[127] conclusion, and performance of the contract. English law spo-

[125] *Highland and Universal Properties* (n 122 above) 418.

[126] See p 104 above.

[127] For an insightful comparison of pre-contractual liability under Dutch law and under the PECL, see C Mak, 'Aansprakelijkheid voor afgebroken onderhandelingen: een vergelijking tussen Nederlands recht en de Principles of European Contract Law' (2002) 51 *Ars Aequi* 62 ff.

radically makes reference to a principle of good faith, or a notion of 'reasonableness',[128] and thus reaches similar results as civil law systems in particular cases, but a general principle of good faith has not been recognised. In relation to specific performance, the only hint at a principle of good faith is given by the requirement of equity that the claimant comes to the court 'with clean hands', which requires among things that he shall have acted in good faith.[129] The scope of good faith, in this respect, is much narrower than in the civil law context. It does not, for example, take into account the economic interests of the defendant, nor does it even suggest a balancing of the interests of buyer and seller. Instead, it focuses solely on the conduct of the claimant and any possible bars to specific performance deriving from that.

Yet, there are signs that the traditional English hostility towards good faith might be abating.[130] Recent case law has shown the courts adopting a more sympathetic stance towards the doctrine of good faith,[131] which may become more prominent with the growing influence of European Directives such as the Unfair Terms Directive and the Consumer Sales Directive. This may be a first step towards acceptance of the doctrine, though its role remains controversial. Arguments based in individualism and legal certainty, supporting the traditional English approach of imposing a duty of good faith only in particular circumstances, vy with countervailing arguments of protection of weaker parties and the prevention of hardship in individual cases.[132] The balance is not an easy one to strike.

This is not the place for a wider discussion of the role of good faith in European contract law.[133] With regard to specific performance in sale of goods law, however, it appears that a more clear-cut case may be made out, at least for a limited role for good faith as a restriction to the availability of the remedy. As shown by *Multi Vastgoed*, the duty of good faith will only in exceptional circumstances deprive a buyer of his right to *nakoming*. Thus, there is no need for excessive fear on the part of common law lawyers that a duty of good faith, if transposed into a uniform European sales law as a bar to specific performance, will undermine the sanctity of contract or the autonomy of the parties. In the majority of cases, the buyer will be able to invoke his right to specific performance without problem and no extra-contractual duty of good faith will prevent

[128] The prime example is the provisions of the Unfair Terms in Consumer Contracts Regulations 1999 (SI 1999/3159), implementing Council Directive (EEC) 93/13 on unfair terms in consumer contracts [1993] OJ L95/29 (Unfair Terms Directive).

[129] R Goode, *The Concept of Good Faith in English Law* (Roma, Centro di Studi e Ricerche di Diritto Comparato e Straniero, 1992) 5.

[130] McKendrick, *Contract Law* (n 90 above) 265.

[131] *Ibid*. Compare case law there mentioned, in particular *Director General of Fair Trading v First National Bank* [2001] UKHL 52; [2002] 1 AC 481.

[132] Compare McKendrick, *Contract Law* (n 90 above) 267–9.

[133] For a comprehensive overview of the subject, see R Zimmermann and S Whittaker (eds), *Good Faith in European Contract Law* (Cambridge, Cambridge University Press, 2000).

him from doing so.[134] In the rare event that it does, it will most likely be to protect the seller against undue hardship, eg in the form of economic loss.[135] The scope of its application may therefore be restricted to particular circumstances, regardless of whether or not a general principle is relied on to achieve this result.

In this respect, it should be noted that one of the most often heard objections to a doctrine of good faith on the part of English lawyers is that it would affect the legal certainty that is such a central value of the common law system. In what the English—perhaps wrongly—like to think is the world's leading financial centre, the predictability of the outcome of a case is thought to be more important than absolute justice.[136] However, seeing that good faith may play only a very marginal role in relation to specific performance, this argument loses much of its weight. The legal certainty provided by a European sales law depends to a much greater extent on the primary conditions for availability of remedies such as specific performance and damages to the aggrieved buyer. The role of good faith, as in many national legal systems in Europe, is a corrective one and its scope depends largely on how happy or unhappy a legal system is with its initial rules.[137] Moreover, the principle will only be resorted to if particular legal doctrines cannot satisfactorily do the job.[138]

4. Conclusion

Over all, it appears that Lord Hoffmann's suspicion can be sustained and that there is indeed an overlap between the considerations taken into account by courts in common law and civil law systems in deciding whether specific performance would be inappropriate in a particular case. The main restrictions on specific performance in sale of goods cases—impossibility and severe hardship—feature in both systems. While they may take a slightly different form—eg civilian systems bring hardship under the general doctrine of good faith—the underlying policy appears similar. Namely, each of the systems seeks to achieve the remedy that is most appropriate not only from the perspective of protection of the performance interest, but also with an eye on economic efficiency. This could be the basis, then, for future harmonisation of this area of law in European systems.

[134] Exclusion by contract of a duty of good faith seems an unlikely event, if at all possible under the law. Express inclusion of an obligation to act in good faith, by contrast, will not necessarily be enforced by the courts either; compare *Walford v Miles* [1992] 2 AC 128 (HL).

[135] *Multi Vastgoed* (n 80 above) *Conclusie van de Advocaat-Generaal mr. Langemeijer* [2.4].

[136] Goode, *The Concept of Good Faith in English Law* (n 129 above) 6.

[137] Compare S Whittaker and R Zimmermann, 'Coming to Terms with Good Faith' in Zimmermann and Whittaker, *Good Faith in European Contract Law* (n 133 above) 669.

[138] *Ibid*, 683.

Nevertheless, even if similarities can be discerned in the restrictions on specific performance, the fact remains that common law and civil law systems adopt different starting points for the availability of the remedy. As has been seen, this may lead to different outcomes in cases that are otherwise very similar. For harmonisation to be successful, therefore, a compromise needs to be made between the two approaches. The next section will consider to what extent this may be achieved.

V. SPECIFIC PERFORMANCE IN EUROPEAN AND OTHER UNIFORM SALES LAWS

To what extent do existing uniform sales laws provide a basis for further harmonisation of specific performance in European sale of goods laws? On the basis of the foregoing, it is thought that the underlying principles of common law and civil law systems are not so far apart as might be perceived at first sight. It will be argued that a similar convergence can be observed in uniform sales laws such as the Principles of European Contract Law (PECL), the Consumer Sales Directive and the Unidroit Principles of International Commercial Contracts (PICC). These instruments find their origins in harmonisation projects between common law and civil law systems, and this is reflected in their content—the majority of their provisions can be traced back to common law or civil law tradition, or to a compromise between the two approaches.[139]

With regard to specific performance, it is obvious that a compromise had to be made because of the different starting premises of common law and civil law systems. On the basis of the above discussions of the availability of the remedy, as well as the theoretical framework set out in chapter three,[140] the 'best solution' appears to be to opt for a general entitlement to specific performance, which corresponds with the civilian approach. While this approach is likely to appear controversial to a common law lawyer, two further arguments can be made that plead in favour of adopting this as the best solution. Moreover, as seen earlier, English law may be starting to pay greater heed to such considerations by moving towards an appropriateness test.

References to the common law approach can be found in the restrictions on specific performance. The compromise, however, may in some uniform laws have been taken too far. It will be argued that, at least in the PECL and the PICC, the restrictions allow for such an inroad to be made upon the general entitlement to specific performance that it may actually harm the interests of the buyer. It appears that too much emphasis has been put on the position of the debtor, rather than on the position of the aggrieved party.

[139] Some of the provisions aim to lay down best solutions and, as such, do not derive directly from national legal systems but instead extrapolate solutions found in these systems. An example is art 6:111 of the PECL, which makes provision for cases of unforeseen hardship and introduces a duty to renegotiate.

[140] Compare ch 3, in particular pp 48 ff.

1. The Basic Principle—General Availability of Specific Performance

Although a stark contrast can be drawn between, on the one hand, the principle-oriented approach of the civil law and, on the other, the pragmatic approach taken by common law systems, if painting with a finer brush, it can be seen that the two approaches are not so far apart after all. In fact, not only do the considerations taken into account by the courts in awarding or denying the remedy show a large degree of similarity, but also, the starting points of the common law and civil law approaches appear to be gradually converging. A tendency towards a general right to specific performance, whilst not originally part of English sales law, is becoming apparent in its shift towards an 'appropriate remedy' test, of which the inadequacy of damages criterion forms a part but is not necessarily the defining element. This corresponds to the civilian approach, as exemplified by Dutch law, where a buyer is generally entitled to a remedy which enforces performance as long as it does not unreasonably harm the interests of the seller.

In the light of this, European sales law is bound to adopt an approach in which the buyer has a general entitlement to specific performance, enforcement of which depends on a balancing of the interests of seller and buyer. Support for this approach can also be found in existing uniform sales laws. Whereas the CISG left the question unanswered because it was, at that time, impossible to reach agreement on the issue,[141] later uniform rules have unanimously struck the balance in favour of general available specific performance, including repair and replacement. The PICC, the PECL and the Consumer Sales Directive, divergent in scope as they may be, all contain provisions that make the remedy available alongside, or even in priority to, damages, termination and price reduction.[142] While sceptics might attribute the inclusion of a general right to specific performance to the predominance of civilian countries participating in the drafting of these instruments, there are autonomous arguments pleading in favour of this approach that justify it being followed in the context of European sales law, as discussed in chapter three.

2. Bars to Specific Performance

Article 9:102 of the PECL gives a neat illustration of the compromise between common law and civil law factors that determine the scope of specific performance. The provision states:

[141] P Schlechtriem and I Schwenzer (eds), *Commentary on the United Nations Convention on the International Sale of Goods*, 2nd English edn (Oxford, Oxford University Press, 2005) 316.

[142] Compare PICC arts 7.2.2 and 7.2.3; PECL art 9:102; Consumer Sales Directive art 3.

Article 9:102: Non-monetary Obligations

(1) The aggrieved party is entitled to specific performance of an obligation other than one to pay money, including the remedying of a defective performance.
(2) Specific performance cannot, however, be obtained where:
  (a) performance would be unlawful or impossible; or
  (b) performance would cause the debtor unreasonable effort or expense; or
  (c) the performance consists in the provision of services or work of a personal character or depends upon a personal relationship; or
  (d) the aggrieved party may reasonably obtain performance from another source.
(3) The aggrieved party will lose the right to specific performance if it fails to seek it within a reasonable time after it has or ought to have become aware of the non-performance.

Sub-section (1) lays down the general right to specific performance. In sub-section (2), the restrictions on this entitlement found in common law and civil law systems can be recognised. A similar provision can be found in article 7.2.2 of the PICC, in which the restrictions to the right of performance largely correspond with those found in the PECL.

To a certain extent, the provision appears to give an adequate depiction of the common law and civil law restrictions on specific performance in sale of goods cases—article 9:102(2)(a) and (b) repeat the impossibility and severe hardship objections. Sub-section (2)(c), regarding personal services, is unlikely to be of general significance in sale cases. The problem lies in sub-section (2)(d), which denies specific performance where performance may reasonably be obtained from another source.[143] In other words, if the buyer can reasonably make a cover purchase, this will deprive him of his entitlement to specific performance. It is thought that this puts too much of a restriction upon the general availability of specific performance, for two reasons.

First, a restriction of this kind is likely to deny specific performance where it would actually be a more appropriate remedy. Since the restriction applies almost without distinction to all cases in which performance is sought, it does not guarantee that a buyer will be able to enforce performance by the seller where this would appear to be the more appropriate remedy. For example, where the sale is for a set of ordinary chairs, the buyer will not be able to obtain specific performance if substitute goods are available in the market. Instead he may be forced to make a cover purchase (of course he would also have a claim in damages to cover the losses suffered as a result). However, this overlooks the possibility that specific performance could have been possible for the seller at a lesser cost and with less inconvenience to the buyer than the making of a cover purchase. While he may eventually obtain a set of chairs that serves his purposes, he will have to go to considerable trouble to achieve this result. In these circumstances, specific performance would seem more appropriate.

[143] Compare PICC art 7.2.2(c).

The argument that termination and damages are generally the more appropriate remedies in cases where substitutes are available in the market may be true, especially in the commercial context, but it does not justify a general restriction such as this one. It is thought that the first two restrictions, especially the disproportionality/hardship bar to specific performance, catch the majority of situations in which specific performance would be less appropriate than an award of damages.

A second objection to the restriction found in article 9:102(2)(d) of the PECL is that it takes away almost in its entirety the buyer's freedom to choose a remedy. Where substitutes are available, the buyer is bound to make do with damages even if he had preferred specific performance. Only if the buyer and the seller come to a new agreement whereby the seller shows his willingness to perform, will the buyer be able to obtain specific performance. This appears to give too much weight to the interests of the seller who, after all, is responsible for the initial unsatisfactory performance. It is thought that the interests of the buyer should prevail in this respect, and that the choice of remedy should primarily be his.[144]

A solution to this effect can be found in the Principles of European Sales Law (PESL) developed by the Utrecht Team of the Von Bar Group.[145] Article 4:202 of the draft Principles provides that

> [t]he seller may not refuse to remedy the lack of conformity merely because the buyer could reasonably have it remedied from another source.

The commentary defines this as a specific deviation from article 9:102(2)(d) of the PECL, necessary on the ground that such a restriction would make the remedy of repair meaningless. After all, it would in most cases be possible for the buyer to obtain repair or replacement elsewhere.[146] In order to safeguard the buyer's right to performance, and to promote cure in cases of non-conformity, a deviation from the PECL, as suggested in the PESL, is in accordance with the criticisms made above. Fears that this may result in cumbersome court proceedings by buyers seeking to enforce repair or replacement against unwilling sellers would seem unfounded. In situations where a seller (unjustly) refuses performance, other remedies such as termination or price reduction would become available to the buyer. In cases where the defect is minor or can be easily cured, buyers are likely to choose one of these alternatives rather than to go down the judicial route.[147]

[144] See also ch 5, pp 123 ff.

[145] For more information, www.sgecc.net and www.copecl.org. The Utrecht Team of the Von Bar Group deals with certain long-term contracts, sales and services. Their solution has been copied also in art III-3:302 of the DCFR.

[146] See comment E to art 4:202 of the PESL.

[147] *Ibid.*

VI. CONCLUSION

Common law and civil law start from different premises—specific performance is a discretionary remedy in English law, whereas it is generally available in civilian systems such as the Dutch and the German. Nevertheless, this chapter has shown that there are signs of convergence between the systems. A tendency to look at the appropriateness of the remedy, which would increase the protection of the performance interest of the buyer, can be observed in English law. At the same time, civil law systems are starting to pay greater heed to economic considerations that may limit the scope of specific performance.

To a certain extent, therefore, Lord Hoffmann's statement in *Co-operative Insurance Society* as to the functioning of specific performance in common law and civil law systems has proved right.[148] Nevertheless, the fact remains that the systems start from different premises, and that this may lead to different outcomes in individual cases. In order to achieve harmonisation of European sales laws, therefore, a compromise will have to be made.

The 'best solution' appears to be to adopt a general entitlement to specific performance for the buyer, accompanied by appropriate restrictions in order to safeguard the interests of the seller. This, arguably, protects the buyer's performance interest to the greatest possible extent, ensuring that he will only be denied performance if another remedy is more appropriate. A test of hardship or disproportionality may serve to protect the interests of the seller—it ensures that no order for specific performance will be made against him where it would be too onerous on him, for example, because it would force him to continue trading at a loss. In such a case, a remedy in damages is thought to be more appropriate.

While the case for a general entitlement to specific performance finds support in uniform rules applying to sale of goods law, some tension remains between the common law and civil law attitudes to the availability of the remedy. Nevertheless, rules such as found in the PECL, the PICC, CISG and the Consumer Sales Directive form a basis for future harmonisation. The next step is to determine whether the scope of specific performance can be extended to the related performance-oriented remedies: repair and replacement.

[148] Above, n 3.

5

Repair and Replacement

I. INTRODUCTION

According to the recital preceding the Consumer Sales Directive,

> in the case of non-conformity of the goods with the contract, consumers should be entitled to have the goods restored to conformity with the contract free of charge, choosing either repair or replacement, or, failing this, to have the price reduced or the contract rescinded.[1]

A FURTHER EXPRESSION OF this statement is found in what is, arguably, the most controversial provision of the Directive—article 3, which lays down a buyer's right to demand repair or replacement, and, more importantly, imposes a hierarchy upon the remedial scheme. The unconventional suggestion of introducing a hierarchy of remedies which places repair and replacement at the top has created some commotion in legal circles. It has not been taken up by all of the national legislators and it is indeed a point of argument whether it should be adopted. Two points require justification. First, why should the buyer be free to opt for repair or replacement if he so wishes? Secondly, why should his choice initially be limited to performance-oriented remedies? The first question will be discussed in this chapter. The question of the hierarchy of remedies appears more closely related to the interests of the seller and will therefore be discussed in the next chapters, which deal with the seller's right to cure.

Before turning to the question of the buyer's freedom to choose between the remedies, the general framework in which repair and replacement operate needs some elaboration. To what extent can they protect the performance interest of the buyer? The point will be addressed at two levels. First, it will be argued that the two remedies in general are able to give the buyer the performance that he contracted for, at least in the sense that they achieve the result that the buyer objectively could have been entitled to expect under the contract. In this respect, there is a resemblance with specific performance. The second strand of the argument turns on the question to what extent this resemblance is reflected in the scope of the remedies. There is a difference between specific performance, on the one hand, and repair and replacement, on the other. While the former relates to the performance of primary rights arising from the contract, the buyer's entitlement

[1] Directive (EC) 99/44 of the European Parliament and of the Council on certain aspects of the sale of consumer goods and associated guarantees [1999] OJ L171/12 (Consumer Sales Directive) recital 10.

to repair or replacement only arises upon breach. In this sense, the remedies may be regarded as secondary obligations of the seller—ie they do not find their direct origin in the contract but instead they are a consequence that the law attaches to breach of the primary conformity obligations of the seller laid down (expressly or impliedly) in the contract. However, it is thought that the practical connotations of this distinction are negligible. The nature of the remedies, ie their focus on obtaining performance for the buyer, puts them in the same league with specific performance. Therefore, it will be argued that similar principles can be applied to determine their scope.

Thus, extending the line of reasoning of the previous chapter, it will be argued that repair and replacement operate under similar principles to specific performance—on the one hand the protection of the performance interest, on the other hand the restrictions found in efficiency considerations. The next step is to determine what the effect will be on the availability of the remedies. Two questions spring to mind: (i) Should the buyer have a general entitlement to repair or replacement upon breach by the seller of his conformity obligations? And (ii) if the buyer opts for a performance-oriented remedy, should he have the choice between repair and replacement, or should the choice be the seller's?

The answer to these questions is not straightforward. Arguably, the choice should lie with the buyer, for if he has the freedom to choose the remedy, he will have a stronger position to obtain the remedy that he wants from the seller. Especially in consumer sales, where the buyer may count on a certain level of protection, it is thought that he should be able to obtain the remedy that best protects his performance interest. Sellers should not be put in a position where they can easily manipulate the buyer into accepting a lesser remedy. Nevertheless, at the same time, the interests of the seller cannot be ignored. Depending on the circumstances, efficiency considerations may plead in favour of restricting the buyer's freedom of choice and giving greater influence to the seller's preferences.

Therefore, while the stand taken will initially be in favour of the buyer, giving him a free choice of remedy, the second part of the chapter will explore restrictions on this freedom of choice that the seller may rely on in his defence. Two main factors emerge that may limit the availability of repair and replacement: impossibility and disproportionality. It will be argued that these coincide with the restrictions on specific performance identified in the previous chapter.

A final note on the scope of the comparison made in this chapter. Because of the relative novelty of the remedies in English law, very little material is available that relates to the functioning of repair and replacement in England. From a practical perspective, therefore, the comparison will focus on Dutch and German law, as amended by the Consumer Sales Directive, as well as on the Principles of European Contract Law (PECL) and the Vienna Convention on Contracts for the International Sale of Goods (CISG).[2] As far as theoretical

[2] UN Convention on Contracts for the International Sale of Goods (adopted 11 April 1980, entered into force 1 January 1988) 1489 UNTS 3 (CISG).

questions are concerned, however, the provisions of the Sale of Goods Act 1979 (SGA) that implement the Consumer Sales Directive in the United Kingdom will be given as much weight as the equivalent provisions of Dutch and German law. In any case—seeing the uneasy fit of the European rules with the pre-existing provisions of the SGA—the UK's implementing legislation will add some colour to the discussion.

II. REPAIR AND REPLACEMENT: DEFINITIONS

'*Herstel en vervanging*'. '*Nachbesserung und Ersatzlieferung*'. Repair and replacement. Two remedies that aim to make good a delivery of non-conforming goods by the seller—if not recognised before its implementation, they now form part of all of Europe's sale of goods laws as a result of the Consumer Sales Directive. To what extent their application may be extended to commercial sales is a question that will be discussed later. For now it needs to be determined what their value is as remedies for the buyer in case of non-conformity of goods. To what extent can they protect the performance interest of the buyer?

It is thought that repair and replacement can be put on par with specific performance in at least one respect: they give the buyer the performance that he contracted for. While the remedies, in theory, do not enforce the primary obligations of the seller laid down in the contract, they provide a remedy that enables the buyer to obtain the end result of performance (ie, in sale of goods cases, the delivery of conforming goods). For all purposes, this means that the performance interest of the buyer is protected.[3]

1. Repair

If a seller is requested to repair defective goods, or if he offers to do so, under English law he is obliged to bring goods already delivered to the buyer into conformity with the contract requirements.[4] Presumably, like the German or Dutch concept of repair, this includes situations in which a defect is fixed through replacement of defective components of the goods, as long as the main goods are not replaced in their entirety.[5] For example, a seller may replace a dented car door with another door, or a damaged valve with a new one.[6]

[3] See pp 46, 48–50.

[4] SGA s 61. CJ Miller and others (eds), *Benjamin's Sale of Goods. Special Supplement to the 6th Edition: Sale and Supply of Goods to Consumers Regulations* (London, Sweet & Maxwell, 2003) [1-126]; Compare R Bradgate and C Twigg-Flesner, *Blackstone's Guide to Consumer Sales and Associated Guarantees* (Oxford, Oxford Univeristy Press, 2003) 118.

[5] Compare J Hijma, *Asser V(I) Bijzondere Overeenkomsten. Koop en Ruil*, 6th edn (Deventer, WEJ Tjeenk Willink, 2001) [388]. In relation to CISG, compare P Schlechtriem and I Schwenzer (eds), *Commentary on the UN Convention on the International Sale of Goods*, 2nd English edn (Oxford, Oxford University Press, 2005) 551.

[6] *Ibid.*

It may be argued, however, that repair does not give the buyer *exactly* what he contracted for. For example, it may be said that if a buyer contracted for new goods, he should not have to settle for goods that have been repaired. Nevertheless, if approaching the question from a functional point of view, it should not matter whether the goods have been repaired or not. As long as the goods function according to their contractual description and they measure up to the implied conditions of quality and fitness for purpose,[7] there does not seem to be any reason to say that the goods are not what the buyer contracted for. Situations where repair cannot satisfactorily remedy the defect do occur, but they are rare. For example, repairs may not satisfy the buyer of a new car where the defects are of a serious nature. Serious malfunctions of the car may make the buyer lose his sense of security in driving the car, the effect of which may be worse depending on the number of repairs needed. In this situation, it may be thought that the better remedy is replacement of the car, rather than repair of the defective components. Whether the buyer will be able to uphold this claim, however, depends on how far the court is willing to extend the conformity requirements. Arguably, where defects are of a very serious nature and relate to elements of the car that influence its driving mechanism, it may be thought that the buyer's confidence in the safety of the car has been destroyed and that, therefore, the repairs cannot succeed in bringing the car back to a pristine state.[8] However, such considerations are specifically applicable to vehicles, and they are unlikely to be of equal relevance in relation to other goods. In relation to other types of goods, there are many circumstances in which repair is likely to remedy the defect satisfactorily.

Moreover, as long as there are sufficient safeguards—for example in the form of time limits—that ensure that the buyer obtains repair with as little delay and inconvenience as possible, the remedy should be regarded as giving the buyer exactly what he contracted for. The only situation where this would be different is if, contrary to the contractual description, the goods initially sold to the buyer are not 'new'. If the buyer contracts for new goods, the seller is in breach of the implied condition of conformity with description if he delivers goods that have been repaired before.[9]

2. Replacement

Replacement, in English, Dutch and German law, refers to situations where the goods are replaced in their entirety. A delivery of defective goods is remedied by

[7] SGA ss 13, 14 and 15; art 7:17 *Burgerlijk Wetboek* (*BW*); § 434 *BGB*. Compare also LG Ellwangen, *NJW* 2003, 517–18.

[8] For a factual situation in which this occurred, compare *Bernstein v Pamson Motors (Golders Green) Ltd* [1987] 2 All ER 220 (QBD).

[9] See, eg, *Andrews Bros Ltd v Singer & Co Ltd* [1934] 1 KB 17 (CA). Compare also AG Guest (ed), *Benjamin's Sale of Goods*, 7th edn (London, Sweet & Maxwell, 2006) [11-016].

the delivery of substitute goods which *do* conform to the contract.[10] For example, the buyer of a portable cd player which turns out to be defective may demand its replacement. The buyer, therefore, gets exactly what he contracted for.

With regard to replacement, however, a different problem arises. While the remedy may bear a resemblance to specific performance, in the sense that it requires the seller to deliver goods that conform to the contract description, a subtle distinction sets the remedies apart. Under English law, specific performance is only available in relation to goods that are either specific or ascertained.[11] Where specific goods are concerned, the buyer is only entitled to receive and the seller only entitled to supply the particular item contracted for. Much the same is true for ascertained goods—even if a contract is for unascertained goods at the outset, and the goods are thus not identified at the time the contract is made, before the property can pass to the buyer the goods will have to be identified, ie to become 'ascertained'. Replacement, however, relates to a substitute delivery, and the goods will therefore by definition not be specific or ascertained. Thus, it appears that the remedy may be available only if the unascertained goods offered in replacement can be ascertained. Whether it is in fact possible to ascertain these goods, which would effectively nullify the original ascertainment of the goods supplied in the initial delivery, is a matter of debate. While the problem may be more theoretical than real,[12] it serves to emphasise that the narrow notion of specific performance in English law may occasionally lead to difficulties.

Dutch law, in comparison, while making a distinction between unascertained and specific goods (the sales contract is either a *genuskoop* or a *specieskoop*), does not attach any consequences to this in terms of remedies.[13] Therefore, problems relating to the type of goods for which specific performance, repair or replacement may be ordered are largely non-existent in Dutch sale of goods law. The same is true for Germany, where the distinction between specific and unascertained goods has been made largely redundant as a result of the recent review of the law of obligations. Only in particular situations will the distinction still be of relevance.[14]

[10] *Ibid*, [397]; Bradgate and Twigg-Flesner, *Blackstone's Guide to Consumer Sales and Associated Guarantees* (n 4 above) 88, 118.

[11] SGA s 52(1).

[12] According to Bradgate and Twigg-Flesner, 'common sense can overcome the conceptual objections'; Bradgate and Twigg-Flesner, *Blackstone's Guide to Consumer Sales and Associated Guarantees* (n 4 above) 119. Compare also ch 6, pp 157 ff.

[13] Compare Hijma, *Asser V(I) Bijzondere Overeenkomsten* (n 5 above) [104].

[14] For example where a contract has been made for specific goods, the seller will not be able to resort to the remedy of replacement; compare R Zimmermann, *The New German Law of Obligations* (Oxford, Oxford University Press, 2005) 98–9.

III. REPAIR, REPLACEMENT AND SPECIFIC PERFORMANCE

If repair and replacement, as suggested, offer full protection of the performance interest, a logical consequence would be, in order to determine their scope, to apply the same principles as with the other performance-oriented remedy of the buyer: specific performance. However, as will be recalled, specific performance in essence is not just a remedy of the buyer, it arises directly from the contract and enforces the actual performance that the buyer is entitled to according to its terms.[15] Entitlements to repair and replacement, on the other hand, arise only upon breach of the primary obligations laid down in the contract. One may wonder, therefore, whether a similar approach can, and should, be adopted to determine their scope. Relying on the approach adopted in civil law systems, in which the remedies have been recognised for some time and to which they are therefore more familiar, an argument can be made to link their availability to the scope of specific performance.

Civilian systems tend to regard repair and replacement as sub-forms of the general right of 'specific performance'. For example, in Dutch law the remedies are sub-forms of *nakoming*, whereas in Germany they are regarded as forms of 'supplementary performance', and thus sub-forms of *Leistung*.[16] The scope of the remedies, therefore, is closely linked to the scope of the general remedy of specific performance, and the balancing exercise made in chapter four equally applies. Factors relating to the performance interest of the buyer, and considerations of an economic nature that take account of the interests of the seller, determine the scope of repair and replacement just as they define the scope of the general right of specific performance.

Since the remedies of repair and replacement appear to have the same objective as specific performance—ie to give the buyer the performance that he contracted for—it appears right that their scope should be regulated in a way similar to that of specific performance. It is suggested that a similar approach can be adopted in English law. While there is a theoretical problem deriving from the distinction between primary and secondary obligations, this can be overcome by adopting a functional approach to harmonisation, which focuses on the results that the remedies seek to achieve.

First, a brief look at the problematic aspect—the distinction between primary and secondary obligations. Specific performance is generally regarded as a primary obligation flowing from the contract. In other words, it is an obligation to perform contained in the contract itself, as opposed to a secondary obligation which is triggered by a breach of a primary obligation.[17] The modern source for

[15] See pp 56–7.

[16] Hijma, *Asser V(I) Bijzondere Overeenkomsten* (n 5 above) [384]; Zimmermann, *The New German Law of Obligations* (n 14 above) 99–100. For the Dutch and German terminology, see ch 4, p 90.

[17] Compare E McKendrick, *Contract Law*, 6th edn (Basingstoke, Palgrave Macmillan, 2005) 393.

this distinction is the judgment of Lord Diplock in *Photo Production Ltd v Securicor Transport Ltd*, in which he states:[18]

> Leaving aside those comparatively rare cases in which the court is able to enforce a primary obligation by decreeing specific performance of it, breaches of primary obligations give rise to substituted or secondary obligations on the part of the party in default, and, in some cases, may entitle the other party to be relieved from further performance of his own primary obligations. These secondary obligations of the contract breaker and any concomitant relief of the other party from his own primary obligations also arise by implication of law—generally common law, but sometimes statute, as in the case of codifying statutes passed at the turn of the century, notably the Sale of Goods Act 1893.

However, whereas specific performance is a primary obligation, repair and replacement appear to fall within the category of secondary obligations. While Lord Diplock's speech, when referring to secondary obligations, seems to relate to the damages remedy only,[19] there is no objection in principle to the extension of the concept to other obligations that arise only upon breach of a primary obligation. The limitation of Lord Diplock's speech to damages is a direct result from the observation that

> [i]n the instant case, the only secondary obligations and concomitant reliefs that are applicable arise by implication of the common law as modified by the express words of the contract.[20]

The common law's answer to breach of a primary obligation is to give rise to a secondary obligation for the contract breaker to pay monetary compensation to the other party. However, this does not preclude the possibility that secondary obligations of a different nature may arise from other sources, eg statute law.[21] Thus, it is suggested that repair and replacement could be regarded as falling within the concept of secondary obligations—they arise upon breach of the (implied) primary obligation to deliver goods that are in conformity with the contract.[22]

This distinction between specific performance and the remedies of repair and replacement could become problematic, depending on the course that English law takes with regard to the former remedy. The relation between the remedies under the new Part 5A of the SGA will be explored in the next paragraph. For now, an important point is that the remedies are linked under the new regime, and a difference in scope would in this light be undesirable. Since a wide scope for repair and replacement was envisaged by the Consumer Sales Directive, it would be problematic if a restrictive scope of specific performance were adopted, for this might stand in the way of the proper functioning of the remedies.

[18] *Photo Production Ltd v Securicor Transport Ltd* [1980] AC 827 (HL) 848–9.
[19] *Ibid*, 849.
[20] *Ibid*.
[21] Compare Lord Diplock's statement above.
[22] SGA ss 13, 14 and 15.

However, the law relating to specific performance is currently in a state of flux, and it has been suggested that a development towards greater availability of the remedy may take place.[23] It is submitted that this may also solve any potential problems with regard to repair and replacement.

As Dutch law shows, for example, the distinction between primary and secondary obligations does not have to lead to the remedies being regarded as separate. Dutch law, to some extent, recognises a distinction between primary and secondary obligations similar to the one found in English law. The conformity requirements laid down in article 7:17 *BW* are not of a performance-oriented nature and can therefore, technically, not be the subject of an action for *nakoming*.[24] It is only because of the additional actions for delivery of missing goods and for repair and replacement of defective goods laid down in article 7:21 *BW* that, in the second instance, actions for *nakoming* are created.[25] The fact that these actions, nevertheless, are labelled actions for *nakoming*, and not mere secondary obligations, can be attributed to the civilian attitude towards performance. To say that repair and replacement should fall under the umbrella of *nakoming* is in line with the civil law's emphasis on the buyer's *right* to actual performance of the contractual obligations, the achievement of which is ultimately safeguarded by these remedies. The right to performance follows from the contract, and the remedies that protect this interest of the buyer, therefore, also flow from the contract itself.

The extension, under English law, of specific performance to include repair and replacement would result in a widening of its scope in another respect. It would then apply not only to cases of non-delivery but also to non-conformity cases. This is in line with the suggestion that English law is moving towards a greater recognition of the performance interest. If it is accepted that these remedies give the buyer exactly what he contracted for, the extension of specific performance and other performance-oriented remedies to non-conformity cases may be seen as a natural consequence of this development. Therefore, the new remedies introduced by the Consumer Sales Directive may be more compatible with English law than it appears at first sight.

Thus, adopting a functionalist approach,[26] the conclusion is that repair and replacement should be treated as sub-forms of specific performance, since they have the same objective, namely to provide the buyer with the performance that he contracted for (or a performance that secures the end result expected under the contract, which could include performance by a third party). In this sense, repair and replacement can be regarded as equivalents of specific performance. At least to the extent that they overlap in time, ie in cases where the buyer's

[23] See ch 4, pp 82 ff.

[24] Hijma, *Asser V(I) Bijzondere Overeenkomsten* (n 5 above) [384].

[25] *Ibid.*

[26] On functionalism, compare R Michaels, 'The Functional Method of Comparative Law', in M Reimann and R Zimmermann (eds), *The Oxford Handbook of Comparative Law* (Oxford, Oxford University Press, 2006) 339.

demand is made *after* a breach of the conformity requirements by the seller, the factors determining the scope of specific performance will be of equal application with regard to repair and replacement.[27]

IV. THE BUYER'S FREEDOM OF CHOICE

As became clear in the previous chapter, the availability and scope of specific performance is determined by an interplay between two main factors: the protection of the performance interest of the buyer and economic considerations, mostly related to efficiency. The latter form a counterweight to the buyer's general claim to performance deriving from the contract and their aim is to ensure that the parties opt for what, in the circumstances, will be the most appropriate remedy. In which place the different legal systems strike the balance between those interests is another matter, and not an altogether straightforward one, as was noted earlier. If a case has been made for specific performance to be generally available,[28] the question remains where repair and replacement fit into the hierarchy.

It will be argued that repair and replacement, like specific performance, should be of general availability to the buyer. In other words, the buyer will be entitled to either of these remedies as of right, immediately upon the seller's breach of his obligation to deliver conforming goods. Moreover, in order to ensure the best protection of the performance interest, it will be argued that the buyer should have a choice between the types of remedy: repair or replacement. Of course, an eye should also be kept on the interests of the seller and, therefore, freedom of choice will not be entirely unlimited. The restrictions on the buyer's freedom of choice will be discussed in the next section.

A preliminary observation—the argument that performance-oriented remedies should be generally available can be taken further, to the extent that they should be principal remedies of the buyer. That is, the buyer will generally be entitled to a performance-oriented remedy sooner than he becomes entitled to any other remedy, such as damages or termination. This is in accordance with the central argument proposed in this book. However, since, as will be seen,[29] the hierarchy of remedies appears to find its main origin in a policy that protects the interests of the seller, the next chapters—on cure—would appear a better place to deal with the arguments that may support such a hierarchy. In the present chapter, therefore, it will be taken as accepted that there *is or should be* a hierarchy of remedies in which performance-oriented remedies are the primary remedies of the buyer.

[27] Technically, specific performance may also be requested before the due delivery date, but the practical significance of this possibility is negligible. See ch 4, p 91.

[28] See ch 4, p 110.

[29] See ch 7, p 201.

1. The Choice between Performance-Oriented Remedies, Damages and Termination

Since repair and replacement share the same aim as specific performance, it seems logical to put them also at the top of the hierarchy. In other words, whether the buyer seeks a remedy for non-delivery or non-conformity of goods, he will generally be bound first to try to obtain performance from the seller. Arguably, the argument made in relation to specific performance—that it offers a better remedy than damages and that it should therefore be available as a first resort for the buyer[30]—can be extended to repair and replacement. After all, the remedies give the buyer the performance that he contracted for, without the risk of under-compensation often associated with damages awards, or the difficulties of assessment that may make an award of damages less practical.[31]

Not surprisingly, in the light of the foregoing, this is in accordance with the approach commonly found in civil law systems. In Dutch and German law, where the remedies are regarded as sub-forms of specific performance, they are available under the same conditions: no default is required, and the buyer is entitled to invoke them immediately after breach.[32]

This is in stark contrast with English law, where the protection of the performance interest has not yet received full recognition and damages are generally considered an adequate remedy. To what extent the Consumer Sales Directive has changed this is debatable.[33] The structure of the remedial scheme for breach of contract in English law, with its emphasis on damages, has proved difficult to reconcile with the Directive's regime, which puts the performance-oriented remedies first. A provision that has sought to clarify the relation between the different remedies is section 48E of the SGA, which sets out the court's powers with regard to the enforcement of the buyer's remedies. It gives the court a certain measure of discretion to choose and enforce the remedy that it deems appropriate and, furthermore, it links specific performance to repair and replacement as a means of enforcement of these remedies.[34] However, the wording of the provision is ambiguous, and it is not instantly clear to what extent the court can exercise its discretion. The link with specific performance might suggest that courts are allowed to take account of the damages remedy, and give a monetary award if this is more adequate than a performance remedy.

This interpretation is undesirable for two reasons. First, if the scope of the performance-oriented remedies is subsidiary to the availability of damages, it is doubtful whether English law has correctly implemented the Directive. Under

[30] See ch 3, p 60.

[31] The risk of overcompensation, on the other hand, may be countered by the limitations to the remedies, in particular disproportionality

[32] Compare art 7:21 *BW*; § 439 *BGB*. See also p 120.

[33] Another striking difference is that the remedies are not generally available in commercial sales; see further pp 142 ff.

[34] SGA s 48E(2).

the regime of the Directive, repair and replacement are generally available if the buyer requests them, subject only to the limitations of impossibility and disproportionality. If the same result is to be achieved under English law, a comparison with the adequacy of damages should not form part of the equation.[35] Secondly, if the adequacy of damages stands in the way of ordering specific performance, it would go against the policy that performance-oriented remedies should be generally available upon the buyer's request, which is generally adopted in other legal systems in Europe. Thus, English law would be out of step by adopting a different approach. This could be problematic for a number of reasons, not least the effect that it would have on legal certainty and consumer protection. After all, was not one of the objectives of the Consumer Sales Directive to lay down 'a common set of minimum rules of consumer law, valid no matter where goods are purchased within the Community'?[36] If the availability of the remedies differs from country to country, it is doubtful to what extent the Directive has actually achieved greater consumer protection.[37]

So does section 48E give effect to the provisions of the Consumer Sales Directive, or does it not? Before looking into this, it is useful to set out the section in full:

> *48E. Powers of the court*
>
> (1) In any proceedings in which a remedy is sought by virtue of this Part the court, in addition to any other power it has, may act under this section.
> (2) On the application of the buyer the court may make an order requiring specific performance or, in Scotland, specific implement by the seller of any obligation imposed on him by virtue of section 48B above.
> (3) Subsection (4) applies if—
>
> (a) the buyer requires the seller to give effect to a remedy under section 48B or 48C above or has claims to rescind under section 48C, but
> (b) the court decides that another remedy under section 48B or 48C is appropriate.
>
> (4) The court may proceed—
>
> (a) as if the buyer had required the seller to give effect to the other remedy, or if the other remedy is rescission under section 48C
> (b) as if the buyer had claimed to rescind the contract under that section.
>
> (5) If the buyer has claimed to rescind the contract the court may order that any reimbursement to the buyer is reduced to take account of the use he has had of the goods since they were delivered to him.
> (6) The court may make an order under this section unconditionally or on such terms and conditions as to damages, payment of the price and otherwise as it thinks just.

[35] Damages may be considered at a second stage, however, in relation to the proportionality test. See pp 132 ff below.

[36] Consumer Sales Directive, recital 5.

[37] Compare ch 2, p 39–40 (this is also true if countries adopt *stricter* measures of consumer protection!).

Whilst on the one hand section 48E(2) extends the scope of specific performance to cases of non-conformity by designating it as the enforcement mechanism for repair and replacement, on the other hand section 48E significantly curtails the discretion of the court in granting the remedy. If the buyer requests any of the remedies under sections 48B or 48C, ie repair, replacement, or price reduction, or if he claims to rescind the contract, sub-sections (3) and (4) provide that the court has the power to substitute the requested remedy with another one if it thinks the other remedy more appropriate. '[T]he other remedy', however, would seem to refer to the Part 5A remedies only and therefore prevents the court from taking into account damages. The self-contained nature of the Part, containing its own code of remedies with no reference to damages, thus stands in the way of the court referring to the traditional inadequacy of damages test for specific performance.[38]

Does section 48E leave room for a different interpretation? The use of the word 'may' in sub-section (2) suggests that maybe it does—if taken literally, the subsection does not oblige the court to make an order for specific performance if so requested, but gives it a certain measure of discretion to deny the remedy. Nevertheless, it seems unlikely that a court would interpret the section in this way. If it did, it is doubtful whether this interpretation would be upheld in the European Court of Justice, should a case ever reach that stage, for it would effectively defy the purpose of the Consumer Sales Directive. Though it has been suggested that the United Kingdom was under no obligation to choose specific performance as a means of enforcement,[39] and that the remedies could have been enforced instead by a substitutionary monetary award,[40] this assumption does not seem to reflect the true purpose of the Directive. The Directive aims to make performance-oriented remedies generally available,[41] and therefore, the court should not be allowed to deny the remedy if the buyer requests it. The self-contained nature of Part 5A is an indication that the English[42] legislature has recognised this and that it does not intend to provide the courts with such a wide discretion.

However, if this is the case, the use of the term 'may' in sub-section (2) seems inappropriate. Would a better formulation of the rule not have been

> [o]n the application of the buyer the court *will* make an order requiring specific performance or, in Scotland, specific implement by the seller of any obligation imposed on him by virtue of section 48B above?

This rule would indicate that the court is obliged to make an order enforcing performance if the buyer is so entitled under the conditions set out in section

[38] Compare DR Harris, 'Specific Performance—a Regular Remedy for Consumers?' (2003) 119 *Law Quarterly Review* 541 at 543.

[39] S Watterson, 'Consumer Sales Directive 1999/44/EC—The Impact on English Law' [2001] *European Review of Private Law* 197 at 212.

[40] *Ibid.*

[41] Compare Consumer Sales Directive, recital 10.

[42] This applies equally to Scots law. Compare SGA s 48A(1).

48B. It would be similar to the provisions found in civilian codes, such as the Dutch article 3:296 *BW*, which provides that the court will make an order for *nakoming* unless the law, the nature of the obligation or a legal act prescribe otherwise.[43]

On the other hand, it may be argued that the provision as it currently stands achieves just that result, and thus that it is in line with the purposes of the Directive. This view could be taken if one interprets the word 'may' in sub-section (2) not as conferring a wide discretion on the court to decide whether or not to grant specific performance, but rather as conferring a more limited discretion.[44] The subsection may indicate that, upon request of the buyer, the court is obliged to grant specific performance in order to enforce repair or replacement, unless it determines that the buyer does not have a right to repair or replacement under the provisions of Part 5A, for example because the requested remedy would be disproportionate. Nevertheless, if section 48E(2) is intended to have this effect, a less ambiguous choice of words might have pre-empted a few problems. By using the word 'may' the sub-section inevitably brings to mind section 52(1) of the SGA, in which the court's discretion to make an order for specific performance is laid down. It is hard to see how, in the light of this terminology, sub-section (2) is not to be read as a direct parallel to that provision.

Still, even if it is clear that section 48E should be interpreted in a way that gives the court no other choice but to make an order for specific performance, thus enforcing a buyer's request for repair or replacement, it is hard to envisage an overnight change of attitude in a matter that is so fundamental to English contract law. Harris, in his note on the new remedial scheme, contends that '[i]t is safe to predict that courts will seek ways to take account of the damages remedy when an order of specific performance is sought under Part 5A'.[45] However, he immediately attenuates this statement by adding that the self-contained nature of the Part stands in the way,[46] and it must be contended that indeed it would be very difficult for a court to justify a deviation from the Part 5A remedies by taking into account the adequacy of damages.

2. The Choice between Repair and Replacement

Once it has been established that the buyer is entitled to a performance-oriented remedy, it is submitted that he should have a free choice between repair and replacement. First, the performance interest of the buyer would seem best protected if the choice of remedy were the buyer's. In that case, the buyer would be

[43] Art 3:296(1) *BW* states: 'Tenzij uit de wet, uit de aard der verplichting of uit een rechtshandeling anders volgt, *wordt* hij die jegens een ander verplicht is iets te geven, te doen of na te laten, daartoe door de rechter, op vordering van de gerechtigde, veroordeeld' (emphasis added). See also ch 4, p 100.

[44] Compare Guest (ed), *Benjamin's Sale of Goods* (n 9 above) [12-102], [12-114].

[45] Harris, 'Specific Performance—a Regular Remedy for Consumers?' (n 38 above) 544.

[46] *Ibid*.

able to choose the remedy that to the best possible extent fulfills the contract and gives him the goods that he contracted for. Moreover, often the buyer will be in a better position to determine whether repaired goods would satisfy his aims, or whether replacement of the goods will be called for. For example, where repair cannot make the goods 'as good as new', replacement is likely to be the preferred remedy of the buyer and in those circumstances he may well be able to insist upon that remedy.[47]

Furthermore, other factors, of a more practical nature, may come into play. The buyer may prefer one remedy over the other for reasons of convenience. For example, a manufacturer who buys machinery for use in his factory will be able to make an assessment of the practical suitability of repair to correct a defect in the machine. This may be much harder to estimate for the seller, who may not be aware of any practical difficulties that may trouble the buyer if a different remedy, such as replacement, is opted for. Thus, where a piece of machinery has been installed, it may be difficult to replace the equipment in its entirety, but much easier to repair the machine or to replace certain components. It is thought that in this situation, the buyer should be free to choose the remedy of repair.

Support for giving the choice of remedy to the buyer can be found in the provisions of domestic sale of goods laws of some of the EU Member States. For example, the buyer's freedom to choose between repair and replacement is reflected in § 439 I *BGB*, which provides:

> As supplementary performance, the buyer may, at his option, demand the removal of the defect or supply a thing free from defects.[48]

Dutch law lists the remedies in article 7:21(1) *BW*, and also leaves the choice between repair and replacement to the buyer.[49]

It may be thought that this wide freedom could impinge upon the rights of the seller. However, there is no reason in principle why the buyer should not be allowed to choose the remedy that would best protect his performance interest or prevent undue inconvenience, as long as there are safeguards to protect the seller against unreasonable behaviour of the buyer. Where there are no safeguards, or where they are considered to be insufficient, it may be thought that

[47] Otherwise, Zimmermann, *The New German Law of Obligations* (n 14 above) 99. However, while the seller may have a better view on which remedies he actually is able to provide, this should not be the concern of the buyer. Initially, the buyer has an entitlement to choose between repair and replacement and it is up to the seller to try to the best of his abilities to effect it. If the buyer chooses a remedy which it turns out the seller is unable to provide, the buyer will then be able to invoke other remedies, such as damages. See further p 132 below.

[48] Original text: 'Der Käufer kann als Nacherfüllung nach seiner Wahl die Beseitigung des Mangels oder die Lieferung einer mangelfreien Sachen verlangen'. Translation available at http://www.iuscomp.org/gla.

[49] Hijma, *Asser V(I) Bijzondere Overeenkomsten* (n 5 above) [383]. That it was the intention of the legislature to make the remedies available at the buyer's option follows from the *travails préparatoirs*; WHM Reehuis and EE Slob, *Parlementaire Geschiedenis van het Nieuwe Burgerlijk Wetboek, Invoering Boeken 3, 5 en 6, Boek 7, Bijzondere Overeenkomsten* (Deventer, Kluwer, 1991) 136.

the buyer's freedom to choose his remedy should be limited. For this reason, the buyer's freedom of choice in Dutch sales law used to be subject to restrictions. Before the implementation of the Consumer Sales Directive, the seller had the right to refuse repair and offer replacement of the defective goods instead or to terminate the contract.[50] This provision applied to consumer sales only, and it was seen as compensation to the seller for the wide range of remedies that the law made available to the buyer on a mandatory basis, ie that could not be contracted out of if this would be to the detriment of the consumer-buyer.[51] Nevertheless, with the introduction of the Consumer Sales Directive, the provision that gave the seller the option to substitute replacement for repair has been abolished. The Directive regards the safeguards for the seller (such as the disproportionality restriction) as sufficient and therefore strikes the balance between the interests of the buyer and the seller in a different place.[52]

While similar considerations should apply in English (and Scots) law, the position there is somewhat complicated by the fact that it is unclear from the wording of the implementing legislation whether the choice of remedy lies with the buyer or with the seller. Section 48B(1) states that the buyer 'may require' the seller to repair or to replace goods if they are defective. The use of this wording suggests that the buyer may not have a right to either of these remedies but may have to accept a different remedy if the seller refuses to provide the requested one. This impression is reinforced by the language used in section 48B(3), which states the circumstances in which the seller is not obliged to carry out the requested remedy, namely in case of impossibility or disproportionality. In these circumstances the buyer 'must not require' the seller to repair or replace the goods, whichever the case may be.[53] Read in combination, the provisions give the impression that it is not a given right of the buyer to be able to demand repair or replacement, and that the choice of remedy may in practice lie with the seller.

The argument made above with regard to the enforceability of repair and replacement within the scheme of the SGA also feeds this impression.[54] If specific performance is not a regular remedy for consumers—as the analysis of section 48E of the SGA appears to suggest—this explains why the availability of repair or replacement to the buyer would be phrased in a tentative way, stipulating that he 'may require' them rather than giving an express entitlement to the remedies. After all, even if the buyer did require either of the remedies, it would still be at the discretion of the court whether or not to enforce the remedy through specific performance.

Nevertheless, it may be that such problems remain theoretical, as long as English courts are willing to look beyond the traditional framework of the SGA

[50] Art 7:21(2) *BW* (repealed).

[51] Hijma, *Asser V(I) Bijzondere Overeenkomsten* (n 5 above) [391].

[52] Compare art 7:21(5) *BW*; § 439 III *BGB*; derived from Consumer Sales Directive art 3(3).

[53] 'May not' would seem more appropriate; compare Guest (ed), *Benjamin's Sale of Goods* (n 9 above) [12-079].

[54] See above, pp 126–7.

and adopt a European approach instead. European law obliges the courts to interpret the new rules in an autonomous, European manner.[55] Moreover, it would be in accordance with the Directive's objective of strengthening consumer protection to place the choice of remedy with the buyer rather than with the seller. As said, this solution would not unduly harm the interest of the seller and, therefore, would also be in accordance with considerations of market regulation.[56]

In the commercial context, if the remedies are available there,[57] the arguments appear also in favour of the buyer's freedom to choose between repair and replacement. Because of the non-mandatory nature of provisions relating to commercial sales, the parties will always be able to determine for themselves where the choice of remedy shall lie. They can incorporate terms into their contract to this effect. Since the discrepancy in bargaining power between commercial parties in general is less great than it is in consumer sales, it is thought that the parties should be allowed to determine their respective duties and obligations in this manner. Nevertheless, in light of the assumption that the buyer will generally be in a better position to determine which remedy is most appropriate, it makes sense to give the buyer an extra tool in the negotiation process in the form of a default rule favouring freedom of choice on his part between the remedies of repair and replacement. Default rules to this effect may stimulate efficient results in commercial dealings.[58]

V. RESTRICTIONS ON THE FREEDOM OF CHOICE

The buyer's freedom to choose between repair and replacement, however, is not absolute. The Consumer Sales Directive provides that the buyer may require the seller to repair the goods or to replace them unless those remedies are impossible or disproportionate.[59] National systems have copied these limitations into their sale of goods laws—section 48B(3) of the SGA, article 7:21(4) *BW* and § 275 I and II *BGB* implement them under UK, Dutch and German sales laws. It is in the nature of the terminology used, however, that it leaves a certain measure of flexibility. Open terms such as 'proportionality', and to some extent also 'impossibility', do not specify to what extent the provisions actually take account of the interests of the seller. In what circumstances is a remedy impossible or disproportionate? Since the impossibility point has been discussed in the previous chapter,[60] and similar considerations apply here, the current section will focus on the proportionality test.

[55] Compare Guest (ed), *Benjamin's Sale of Goods* (n 9 above) [12-114].
[56] See also p 201 and p 207.
[57] English law currently only recognises entitlements to repair or replacement in consumer sales; see p 142.
[58] Compare ch 3, p 62.
[59] Art 3(3) and recital 11.
[60] See ch 4, p 97, 100.

The question can be divided into three parts. First, starting from the provisions of the Consumer Sales Directive, there is a question as to the scope of the proportionality test—Which remedies should be taken into account in the comparison? It may be thought that the test should apply only to the remedy itself. Another possibility would be to make a comparison between repair and replacement and, thirdly, a comparison could be made between repair, replacement and other available remedies (eg including damages, termination and/or price reduction). The wording of the Directive does not give a definitive answer as to which of these options should prevail. Arguably, the answer depends on which scope a legal system allows for specific performance. The best solution, it will be argued, is to enable a comparison at least between repair, replacement and damages so that the courts are able to arrive at the most appropriate remedy in individual cases.

However, this solution would appear to work only in civil law systems, which only in exceptional circumstances deny a request for specific performance or related remedies. If it were applied in English law, the availability of repair and replacement would be limited significantly, for the more restrictive approach to the availability of specific performance would enable the courts to deny a buyer's request for one of the remedies in the majority of cases. In other words, while civilian courts would be reluctant to overrule a request for repair or replacement merely on the basis that damages offer a more cost-effective solution, common law courts would be likely to find this enough justification for denying the remedy even if it meant that the buyer would not see his performance interest protected. An alternative solution in this context could be, if the buyer requests either of the remedies, to allow a comparison only between repair and replacement. This, however, will be argued to be only a second-best solution.

The second point relates to the factors that are taken into account in the proportionality test—To what extent do they coincide with the bars to specific performance? It will be argued that the factors listed in the Consumer Sales Directive fall within the earlier recognised limits on specific performance. The elements of the proportionality test, thus, can be brought under the umbrella of the severe hardship or good faith restriction.

Finally, the third question is whether repair and replacement, with these limitations, should also be made available for commercial sales. In German law, the rules apply to consumer and commercial sales alike, and the same is true for Dutch law. English law, on the other hand, has not formally recognised the remedies in a commercial context. However, it will be argued that the civil law approach offers a better model for future harmonisation. Support for this view, further, may be gleaned for the fact that CISG recognises repair and replacement as remedies of the buyer.

1. The Proportionality of the Remedy

In English law, it appears that, in order to determine whether repair or replacement is a proportionate remedy, two comparisons need to be made.[61] In the first place, it needs to be determined whether the remedy is proportionate on its own. To that effect, a comparison needs to be made between on the one hand the costs to the seller of providing the remedy, and on the other hand the benefits that the buyer derives from receiving the remedy. The same applies in German and in Dutch law.[62] Secondly, a comparison should be made between repair and replacement, weighing out the costs and benefits of both remedies. However, this second part of the test may be criticised for being too narrow. Arguably, damages should form part of the comparison. Other remedies, such as termination and price reduction, may be excluded.

It should be noted that in relation to the concurrent rules on the availability of the remedies in Dutch law, it has been argued that the second-stage comparison is governed by the principle of subsidiarity rather than that of proportionality.[63] The correctness of this approach, however, may be questioned. The subsidiarity principle is concerned with a balancing between different alternatives in order to determine which one offers the least onerous solution. An earlier chapter, however, has shown that, rather than merely looking for the least invasive solution, the search is for a remedy that best protects the interests of the buyer. The general availability of performance-oriented remedies may be justified on this basis.[64] Further, while limitations to the availability of the remedies may weigh the interests of the different parties and, in this context, may look for the remedy that is least onerous, the principle of subsidiarity will then be part and parcel of the proportionality principle. After all, a remedy is unlikely to be proportionate if a less harmful alternative is available. Since in essence the same principle is at work then, it does not seem desirable to differentiate between subsidiarity and proportionality in relation to the weighing of remedies against each other.[65]

a) Proportionality and Damages

Arguably, the proportionality test should take account of other available remedies apart from repair and replacement, in particular damages. This would

[61] Bradgate and Twigg-Flesner, *Blackstone's Guide to Consumer Sales and Associated Guarantees* (n 4 above) 92 ff.

[62] See for example LG Münster, *ZfSch* 2004, 215–17; OLG Karlsruhe, *ZGS* 2004, 465–6; OLG Braunschweig, *NJW* 2003, 1053–4. For Dutch law, see MM Stolp, *Ontbinding, schadevergoeding en nakoming. De remedies voor wanprestatie in het licht van de beginselen van subsidiariteit en proportionaliteit* (Deventer, Kluwer, 2007) 249, 250–51.

[63] Stolp, *Ontbinding, schadevergoeding en nakoming* (n 62 above) 188 ff.

[64] See ch 3, p 60.

[65] Otherwise, Stolp, *Ontbinding, schadevergoeding en nakoming* (n 62 above) 7–8. Compare however L Reurich, 'Risico en proportionaliteit' in WH van Boom and others (eds), *Koop! BW-krant jaarboek 1998* (Deventer, Gouda Quint, 1998) 59, fn 25.

enable the courts to make a more rounded assessment of the appropriateness of the requested remedy. Where repair or replacement would be excessively costly in comparison to, for example, a remedy in damages, the court would be free to make a monetary award instead. It is submitted that, provided certain preconditions are fulfilled, this view should be preferred to the narrow view that makes a comparison only between repair and replacement. The main precondition, however, would be that the proportionality test between performance-oriented remedies and damages starts from the premise that the former type of remedy is available if the buyer requests it, and that it will only be replaced with damages in exceptional circumstances. As seen in the previous chapter, general availability of specific performance is a prerequisite to offering a buyer sufficient protection of his performance interest.

Support for this view can be found in civilian systems. Thus, German law provides, in § 439 III *BGB*, that

> *[w]ithout prejudice to § 275 II and III*, the seller may refuse the form of supplementary performance chosen by the buyer if such performance is possible only with unreasonable expense (emphasis added).

The general provision, § 275 *BGB*, lays down the circumstances in which *Leistung* may be denied—ie in cases of impossibility or where

> performance requires expenditure which, having regard to the subject matter of the obligation and the principle of good faith, is manifestly disproportionate to the obligee's interest in performance.

As seen in the previous chapter, the good faith or severe hardship test may lead to a refusal of the remedy in cases where the buyer's request for it would be disproportionate with regard to other available remedies, in particular damages.[66] The comparison, therefore, includes damages. Seeing that § 439 III *BGB* expressly provides that the same rules should apply to repair and replacement ('without prejudice to § 275 II and III'), the proportionality test will also have to take account of damages.

The fact that the provision also states that 'it is necessary to have regard to . . . the question whether the defect could be remedied by the other form of supplementary performance without material detriment to the buyer' would not appear to change this, though it is of some significance. It is derived from the Consumer Sales Directive, which, though ambiguous in its wording, appears to suggest a narrow basis for the proportionality test—ie the comparison should be between repair and replacement only, and should not include termination or price reduction.[67] However, the Directive does not extend to damages. Therefore, all the provision does is emphasise that termination and price

[66] See in particular *Multi Vastgoed BV/Onroerend Goed Maatschappij Nethou BV*, HR 5 januari 2001, *NJ* 2001, 79; ch 4, p 101, 108.

[67] See below, pp 134 ff.

reduction do not form part of the test. However, it leaves intact the possibility that damages may be taken into account on the basis of § 275 II and III *BGB*.

Similar observations can be made for Dutch law. While the Directive has made adjustments to the hierarchy of remedies, it does not appear to have had an effect on the substance or general scope of the rights of repair and replacement found in the pre-existing version of article 7:21 *BW*. Restrictions on the general right of *nakoming*, of which repair and replacement are regarded as sub-forms, are largely similar to those found in the Directive—impossibility and (under the heading of good faith) proportionality.[68] Thus, article 7:21(4) *BW* provides that repair and replacement are unavailable if they are impossible or if they 'cannot be demanded of the seller'. Making the link back to the general restrictions on *nakoming*, the proportionality requirement also appears to envisage a comparison that takes account of damages. *Multi Vastgoed* is still good law and is of general application to consumer as well as commercial cases.[69]

The adoption of a more limited comparison in English law, therefore, appears odd. Why should the comparison be more limited than in civilian systems, especially since that is where the remedies of repair and replacement find their origin? It appears that the narrow view on the substance of the proportionality test is linked to the generally more restrictive view towards the availability of specific performance in English law. It guarantees that repair and replacement are not denied merely on the basis that the court finds that damages are a more cost-effective solution, regardless of whether a monetary award would sufficiently protect the performance interest of the buyer.[70] This appears to be a second-best solution, inspired purely by the restrictive approach that English law takes towards specific performance, and there is little other justification for it. The Directive itself does not appear to stand in the way of a proportionality test that takes account of damages in comparison to repair and replacement. Moreover, the need for a restrictive approach appears questionable in the light of criticisms relating to the limited scope for specific performance in English law, which appear to steer towards a reconsideration, and potential expansion, of the scope of the remedy.[71]

b) Proportionality and Termination or Price Reduction

With regard to termination (or, in the terminology of the Directive, rescission) and price reduction, however, a case may be made for a narrower interpretation. The arguments are not all one way, however—the wording of the

[68] See ch 4, pp 100 ff.

[69] *Multi Vastgoed* (n 66 above). See MBM Loos, *Consumentenkoop* (Deventer, Kluwer, 2004) 55. See also ch 4, p 101 and below, p 138, 144.

[70] Compare above, pp 124–5.

[71] See ch 4, pp 82 ff.

Consumer Sales Directive is very ambiguous in this respect. If any solution is to be found, it is on grounds of policy.

Bradgate and Twigg-Flesner list a number of arguments based on the wording of the Directive that allegedly could support the narrow view.[72] Nevertheless, these appear somewhat contrived. First, it is said that the location of the proportionality test in the middle of article 3(3), which is concerned solely with repair and replacement, points in this direction. Price reduction and rescission are introduced in article 3(5). According to Bradgate and Twigg-Flesner, '[i]f it had been intended to apply the disproportionality test to all the remedies, it would have made more sense to include it in a separate sub-paragraph following Article 3(5)'. This argument seems weak mainly because it completely ignores article 3(2), which actually introduces rescission and price reduction at the same time as it introduces repair and replacement. While the provision refers to paragraph (3) for the availability of repair and replacement, and paragraphs (5) and (6) for the availability of the other remedies, there is no reason to assume that this excludes rescission and price reduction from comparison made with regard to the disproportionality test in paragraph (3). The provision merely sets out the range of available remedies and it refers to the rules that regulate their availability—but it does not indicate that these rules exclude reference to the other available remedies. The location of the proportionality test, in itself, therefore does not seem to give strong support to the narrow view.

In fact, the reference to 'the alternative remedy' in article 3(3) is ambiguous as to what it includes. The provision requires a comparison to be made between the costs of the buyer's chosen remedy and 'the alternative remedy' which, according to Bradgate and Twigg-Flesner, in its context in article 3(3), seems to suggest a comparison of repair with replacement and vice versa.[73] If a wider comparison, between repair and replacement and other remedies, had been intended, different wording would have been more appropriate. For example, the provision could have stated 'another' or 'any other' remedy. However, this does not appear conclusive in itself. The Dutch provision implementing article 3(3) of the Directive, for example, does speak of 'another right or another claim',[74] instead of referring to 'the alternative remedy'. Still, the context in which the provision is to be read is not any clearer than the Directive. On the basis of the discussion of specific performance in the previous chapter, one

[72] Bradgate and Twigg-Flesner, *Blackstone's Guide to Consumer Sales and Associated Guarantees* (n 4 above) 93.

[73] *Ibid.* Compare also MC Bianca and S Grundmann (eds), *EU Sales Directive: Commentary* (Antwerp, Intersentia, 2002) 162, the text of which suggests that 'the alternative remedy' refers to the remedy of replacement only.

[74] Art 7:21(5) *BW*: 'Herstel of vervanging kan bij een consumentenkoop van de verkoper niet gevergd worden indien de kosten daarvan in geen verhouding staan tot de kosten van de uitoefening van *een ander recht of een andere vordering* die de koper toekomt, gelet op de waarde van de zaak indien zij aan de overeenkomst zou beantwoorden, de mate van afwijking van het overeengekomene en de vraag of de uitoefening van een ander recht of een andere vordering geen ernstige overlast voor de koper veroorzaakt' (emphasis added).

would expect at least that a comparison between repair and replacement and the damages remedy would be allowed, though no further hint is given as to the inclusion of rescission and price reduction in the comparison. The terminology, therefore, could apply equally well to a wide comparison and does not unambiguously point to a narrow comparison only between repair and replacement.

Finally, the fact that recital 10 emphasises the primary character of repair and replacement, perhaps signifying that any comparison made should be made between them,[75] appears weak authority for the narrow view. The mere circumstance that rescission and price reduction are available only when repair and replacement are either impossible or disproportionate does not exclude them from the scope of the proportionality test. While the balance may generally be struck in favour of repair and replacement—since they give the buyer the actual performance that he contracted for[76]—it should be possible to deny these remedies where they are disproportionate in comparison to rescission and/or price reduction.

Article 3(5) may, nevertheless, also lend some support to the wider view, which includes price reduction and rescission in the comparison. However, the authority for this, also, is weak. Bradgate and Twigg-Flesner argue that, while a buyer will not be entitled to repair or replacement if these are impossible or disproportionate, it is hard to see how both could be disproportionate, or how, if one were impossible, the other could be considered disproportionate. Therefore, the only circumstances in which both would be unavailable would be where they were both impossible. However, since article 3(5) does not refer to both being impossible but to the consumer being entitled to neither remedy, it would make more sense if the proportionality test admitted a comparison between repair and replacement on the one hand, and rescission and price reduction on the other hand.[77] Nevertheless, their argument fails to recognise that instances of impossibility or disproportionality are not the only occasions in which a buyer may not be entitled to repair or replacement. There is also the situation in which a buyer has requested either repair or replacement, and these have not been successful. In that case, the buyer may resort to rescission or price reduction. In the light of this, it is doubtful whether article 3(5) had in mind the proportionality test and whether, therefore, the provision can be cited in support of the wide view. Keeping in mind the Directive's two-tier hierarchy of remedies, it is not unlikely that the wording of the provision mainly seeks to emphasise the secondary nature of the remedies of rescission and price reduction.

According to Bradgate and Twigg-Flesner, '[p]erhaps the strongest reason for favouring the narrow view is policy'.[78] They argue that if the wider view were

[75] Bradgate and Twigg-Flesner, *Blackstone's Guide to Consumer Sales and Associated Guarantees* (n 4 above) 93.

[76] See also above, p 117.

[77] Bradgate and Twigg-Flesner, *Blackstone's Guide to Consumer Sales and Associated Guarantees* (n 4 above) 93–4.

[78] *Ibid*, 94.

adopted, which would include rescission and price reduction in the comparison, the consumer would generally be restricted to those remedies and would not be able to obtain repair or replacement. After all, those remedies, especially price reduction, are likely to be available at lower cost to the seller than repair or replacement.

To the extent that the argument hinges on the assumption that price reduction would provide a more cost-effective solution, it appears to be a strong indication in favour of the narrow view. Only one rider needs to be added—namely, that there is no evidence that this is the case in practice. Therefore, where repair and replacement can be achieved at the same or lower cost than the money that the seller would lose in case of price reduction, they would not appear to be disproportionate. Moreover, in cases where the remedies are available at equal cost, repair and replacement would seem preferable. After all, they provide the buyer with a true remedy (ie they cure the defect in the goods), whereas price reduction does not involve any action on the part of the seller to make good the defect in the goods. Thus, where businesses are able to cut costs by repair or replacement of defective goods, and if they can do so on a large scale, it may be more profitable than price reduction. There may, therefore, be instances in which price reduction does not result in a more cost-effective outcome.

Whether the same argument applies to termination or rescission is debatable. Like price reduction, it does not give the buyer the performance that he contracted for—instead the obligations of the parties come to an end and the buyer may claim damages in compensation of his performance interest. The fact that the remedy falls short of giving the buyer the performance that he contracted for could plead in favour of regarding it purely as a second-stage remedy and treating it in similar fashion as price reduction. Thus, it would make sense not to include it in the proportionality test. However, a counter-argument would be that termination is hardly ever invoked on its own, but is generally accompanied by an additional remedy in damages. To this extent, it could be argued that the effect of the remedy is similar to damages and that it should therefore receive the same treatment as that remedy. This would mean that, in national legal systems, the general attitude towards the protection of the performance interest determines whether the remedy is taken into account in the proportionality test. In common law systems, a narrow view would be adopted, for to do otherwise would enable the courts to deny repair or replacement in every case where damages are deemed to be inadequate or, if the developments in this direction continue, inappropriate. In civil law systems, termination could be taken into account in the proportionality test, for specific performance would anyhow be denied only in exceptional circumstances.[79]

The better view, it is submitted, is to leave termination out of the proportionality test altogether. While it may often be linked to a monetary remedy (eg compensatory damages), it does not have to be, for the buyer is not obliged also

[79] Compare ch 4, p 99.

to make a claim for damages. On its own, it is hard to determine whether termination is a more cost-effective remedy than repair or replacement. After all, it releases the parties from their obligations, leaving them free to take whatever action they deem appropriate—but it is outside the scope of the proportionality test to make an enquiry into the parties' likely course of action after termination. Whether the buyer intends to go into the market to make a cover purchase, or whether he gives up the transaction altogether are not factors that can be taken into account at this stage. The buyer may not even have made up his mind on this, since his primary aim is to obtain repair or replacement. Therefore, termination should be seen purely as a second-stage remedy and no enquiries should be made about it in relation to the restrictions on repair and replacement.

2. Elements of the Proportionality Test

Which factors, then, should be taken into account in the proportionality test in consumer sales? It appears that the starting point is similar to that of the severe hardship or good faith restriction on specific performance—the costs of the remedy. According to article 3(3) of the Consumer Sales Directive, '[a] remedy shall be deemed to be disproportionate if it imposes costs on the seller which, in comparison with the alternative remedy, are unreasonable'. It also lists a number of factors that may be taken into account in determining this: the value that the goods would have if there were no lack of conformity; the significance of the lack of conformity; and whether the alternative remedy could be completed without significant inconvenience to the consumer. While these factors do not directly correspond with any of the factors encountered in the discussion on specific performance, it has to be remembered that the cases there discussed did not relate to consumer sales per se. For example, cases such as *Co-operative Insurance Society* and similar cases from other jurisdictions focus on economic interests of a commercial nature, rather than on the interests of individual consumers. Nevertheless, each of the factors listed in relation to consumer or commercial sales relates to situations in which an order for specific performance or another performance-oriented remedy would be too onerous on the seller. In this respect, therefore, it is thought that they can all be brought under the umbrella of the general severe hardship or good faith test for specific performance.

A brief discussion of each of the factors that make up the proportionality test in consumer sales will serve to show their potential scope. It will be argued that the restrictions should be interpreted so as to limit the buyer's entitlement to repair or replacement only in exceptional circumstances. This test may even be slightly more restrictive than the one derived from *Multi Vastgoed*, which does not apply exclusively to consumer sales.[80] After all, consumer buyers in general

[80] *Multi Vastgoed* (n 66 above). See above, p 133.

have a greater interest in obtaining actual performance—the 'consumer surplus'—than commercial buyers do.[81] The restrictive nature of the test, moreover, is reflected in recital 11 of the Directive, which states: 'In order to determine whether the costs are unreasonable, the costs of one remedy should be *significantly higher* than the costs of the other' (emphasis added).[82]

A preliminary comment—the factors here listed are relevant to both stages of the proportionality test, ie the proportionality of the remedy in itself and in comparison with other available remedies. The first stage of the test—which focuses on the proportionality of the chosen remedy itself—involves a cost/benefit analysis between the interests of the seller in providing, and of the buyer in obtaining the remedy. The second stage of the test balances repair, replacement and damages against one another. It requires an assessment of the cost/benefit balance of the requested remedy and the other remedies, followed by a comparison of the costs and benefits of each.

a) Value of the Goods

The first factor, the value of the goods, appears to be a good practical indicator of the proportionality of the chosen remedy, for it lays down some fairly straightforward rules of thumb as to the application of the test. Thus, as a general rule, low value consumer goods which are produced on a large scale will lend themselves best to replacement. Repair is likely to be disproportionate in such cases, for the costs of the remedy may well exceed the value of the goods. For more sophisticated goods, such as electronic equipment, mobile phones, and computers, however, repair may usually be the more appropriate option. One reason is that the remedy may be cheaper. Should a seller be obliged to offer replacement of such goods, he would be left with the defective items on his hands and, even if these can be repaired, they cannot generally be resold as 'new' at their full price.[83] Furthermore, it is thought that repair may be proportionate, even at high cost to the seller, where goods that would have been of high value had they conformed to the contract, have been rendered useless by the particular defect.

The value of the goods, however, will hardly ever be determinative on its own. The next factor, the significance of the defect, overlaps to a certain extent with this factor.[84] A minor lack of conformity, for example, is unlikely to be sufficient justification for an expensive repair even where the goods are of high

[81] Loos, *Consumentenkoop* (n 69 above). Also ch 3, p 61.

[82] Few specific data are available as to what would qualify as 'significantly higher'. A difference of 20% appears to be enough in German law (LG Ellwangen, *NJW* 2003, 517), though it has also been suggested that a 10% discrepancy would suffice (G Bitter and E Meidt, 'Nacherfüllungsrecht und Nacherfüllungspflicht des Verkäufers im neuen Schuldrecht' (2001) 22 *ZIP-Zeitschrift für Wirtschaftsrecht* 2114 at 2122).

[83] Bradgate and Twigg-Flesner, *Blackstone's Guide to Consumer Sales and Associated Guarantees* (n 4 above) 94.

[84] *Ibid*, 95.

value. This factor, thus, puts a strong restriction on the buyer's freedom to choose a remedy. Still, as will be seen, the consumer may expect a more lenient treatment in this respect than the commercial buyer.

b) Significance of the Lack of Conformity

In a Dutch case,[85] a consumer-buyer sought termination of a contract for the purchase of a sofa after the upholstery had started to show defects. The price of the covers was *f*500, whereas the price paid for the entire sofa was approximately *f*2250. In the light of what were, in the opinion of the court, relatively insignificant costs of repair, termination of the contract was held to be a disproportionate remedy. Though the case appears to have a stronger affiliation with cure,[86] it does give some indication as to the circumstances in which repair is deemed an appropriate remedy. Apparently, the fact that the costs of the remedy made up almost a quarter of the contract price did not dissuade the court from making an order for repair.

Thus, it can be seen that it may sometimes be proportionate to request repair from the seller, even if the costs of the remedy amount to a significant part of the contract price. It should be noted here that the actual comparison should be between the costs of repair and the *value* of the goods in their conforming state. The contract price is only relevant to the extent that it represents the true value of the goods. In relation to a sofa, the indication of its value should be the market price, ie the price for which a sofa of that type can normally be obtained in the market at the time of the breach. Where, as here, the defect is relatively minor in nature and can be repaired easily, while the value of the goods is relatively high, repair is the most appropriate remedy for both parties.

Nevertheless, in comparison to the *Multi Vastgoed* case,[87] it is somewhat surprising to see a court award repair where the cost of the remedy is not a mere three or four per cent of the contract price, but amounts to almost a quarter of it. Two explanations may be given for this divergence. First, the constructor in *Multi Vastgoed* had made express guarantees with regard to the quality of the building. He was defeated by his own warranties and had to provide the more expensive remedy. Secondly, and of more general application, the courts will be inclined to attach greater value to the performance interest of a consumer than to that of a commercial buyer. In the case regarding the sofa, therefore, the court would have started out from a stronger premise to order repair, had the buyer requested it, than it would have in a commercial case.

[85] Unreported, 14 april 1994 (Kantongerecht Tilburg, The Netherlands).

[86] Moreover, it is debatable whether termination should be subject to a similar good faith restriction as specific performance. Compare Loos, *Consumentenkoop* (n 69) 55–6.

[87] *Multi Vastgoed* (n 66 above).

c) Inconvenience to the Buyer

The costs of repair or replacement, the value of the goods had they not been defective, and the significance of the lack of conformity, thus, are the factors that determine the proportionality of the remedy. All of these, nevertheless, can and should be outweighed by the one remaining factor of the disproportionality test: the degree of inconvenience caused to the buyer by the provision of the particular remedy. This is the factor that, instead of focusing on the economic interests of the seller, relates back to the starting point of the Directive's remedial scheme, namely the protection of the buyer.[88]

The inconvenience criterion may enable a consumer to obtain a remedy that would otherwise have been considered disproportionate.[89] A situation where the inconvenience caused to the buyer may entitle him to a 'disproportionate' remedy is where the fact that the buyer will have to do without the goods for some time while waiting for their repair or replacement causes him unreasonable difficulty. An example may be the purchase of a lap-top computer by a student. If there is a problem with the computer, for example the screen is defective, the buyer will usually have to return it to the seller who then either carries out the repair himself, or sends the computer back to the manufacturer in order for it to be repaired. The costs of this will generally be lower for the seller than the costs associated with replacement. While the repairs are made, however, the buyer may experience considerable inconvenience by not having the laptop at his disposal. Unless the seller offers a temporary substitute, this may be sufficient ground for the buyer to demand replacement even where the other factors (value of the goods, significance of the lack of conformity) would have pointed towards a different remedy.

Nevertheless, while it is important to ensure that the buyer is not harmed by the seller's initial failure to perform correctly and subsequent attempts to remedy such failure, it should be noted that the awarded remedy should also not put him in a better position than he would have been in had the contract been fulfilled satisfactorily in the first place. The buyer's choice of remedy may therefore, for example, be limited where he has had use of the defective goods for a significant period of time. Thus, in a Dutch case concerning a defective washing machine,[90] a limitation of the buyer's remedies to price reduction or damages seemed appropriate. Having had use of the machine for 2½ years prior to the decision of the tribunal, a replacement order would have left the buyer with a new washing machine and the additional, free use of the defective machine for this period of time. The tribunal did not need to make a decision on this point as the buyer changed his claim to one for damages in the course of the proceedings.

[88] Bradgate and Twigg-Flesner, *Blackstone's Guide to Consumer Sales and Associated Guarantees* (n 4 above) 95.

[89] *Ibid.*

[90] Geschillencommissie Thuiswinkel, 22 november 2005 en 11 april 2006 [2006] *Tijdschrift voor Consumentenrecht* 171.

However, a decision to this effect would seem to fit with the proportionality exception to the remedy of replacement.[91]

The inconvenience test, therefore, confirms that the interests of the buyer are of utmost importance in determining whether a remedy will be deemed disproportionate or not. What is striking, however, is that it is mentioned so explicitly in an instrument like the Consumer Sales Directive, while instruments relating to commercial sales (eg CISG) do not stipulate that a remedy may be disproportionate if another remedy 'could be completed without significant inconvenience' to the buyer. This would seem to give a strong indication to the courts to award an alternative remedy, as long as it does not cause significant inconvenience and, thus, to place the interests of the seller higher than those of the buyer. An explanation, however, may be that the Directive merely seeks to emphasise the importance of not causing inconvenience to the consumer when providing a remedy, but that it does not intend to suggest that another remedy should be opted for simply because it is not inconvenient. The other criteria will determine the proportionality of the remedy, and the inconvenience factor is merely there to rein those in if necessary. In this respect, the explicit mentioning of it may be regarded as another indication that consumers' interests are taken seriously, sometimes more explicitly than the interests of commercial parties.

3. Repair and Replacement in Commercial Sales

The discussion, up to this point, has focused on repair and replacement as remedies in consumer sales. However, while English law only makes the remedies available in this context,[92] no good reason appears to exist to limit the scope of the remedies to consumer contracts and to exclude them from commercial transactions. In fact, other systems do extend the scope of repair and replacement to the commercial sphere. For example, § 439 *BGB* and article 7:21 *BW*, which make the remedies available, are of general application respectively in German and in Dutch law. Furthermore, CISG—which applies to international commercial sale of goods contracts—lists the remedies as available.[93] Therefore, should repair and replacement not also be made available for commercial sales in English law?

a) The Availability of Repair and Replacement in Commercial Sales

The limitation of the right to demand repair or replacement of non-conforming goods to consumer sales in English law has been questioned. According to Beale, 'it seems to be a rule that would be suitable for many commercial sales, and . . .

[91] See MBM Loos [2006] *Tijdschrift voor Consumentenrecht* 171 at 173.

[92] That is, in the absence of express stipulation by the parties that recourse may be had to repair and/or replacement.

[93] See CISG art 46(2) and (3).

many sales contracts contain express provisions to a similar effect'.[94] Moreover, as the process of harmonisation of European contract law intensifies, the time may come to bring English law into line with these systems. In a global economy, or even within the regional economy of the European Union, England would not seem to benefit from being an outsider.[95] However, it is likely that the fact that its laws are out of step with other legal systems on significant issues such as the remedies in sale of goods law will only serve to strengthen this image. There may, therefore, be good reason for adjusting the remedial scheme in the sale of goods law and bringing it closer to the continental systems.

Also, autonomous reasons plead for an extension of the remedies of repair and replacement to commercial sales. First, repair and replacement, like specific performance in its narrow sense, avoid situations of under-compensation, to which the damages remedy is often prone.[96] Secondly, the case law shows that the remedies are not entirely unheard of in commercial practice.[97] From a viewpoint of legal certainty, it would be desirable for the law to reflect this, for it would make it easier for sellers and buyers to understand their rights. Especially small businesses may benefit from such provisions. After all, rules of commercial sales law are of a default nature and the parties are therefore free to replace them with their own contractual provisions.[98] In situations where there is a striking inequality of bargaining power, eg where a small business enters into a transaction to purchase goods from a multi-national supplier, a small business may profit from a legal backup of the remedies of repair and replacement. An exclusion of the remedies may have to satisfy the reasonableness test of UCTA,[99] thus protecting the weaker contracting party against unfair exclusion clauses.

b) Restrictions on Repair and Replacement—The Proportionality Test in Commercial Sales

If repair and replacement are made available in commercial sales, they will of course be subject to restrictions, for the buyer's entitlement has to be weighed against the justifiable interests of the seller. But what form do these restrictions take? There are at least three possibilities. First would be to adopt the same standards as in consumer sales, ie impossibility and disproportionality. This is

[94] H Beale, 'English Law Reform and the Impact of European Private Law' in S Vogenauer and S Weatherill (eds), *The Harmonisation of European Contract Law* (Oxford, Hart Publishing, 2006) 31, 33. Beale makes an exception, however, stating that the remedies may not be suitable for commodity sales; *ibid*, p 33, fn 16.

[95] The argument applies to the UK as a whole. Compare E McKendrick, 'Good Faith: A Matter of Principle?' in ADM Forte, *Good Faith in Contract and Property* (Oxford, Hart Publishing, 1999) 39 at 59.

[96] Compare ch 3, p 61 ff, ch 4, pp 88–9.

[97] For example *British Fermentation Products Ltd v Compair Reavell Ltd* [1999] 2 All ER (Comm) 389 (QBD).

[98] This freedom may, however, be curtailed by the Unfair Contract Terms Act 1977 (UCTA).

[99] UCTA s 6(3).

the solution adopted in German law, reflecting the origin that the recent reform of the law of obligations has in the Consumer Sales Directive. The second option would be to adopt the approach of Dutch law. Article 7:21(1) *BW* provides that repair is available 'as long as the seller can reasonably give effect to it', whereas replacement is available 'unless the lack of conformity is too minor to justify it'. Finally, the third option is that found in article 46(2) and (3) of CISG. Repair may be required of the seller 'unless this is unreasonable having regard to all the circumstances', while the buyer may require delivery of substitute goods 'only if the lack of conformity constitutes a fundamental breach of contract'.

While each system uses slightly different wording, the restrictions on repair and replacement appear to show great similarities. Impossibility, quite naturally, is a reason for denial of the remedies in all of the systems, and is in accordance with the general limitations to specific performance.[100] The references to the 'reasonableness' of requiring the seller to provide the remedy, or the 'minor' nature of the lack of conformity are reminiscent of the severe hardship, good faith or proportionality restrictions on specific performance, or repair and replacement in consumer sales. It is submitted, therefore, that the restrictions on repair and replacement in commercial sales reflect similar standards to those applied in consumer sales. Moreover, at a general level, both find their origin in the limitations to specific performance.

Nevertheless, while impossibility and proportionality may set the standard, the application of the restrictions in the commercial context may vary slightly from their application in consumer sales. For example, while two of the factors listed for the proportionality test in consumer sales were the value of the goods and the significance of the lack of conformity, they may apply in a different manner in commercial sales. Since the amounts at stake in commercial sales will generally be much higher than those in consumer sales, a case may be made for restricting the proportionality test to replacement, even though a case may technically concern repair taking the form of replacement of defective components. A good illustration of such a case is given by the Dutch case *Multi Vastgoed*.[101] A main determinant in such cases, according to the Dutch courts, was whether repair was disproportionate, taking into account the economic efficiency of the remedy in the light of considerations relevant to the running of a business. In this respect, the *Gerechtshof* (Court of Appeal) made a comparison between the value of the building on the one hand, and the costs of repair on the other hand. The court appeared inspired by article 7:21(1)(b) *BW*, which provides that a buyer is entitled to repair 'provided that the seller may reasonably effect it'.[102]

[100] See ch 4, p 97, 100.

[101] *Multi Vastgoed* (n 66 above).

[102] In Dutch: de koper kan eisen 'herstel van de afgeleverde zaak, mits de verkoper hieraan redelijkerwijs kan voldoen'.

The costs of repair amounting to less than three to four per cent of the value of the overall project,[103] the Court deemed repair to be a proportionate remedy.

Whether this is an appropriate test in building cases, however, is debatable.[104] The costs of repair will usually be insignificant in comparison to the much higher value of the building. Repair, therefore, will almost never be a disproportionate remedy. It may be thought that building cases of this sort should be dealt with under article 7:21(1)(c) *BW*, which deals with replacement, rather than under paragraph (b). The test there is whether the defect is not too minor to justify replacement.[105] This test may give a better indication of the reasonableness of replacement of a component of immovable goods than the comparison between costs of repair and the value of moveable goods.[106]

Another point that may lead to controversies in this respect is the question whether a seller may insist on repair if a buyer requests replacement. If the significance of the lack of conformity is the determining criterion, as it is in Dutch law and under CISG, the fact that repair is possible is a strong indication that the defect is too minor in nature to justify replacement, or in other words, that it does not amount to a fundamental breach.[107] It is submitted that this is the correct approach in cases where the defective goods are mere components of a larger object. An illustration of this is given by *Marques Roque Joachim v La Sarl Holding Manin Riviere*.[108] This CISG case concerned a contract for the sale and dismantlement of a second-hand aircraft hangar. The French seller and the Portuguese buyer agreed that payment should take place in three instalments. The buyer paid the first two of these, but refused to pay the third, alleging the non-conformity of some metallic elements, which could not be used for the reassembling of the hangar. The seller repaired the defective elements and sought to re-deliver them to the buyer. The buyer, however, refused to accept delivery and alleged that the seller had contractually agreed to supply new metallic elements. The seller then commenced an action to recover the balance of the price. The buyer in turn claimed avoidance of the contract, a refund of the instalments paid, and damages. Both the lower court and the Court of Appeal ruled in favour of the seller, holding that the lack of conformity did not constitute a fundamental breach of contract in the sense of article 25 of CISG. The lack of conformity related only to part of the hangar and the seller had been able to repair the defective elements satisfactorily. Therefore, the buyer was not allowed to avoid the contract. Moreover, since the lack of conformity did not

[103] Still a significant amount, *f*6.000.000 (approx £1,700,000).

[104] Compare MA Leijten, 'Tekortkoming: nakoming of schadevergoeding?' [2001] *Bedrijfsjuridische berichten* 43 at 46.

[105] In Dutch: de koper kan eisen 'vervanging van de afgeleverde zaak, tenzij de afwijking van het overeengekomene te gering is om dit te rechtvaardigen'.

[106] Leijten, 'Tekortkoming: nakoming of schadevergoeding?' (n 104 above).

[107] Hijma, *Asser V(I) Bijzondere Overeenkomsten* (n 5 above) [398]. Schlechtriem and Schwenzer, *Commentary on the UN Convention on the International Sale of Goods* (n 5 above) 544.

[108] Unreported, 26 April 1995 (Cour d'Appel de Grenoble, France); available at www.unilex.info.

constitute a fundamental breach, the buyer would also not have been entitled to replacement.

Apart from situations such as these, it appears that the factors applicable in commercial sales are largely similar to those applicable in consumer sales. Where the goods suffer from a more serious defect, which affects the goods as a whole, the breach will be regarded as fundamental and replacement will be available. An example is the sale of flowers which should have flourished the whole summer but did so only for a small part of it.[109] Similarly, where repair is sought in relation to the goods as a whole, and not just in relation to particular components, it will be available unless it would be disproportionate to require the seller to effect it. The general test of proportionality adopted for consumer sales, therefore, appears relevant also to the majority of commercial cases.

VI. CONCLUSION

The remedies of repair and replacement show a strong connection with specific performance. They aim to give the buyer the performance that he contracted for, and thus are able to protect his performance interest to the fullest. In the light of this connection, it has been argued in this chapter that the availability of the remedies should be governed by similar principles to those identified in relation to specific performance.

The choice of remedy should lie with the buyer, which means that repair and replacement should initially be generally available. Whether the choice of remedy is left to the buyer or the seller is a matter of policy. It is thought that the buyer will generally be in a better position to decide which remedy best protects his performance interest. Therefore, the choice should be in his hands. The interests of the seller may be protected by placing restrictions on the availability of the remedies, which guarantee that the buyer will not be able to obtain a remedy if it would be disproportionate to require the seller to effect it.

General restrictions on repair and replacement resemble the main limitations identified in relation to specific performance in sale of goods law. Whereas the common denominators in that context are impossibility and severe hardship, ie good faith, the restrictions on repair and replacement are generally brought under the headings of impossibility and disproportionality. In practice, the limitations appear to take account of similar considerations to those applying with regard to specific performance. Thus, the economic interests of the seller form the main counterweight to the availability of performance-oriented remedies for the buyer.

While English law has experienced some difficulty in trying to get to terms with the functioning of the remedies, it is thought that ongoing developments in

[109] Unreported, 1 July 1994 (Oberlandesgericht Innsbruck, Austria); also available at www.unilex.info.

relation to specific performance may iron out some of these problems. For example, if a wider scope for specific performance is adopted, the courts may have room to take account of the damages remedy in deciding whether repair or replacement is a proportionate remedy. At the moment, to allow them such scope would almost certainly result in the practical unavailability of repair and replacement in all cases where damages are deemed 'adequate'. Nevertheless, the solution to leave damages altogether out of the equation may be a short-term solution, but it is not recommended for the long term. It prevents the courts from denying repair or replacement in those (exceptional) circumstances where damages would be a more appropriate remedy. The current attitude to repair and replacement in English law, therefore, appears to represent only a second-best solution.

Having thus set the framework for the potential harmonisation of the law relating to the performance-oriented remedies of the buyer, the next step is to consider the position of the seller. The following chapter will seek to determine whether the seller has, or should have, an entitlement to insist upon performance after an initially defective performance.

6

The Seller's Right to Cure

I. INTRODUCTION

TO WHAT EXTENT should the performance of contracts be encouraged, even after an initially defective performance? There are indications in different legal systems that a buyer's right to specific performance may be counterbalanced by another performance-oriented remedy: the seller's right to cure. This is, in a sense, the mirror image of the buyer's entitlement to specific performance. Whereas the latter enables the buyer, regardless of the preference of the seller, to enforce his contractual right to performance, cure allows the seller to insist upon performance in situations where the buyer may prefer a different remedy. In other words, the seller may be given a chance to make good a non-delivery, or to repair or replace defective goods before the buyer will be allowed to terminate the contract or claim damages.

Nevertheless, the extent to which European legal systems entitle the seller to cure a defective performance varies significantly between jurisdictions. While policy reasons such as the minimisation of economic loss may plead in favour of allowing cure, some systems pay little heed to this and instead make it possible for the buyer to end the contract immediately upon the seller's failure to perform, even if it occurs before the due delivery date. It will be argued that this approach is undesirable and even incorrect, not only for policy reasons, but also because an analysis of domestic sales laws suggests that the seller has a *right* to cure, at least up until the contractual delivery date. As the buyer has a contractual interest in receiving performance, so the seller has an interest in effecting performance. Where the seller still has time to give effect to this within the contractually agreed time period for performance, he should be allowed to do so, and the buyer should at this point not be entitled to interfere with the seller's right to perform.

An argument will also be made in favour of the right of a seller to effect cure after the due delivery date, although it is conceded that an extension of the right to cure after this date is controversial. At this point in time, the seller's failure to perform will be regarded in a different light, since the time for performance has passed. It may thus give rise to entitlements of the buyer, for example to terminate the contract and to claim damages. Nevertheless, it will be argued that policy reasons may support a right to cure in this situation, at least for a limited time after the original date on which the seller should have delivered the goods.

Finally, a word needs to be said on regimes that encourage informal attempts at cure. While these may be an alternative to systems that give the seller a right to cure, it will be argued that they cannot guarantee to a sufficient degree that cure is enabled in appropriate circumstances. The main reason for this is that, in those systems, the choice for cure ultimately remains at the buyer's discretion. The incentives for buyers to opt for cure, however, may not be sufficient to promote cure even where it would be the appropriate remedy.

II. POLICY ISSUES

Two main policy reasons plead in favour of the recognition of a right to cure for the seller.[1] First, it promotes the objectives of contract law, for example to ensure performance of the contract. If the seller is given a second chance to perform, this forms an extra safeguard for the parties to ensure that actual performance of the contract is achieved, the likelihood of which would be far less if the buyer were entitled to terminate the contract at the moment of the defective performance.[2] Secondly, it is in line with the policy to avoid economic waste. Termination of a contract upon breach may cause losses for both parties: the buyer may incur extra costs if the defective performance forces him to go out into the market and make a cover purchase, while the seller, upon termination by the buyer, may lose any benefit expected from the performance of the buyer's obligations (eg payment of the price) and may have incurred expenditure which is wasted now that he does not have a second chance to perform.[3] In this light, cure could well play a useful role in preventing such waste and achieving an economically efficient solution.

Considerations of economic policy are especially important in the European context, with the European Union being mostly an economic co-operation between the Member States.[4] These considerations may even outweigh the policy of consumer protection. For example, with regard to the hierarchy of remedies laid down by the Consumer Sales Directive,[5] which makes repair and replacement primary remedies in consumer sales, it has been said that '[t]he rule really is about reducing costs of remedies'.[6] Thus, to the extent that the Directive has given rise to a right to cure for the seller, it appears to be inspired by considerations of an economic nature rather than by consumer protection policy. However, while this may be the true inspiration for the Consumer Sales

[1] See also ch 3, p 57, 59.

[2] A Apps, 'The right to cure defective performance' [1994] *Lloyd's Maritime & Commercial Law Quarterly* 525 at 554.

[3] *Ibid*, 555.

[4] See ch 2, p 22.

[5] Directive (EC) 99/44 of the European Parliament and of the Council on certain aspects of the sale of consumer goods and associated guarantees [1999] OJ L171/12 (Consumer Sales Directive).

[6] S Grundmann, 'Consumer Law, Commercial Law, Private Law: How can the Sales Directive and the Sales Convention be so Similar?' [2003] *European Business Law Review* 237 at 243.

Directive, that does not mean that a right to cure is necessarily at odds with consumer interests. Cure, whether in the form of repair, replacement or (delayed) delivery,[7] protects the performance interest of the buyer and ensures that he receives the performance that he contracted for. To the extent that the provisions on cure contribute to this goal, they are as much in favour of the consumer-buyer as they are in favour of the seller.

However, even if there are strong policy reasons that plead in favour of a right of cure, it may be difficult to integrate such a right into the sales regime of a particular legal system. The provisions on cure necessarily interact with other provisions in any sales regime, such as those relating to delivery, rejection and termination, and it may be that these frustrate the possibility for the seller to cure a defective performance. The English sale of goods regime, for example, appears to include an almost unlimited right for the buyer to reject goods that do not fulfill the implied conditions of sections 13–15 of the Sale of Goods Act 1979 (SGA) and to repudiate the contract for breach, thus allowing little or no room for the seller to cure. Under the UN Convention on Contracts for the International Sale of Goods (CISG),[8] on the other hand, where the availability of rejection and termination (or avoidance, to stick with the terminology of the Convention) is subject to less strict rules, a right to cure would seem to encounter less scope for obstruction.[9]

Arguments to do with the structure of the remedial scheme, however, should not stand in the way of the introduction of a broader right to cure in European sale of goods laws. It is time for a re-assessment of the scope of cure in the different regimes that have bearing on sale of goods transactions within Europe. The trend, it will be argued, should be towards wider availability of cure. This has already been the approach in international instruments, such as the Principles of European Contract Law (PECL) and CISG, which make cure available before and also, within certain limits, after the contractual date of delivery.[10] It is thought that this approach comes closest to achieving the policy objectives discussed in chapter three. A widely available remedy of cure promotes performance of the contract, thus ensuring maximum protection of the performance interest, and it enables the parties to resolve their dispute with the smallest possible economic losses.[11]

[7] See pp 117 ff. Even if a delay, technically, may be incurable, it will be argued that there are circumstances where the seller may still be able to give the performance that he contracted for. See below, p 169.

[8] UN Convention on Contracts for the International Sale of Goods (adopted 11 April 1980, entered into force 1 January 1988) 1489 UNTS 3 (CISG).

[9] Compare M Bridge, 'The Vienna Sales Convention and English Law: Curing Defective Performance by the Seller' in LL Andersen, J Fejø and R Nielsen (eds), *Festskrift til Ole Lando* (Copenhagen, Gadjura, 1997) 83 at 98.

[10] See below pp 164 ff, pp 167 ff.

[11] Ch 3, pp 48, 59–60.

III. CURE BEFORE THE DUE DELIVERY DATE

The seller's right to cure, in all legal systems, finds its limits in the entitlement of the buyer to terminate for breach of contract. Regardless of whether a breach occurs before or after the date contractually agreed upon for performance, when the buyer is entitled to terminate for breach and decides to exercise this right, the seller's right to cure automatically comes to an end. The two rights are incompatible, since one requires the contract to be kept alive, whilst the other brings the contract to an end and it 'releases both parties from their obligation to effect and to receive future performance'.[12]

However, there is hardly any uniformity amongst the different systems as to *when* a buyer becomes entitled to terminate. Does an unsatisfactory performance before the due delivery date amount to a repudiatory breach? Or does the fact that the time for performance has not yet expired mean, on the contrary, that the seller should be given a second chance to perform within the time left? And what should be the position where the time for performance has expired? Has the seller altogether lost the opportunity to cure?

It is submitted that, as a matter of principle, the seller should have a right to cure, at least where he still has time to do so before the contractual date of delivery—in that case, he is not in breach and the buyer is not entitled to terminate. In other words, in these circumstances, the seller is still entitled to perform under the contract and thus to cure his defective performance. Support for this proposition may be found in German and Dutch sale of goods law, which operate on the basis that an obligation does not become exigible or actionable until the agreed time for performance and that, as a consequence, the buyer does not become entitled to terminate the contract until that time.[13] A similar analysis may be made of English law, although the issue is controversial there. The better view, arguably, defends cure on the ground that English law is regulated by two fundamental contractual remedial principles: first, the right of the aggrieved party to whom the defective performance is tendered to withhold his or her own performance until a correct performance is tendered, and secondly, the right of the aggrieved party to terminate the contract for breach.[14] The right to cure is available while the parties are operating under the first principle, but ceases to be available when the second principle is triggered.[15] As in Dutch and German law, it appears that the second principle—that of termination—only becomes effective after the due delivery date. It will be argued, therefore, that at least at the level of underlying principles, there is a basis for harmonisation.

The way forward from there is to determine to what extent these principles find expression in the national sale of goods laws in Europe. It will be argued

[12] Compare PECL art 9:305(1).
[13] See further below, p 154.
[14] Apps, 'The right to cure defective performance' (n 2 above) 526.
[15] *Ibid.*

that, currently, the Dutch and German regimes have an advantage over English law in that they ensure a time for seller's cure before the contractual delivery date. The position under English law, by contrast, is tainted by numerous uncertainties, making it doubtful whether a seller can insist upon a second chance to perform. The main problem lies in the relationship between the buyer's right to reject defective goods and his right to terminate for breach. However, on the basis that the sale of goods law in England is governed by similar principles to those that operate in Dutch and German law, it will be argued that these rights should be regarded as independent, thus leaving room for cure.

Reference should also be made to international instruments relating to the sale of goods. The approach taken to breach under CISG suggests that the possibility of cure could be taken into account as a factor in determining whether a breach is 'fundamental' and thus entitles the buyer to terminate. In other words, where defects are 'curable', the seller should be allowed a second chance to perform. While this approach has some merit, it may have significant disadvantages. For example, there may be concerns as to the level of legal certainty that it ensures. Under international instruments such as CISG and the PECL, however, the seller's right to cure before the delivery date is more or less independent from the right to terminate. The right to cure is generally available before that date, the only exception being where there is an anticipatory breach.[16] The question of 'fundamental' breach, thus, is mainly of relevance to the possibility of cure after the delivery date and, for that reason, it will be discussed in the next paragraph, which deals with the time period for cure.

1. Cure in the Light of the Relationship Between the Right to Withhold Performance and the Right of Termination

Under the Dutch *Burgerlijk Wetboek* (*BW*), a creditor can only claim damages or terminate the contract if the debtor is *in verzuim*.[17] This term could be translated as 'in default', meaning that performance is somehow unsatisfactory and also signifying that, as a result of this, the debtor is in breach and the creditor is entitled to a remedy. The notion of breach (in Dutch: *wanprestatie*) is similar to the English one, which relates to the non-performance or defective performance of a contract and which generally entails that certain remedies become available to the aggrieved party.[18] The difference, however, is that, while an unsatisfactory performance under English law may almost immediately be classified as a breach, the default requirement of the *BW* implies that an additional step needs to be taken for a bad performance to qualify as a breach under Dutch law. What this step involves is clarified in article 6:81 *BW*, which provides:[19]

[16] CISG arts 37 and 48; PECL art 8:104.

[17] Arts 6:74(2) and 6:265(2) *BW*.

[18] Unless the breach is too minor in nature; compare SGA s 15A.

[19] In Dutch: 'De schuldenaar is in verzuim gedurende de tijd dat de prestatie uitblijft nadat zij opeisbaar is geworden en aan de eisen van de artikelen 82 en 83 is voldaan'.

> Except to the extent that the delay cannot be imputed to him or performance is already permanently impossible, the debtor is in default during the period that the performance is not rendered, *once it has become exigible and the requirements of articles 82 and 83 have been met* (emphasis added).

Articles 6:82 and 83 *BW*, to which the provision refers, contain technical requirements relating to the circumstances in which a written warning is required for the debtor to be put in default. In general, it will be necessary to give written notice to the debtor, in which he is granted a reasonable time for performance. If he fails to perform within this period, he will then be in default and the aggrieved party will be entitled to claim damages or to terminate the contract.

The default requirement lays bare a fundamental remedial principle of Dutch contract law. It emphasises that a creditor will not be entitled to demand a remedy from the debtor as long as the debtor's obligation has not become 'exigible' or 'actionable' (in Dutch: *opeisbaar*). This will normally be the case where the time for performance has not yet expired. For defective performance cases in the sale of goods law it means that, where a seller still has time to perform, the buyer will not have an actionable right to insist upon performance or to claim any other remedy. It does not mean that the buyer does not have an entitlement to performance,[20] but merely that he will be unable to enforce it. The only circumstance in which this will be different is where the defective performance amounts to an anticipatory breach. In that case, the creditor will be able to invoke his remedies even before the claim has become exigible, and the default requirement does not apply.[21]

The new German law of obligations appears to operate under similar principles. § 323 I *Bürgerliches Gesetzbuch* (*BGB*) provides[22]:

> If under a synallagmatic contract the obligor fails to effect performance when due or to perform in accordance with the contract, the obligee may terminate the contract, if he has fixed, to no avail, an additional period of time for performance.

This corresponds to the default requirement found in Dutch law. As under that regime, the provision appears to apply only to cases where performance has become exigible. While the wording is not entirely unambiguous, it would seem that 'when due' refers not only to cases of delay, but also to the time at which the quality of performance is assessed. Zimmermann shares this view, referring to the situation 'where the debtor does not perform, or does not perform properly,

[20] Under Dutch and German law, he may have such an entitlement, for specific performance is a primary obligation under these systems. Compare J Hijma, *Asser V(I) Bijzondere Overeenkomsten. Koop en Ruil*, 6th edn (Deventer, WEJ Tjeenk Willink, 2001) [373]. See ch 3, pp 56–7.

[21] Compare art 6:80 *BW* on the requirements for anticipatory breach.

[22] In German: 'Erbringt bei einem gegenseitigen Vertrag der Schuldner eine fällige Leistung nicht oder nicht vertragsgemäß, so kann der Gläubiger, wenn er dem Schuldner erfolglos eine angemessene Frist zur Leistung oder Nacherfüllung bestimmt hat, vom Vertrag zurücktreten'. Translation from www.iuscomp.org/gla.

at the time when he has to effect performance'.[23] It is also in line with § 271 II *BGB*, which provides that where a time for performance has been agreed upon, the debtor may perform before the end of this time period but the creditor cannot demand performance until the time for performance has arrived.[24] Thus, the buyer is not entitled to terminate the contract before the due delivery date. The only exception to this rule is where there is a situation of anticipatory breach, a concept that has now been introduced into the German Code. § 323 IV *BGB* provides that the creditor may terminate the contract before performance becomes due if it is obvious that the preconditions for termination will be satisfied.[25]

Are these principles entirely foreign to English law—or is it possible to hold that a defective performance before the due delivery date does not always automatically amount to a breach for which the buyer is entitled to terminate? The Sale of Goods Act 1979 does not provide a straightforward answer to this question, for it does not specify at what point in time the seller commits a repudiatory breach of condition in relation to the quality or fitness of goods.[26] However, contract principles in English law appear to lend support to the rule, similar to that found in Dutch and German law, that a creditor does not have an actionable right to enforce performance before the date on which performance becomes due. Before the contractual delivery date, therefore, the seller's failure to perform satisfactorily does not amount to a repudiatory breach, and the only remedy of the buyer is to withhold the performance of his own obligations whilst waiting for the seller to make a new attempt at performance. Other remedies, such as the right to terminate, only arise when the seller's obligations can no longer be performed in accordance with the contract.[27] Thus, it appears that the right to terminate is unavailable to the buyer if there is still time to perform. Further support for this proposition is given by Beale:[28]

> [The right to withhold performance until the other party has performed or is ready to do so] does not depend on any right to 'terminate' the contract in the sense of justifiably refusing ever to perform it. This may be confusing to a reader familiar with the notion that 'a contract may be terminated for breach of condition.' It is quite correct that A's unwillingness or failure to perform an obligation when its performance is a condition may give B the right to terminate, but that right cannot arise until the time for performing the contract has expired. The only circumstances in which B may terminate before this are either if the agreement expressly gives him the power to do so or if A repudiates the contract . . . Merely failing to perform is not a repudiation, and is not even a breach until the date set for performance has passed.

[23] R Zimmermann, *The New German Law of Obligations* (Oxford, Oxford University Press, 2005) 70.

[24] Compare W Ernst in W Krüger (ed), *Münchener Kommentar zum Bürgerlichen Gesetzbuch*, vol 2a, 4th edn (München, CH Beck, 2003) § 323, fn 46.

[25] In German: 'Der Gläubiger kann bereits vor dem Eintritt der Fälligkeit der Leistung zurücktreten, wenn offensichtlich ist, dass die Voraussetzungen des Rücktritts eintreten werden'.

[26] M Bridge, *The Sale of Goods* (Oxford, Oxford University Press, 1997) 198. See also below, p 159.

[27] Apps, 'The right to cure defective performance' (n 2 above) 528.

[28] H Beale, *Remedies for Breach of Contract* (London, Sweet & Maxwell, 1980) 20–21.

Thus, a defective performance before the due delivery date will not automatically amount to a repudiatory breach and the buyer will not be entitled to terminate the contract or claim damages. His only remedy will be to withhold performance of his own obligations (eg, payment of the price) in the hope that this will coerce the seller to perform. The seller, therefore, retains his right to perform, ie he is entitled to exercise a right to cure.

An important limitation must, nevertheless, be taken into account. It relates to the nature of the breach. It may be thought that the fact that the seller voluntarily decides to perform before the contractual delivery date could be interpreted as a waiver of some sort—by choosing to perform early, the seller takes on the obligation to perform satisfactorily before the contractual delivery date and, in doing so, he should also accept the possibility that the buyer may invoke remedies if the performance does not live up to the contractual standards. Essentially, by performing early the seller runs the risk of creating an anticipatory breach of contract, and in doing so he exposes himself to the possibility of the buyer terminating the contract, in which case the right to cure will be lost.

Nevertheless, this view is unpersuasive for two reasons. First, one should ask the question whether a delivery of defective goods should be interpreted as showing an unwillingness on the part of the seller to perform the contract satisfactorily. Where there is still time to perform, it seems far-fetched to say that the simple fact of defective performance indicates that the seller is unwilling to try again and cure the defect before the due delivery date. Only if the defect is sufficiently serious, or if other factors indicate the seller's unwillingness to perform, can the seller's behaviour be interpreted as an anticipatory breach on the grounds of which the buyer is entitled to terminate. Secondly, contract theory pleads in favour of keeping the contract alive where performance is still possible. As seen above,[29] such a policy may lead to cost-effective outcomes for both parties. In this light, also, it is submitted that the mere fact of a defective performance is not sufficient to indicate an intention on the part of the seller to no longer be bound by the contract—if it were, the seller would never be entitled to cure.[30]

The right to withhold performance, thus, regulates the remedies of the parties before the due delivery date. Still, while this approach, in principle, is valid for each of the legal systems under consideration, English law contains some peculiarities that may prevent the practical application of the rules of sale of goods law from resulting in a right of cure for the seller. In effect, the scope of anticipatory breach may appear wider under English law than it is in the Dutch or German systems, thus limiting the scope for cure. There are two restricting factors in particular: first, the fact that authority for a right to cure only exists with regard to defective tenders and not with regard to deliveries of defective goods; and secondly, the unfortunate drafting of the Sale of Goods Act that

[29] See p 150; also ch 3, p 69.
[30] See Apps, 'The right to cure defective performance' (n 2 above) 548.

links rejection to termination, leaving no room for cure where goods have been formally rejected. It is submitted that each of these restrictions is open to serious criticisms and that they should not stand in the way of bringing English law closer in line with other European sale of goods laws.

2. Cure, Tender and Delivery

One of the main points of criticism of the English cure regime is that, in relation to replacement, it would appear to apply only to defective tenders, not to defective deliveries.[31] This approach seems too restrictive. In fact, the distinction between tenders and deliveries is mostly technical in nature, a necessary step to identify the contract goods where this has not been done at the time of conclusion of the contract. But does this really have an impact on the question whether cure should be allowed or not? Three routes are open. First, it may be thought that appropriation to the contract is definite and therefore that cure, in the form of replacement, is impossible in relation to specific or ascertained goods. In other words, if goods are specific or if they have been appropriated to the contract (ie they have become ascertained) cure is not an option. The seller only may only be entitled to cure if the goods are unascertained. Secondly, it may be thought that appropriation as such does not preclude cure. The fact that the contract goods have been identified is not irrevocable and the seller may be allowed to make a second tender where the initial performance was defective, as long as the buyer has not accepted the tender. Thus, even in relation to ascertained goods, cure may be possible. Thirdly, as with the second option, cure may be allowed, but now this is extended to situations where the buyer *has* accepted the tender, ie where he has taken delivery of the goods. While English law seems to follow the second route, it is arguable that there is room for adopting the third approach, and to extend the scope of cure to deliveries.

Section 61(1) of the SGA contains the definition of delivery under English law: it is a 'voluntary transfer of possession from one person to another'.[32] For a buyer to take delivery of goods it is required that the seller yields effective control over them, 'coupled with the abandonment by the seller of an intention to exercise effective control and the simultaneous assertion of such an intention by the buyer'.[33] Tender, by contrast, signifies the delivery of goods by the seller, without requiring that the buyer must also receive them.[34] A similar distinction can be made in relation to delivery or tender of documents, such as shipping documents. While the main focus of the thesis is on cases concerning defective

[31] Repair may be possible for it does not require the seller to tender or deliver *different* goods.

[32] A similar definition can be found in the Dutch *BW* in art 3:90(1). The provision states: 'De levering vereist voor de overdracht van roerende zaken, niet-registergoederen, die in de macht van de vervreemder zijn, geschiedt door aan de verkrijger het bezit der zaak te verschaffen'.

[33] Bridge, *The Sale of Goods* (n 26 above) 202.

[34] Compare *Caradoc Nurseries Ltd v Marsh* (1959) 19 DLR (2d) 491.

goods, in the present context it may be appropriate to make a comparison with cases dealing with defective documents. After all, the issue relates to the transfer of possession in goods, which does not necessarily have to take the form of physical transfer but which may also take place by handing over certain documents (eg a bill of lading).

Leaving aside specific goods, for which cure in the form of replacement in any case would seem an impossibility, the main problem with the distinction between tenders and deliveries in English law appears to lie in the notion of ascertained goods. It may be thought that the fact that goods have been ascertained puts the seller in the same position as he would have been in had the goods been specific—these particular goods have been linked to the contract and a delivery of substitutes has therefore become impossible. Replacement, thus, would seem possibly only with regard to unascertained goods. As a consequence, cure appears to be precluded in cases where the buyer has taken delivery, for he has then received the goods, which implies that, at this point or earlier, they have become ascertained. Nevertheless, two criticisms may be made against this. First, it is arguable that appropriation of goods is not irrevocable in case the tender is *defective*. Secondly, while the reasoning applied to defective tenders may not suffice to justify cure in relation to defective deliveries, it will be argued that there are other grounds on which an appropriation of goods may be overturned in such cases.

Under English law, defective tenders do not appear to constitute an irrevocable ascertainment of goods. There is authority for the rule that an initial defective tender of previously unascertained goods should not bind the seller and prevent him from having a right to cure. For example, in *Borrowman Phillips & Co v Free & Hollis*[35] a cargo of maize was refused by the buyers on the ground that the shipping documents had not been tendered with it. When, subsequently, the sellers made a second tender, using a different ship but still within the time for performance, the question was whether they were entitled to do so and whether the buyers were bound to accept the tender. The buyers, relying on the doctrine of election, contended that the sellers had lost the opportunity to tender for a second time because they had already tendered once, and had insisted upon that tender. The Court of Appeal rejected this argument of the buyers.

The point of election was dealt with in detail by Lord Justice Brett. In relation to the first tender, the cargo of a ship called the *Charles Platt*, he held that

> [i]t may be that, where goods which fulfil the terms of a contract are appropriated for sale in performance thereof, there is an election by the vendor which is irrevocable; but here the contention for the defendants is that the cargo of the *Charles Platt* was not in accordance with the contract.[36]

In other words, only a satisfactory tender amounts to an irrevocable election. Where the goods are defective, the tender is not definitive, and consequently, the

[35] *Borrowman Phillips & Co v Free & Hollis* (1878) 4 QBD 500 (CA).
[36] *Ibid*, 504.

seller retains the right to cure. This view has since found support in other cases, most famously in The Kanchenjunga, where Lord Goff of Chieveley stated:

> If the time for delivery has not yet expired, the seller is still entitled to make a fresh tender which conforms with the contract, in which event the buyer is bound to accept the goods so tendered.[37]

Support for the seller's right to cure a defective tender can also be found in the literature. As pointed out by Bridge,[38] early editions of *Benjamin on Sale* recognised that

> an appropriation and tender of goods, not in accordance with the contract, and in consequence rejected by the purchaser, is revocable, and the seller may afterwards, within the contract time, appropriate and tender other goods which are according to the contract.[39]

Moreover, the right to cure a defective tender appears to be in accordance with the provisions of the SGA. After all, it is unlikely that a non-conforming tender in itself constitutes a (repudiatory) breach on the grounds of which the buyer would be allowed to terminate the contract.[40] As Bridge points out, the SGA does not specify at what time the condition as to quality or fitness of the goods—breach of which may give rise to a right to reject or terminate—should be fulfilled. However, it is unlikely that this should be before the time of sale or, which in practice will be the same thing, delivery.[41] If Bridge is correct, it must be concluded that the seller at least has the opportunity to make a second *tender* before the stipulated date of delivery.

The point becomes troublesome in relation to cases where the buyer has taken *delivery* of the goods. It is here that, unfortunately, the SGA and related case law leave us in the dark. There is no binding authority as to which rule should apply in such cases, though it has been recognised that the rule may not necessarily be the same as for defective tenders. As pointed out by Lord Justice Brett in *Borrowman*,

> I have only to add that a different rule might have been applied, if the defendants had *accepted* the cargo of the *Charles Platt*; it is possible that the tender of the plaintiffs could not in that case have been withdrawn[42] (emphasis added).

[37] *Motor Oil Hellas (Corinth) Refineries SA v Shipping Corporation of India (The Kanchenjunga)* [1990] 1 Lloyd's Rep 391 (HL) 399. Compare *Empresa Exportadora de Azucar v Industria Azucarera Nacional SA (The Playa Larga)* [1983] 2 Lloyd's Rep 171 (CA) 186; *SIAT di del Ferro v Tradax Overseas SA* [1980] 1 Lloyd's Rep 53 (CA) 62–3; *McDougall v Aeromarine of Emsworth Ltd* [1958] 2 Lloyd's Rep 345 (QBD); *EE & Brian Smith (1928) Ltd v Wheatsheaf Mills Ltd* [1939] 1 KB 302 (KBD) 314; *Ashmore & Son v CS Cox & Co* [1899] 1 QB 436 (QBD) 440–41.

[38] Bridge, *The Sale of Goods* (n 26 above) 200–01.

[39] WCA Ker (ed), *Benjamin on Sale*, 6th edn (London, Sweet & Maxwell, 1920) 402.

[40] Bridge, *The Sale of Goods* (n 26 above) 198.

[41] *Ibid.*

[42] *Borrowman Phillips & Co v Free & Hollis* (n 35 above) 505. Acceptance, in this context, appears to refer to the appropriation of the goods and not to acceptance in its technical sense, which limits the buyer's remedy to damages.

Thus, he emphasised that there could be a distinction between situations where there had only been a tender of goods and cases in which that tender had actually been accepted; in the latter situation, the sellers may be held to this tender and thus not allowed to cure by making a second tender. However, the statement was made *obiter*[43] and can thus not be conclusive for this point of view.

Nevertheless, it is submitted that the fact of delivery does not preclude cure by the seller. In case of delivery of defective goods, the general rule is that the buyer may reject the goods, in which case the original appropriation is nullified and the rights of the parties are (for the most part) regulated as if no appropriation had been made and no delivery had taken place.[44] In other words, the appropriation of the goods, while initially valid, is conditional only and it can be undone by the buyer's rejection of the goods. It is submitted, therefore, that there should be no distinction as to the possibility of cure in cases where a tender of goods has been made or cases where the goods have been delivered. In other words, if the governing principle is that before the due delivery date the seller's obligation is not exigible and the buyer may only rely on his right to withhold performance, this is no different in cases of defective delivery than it is in cases of defective tender. The only persuasive reason to distinguish between tender and delivery, thus, would be where a defective delivery would sooner satisfy the requirements of anticipatory breach.

3. Cure between Rejection and Termination

Is it established, then, that a delivery of defective goods does not automatically amount to an anticipatory breach? According to Lord Devlin,

> [a] tender of . . . goods under a contract for the sale of goods . . . in a condition that does not comply with the terms of the contract is not a breach of contract. What creates the breach in such a case is the failure to tender within the contract time [goods] in a condition that *does* comply with the contract.[45]

If tender and delivery, as suggested, should be treated in a similar fashion, the same may be said with regard to a delivery of defective goods—the fact of defective delivery in itself does not amount to a (repudiatory) breach. However, there is a difficulty. Whereas the refusal to accept a defective tender does not have any direct consequences with regard to the remedies of the buyer, the traditional approach of English law with regard to the rejection of a delivery of defective goods is a different one. To refer to Lord Devlin again, it has been said that '[a] right to reject is, after all, only a particular form of the right to rescind the

[43] *Borrowman Phillips & Co v Free & Hollis* (n 35 above) 505. Brett LJ expressly stated: 'I wish it however to be understood, that this is a point upon which I express no opinion'.

[44] R Goode, *Commercial Law*, 3rd edn (London, LexisNexis, 2004) 214.

[45] Lord Devlin, 'The Treatment of Breach of Contract' [1966] *Cambridge Law Journal* 192 at 194.

contract'.[46] If this is right, a delivery of defective goods may give rise to rejection *and* termination.

It is submitted that this is too strict a limitation on the seller's right to cure. Taking into consideration the remedial principles of English contract law, it is thought that rejection should be regarded as a sub-form of the right to withhold performance rather than a particular manifestation of the right to terminate. If it is right that the seller's obligation to perform is not exigible before the date of delivery, the buyer will not be able to terminate the contract where an early delivery by the seller is unsatisfactory. A rejection of the goods by the buyer, therefore, should be regarded as a mere indication that he is dissatisfied with the goods and that he intends to withhold his own performance (eg payment of the price) until the seller delivers goods that do conform to the contract.

While Dutch and German law do not rely on a technical concept such as the right to reject found in English law, the approaches found in these systems in principle support the argument that any indication of refusal of the goods by the buyer can only be seen in the light of his right to withhold performance. Only where the delivery of defective goods before the contractual time for performance amounts to an anticipatory breach will the buyer be entitled to terminate the contract. In general, however, the fact that performance is not exigible before that date means that a defective performance will not bind the seller and that he has a right to perform, ie to effect cure.

Nevertheless, while the Dutch and German Codes are quite unambiguous in their meaning, it should be conceded that English sale of goods law leaves doubt as to the correct interpretation of the rules on rejection and termination. For example, the SGA is mostly silent on whether rejection will always automatically be followed by termination, and where it does mention the two, the wording of the provisions is far from clear-cut. Section 11(3) of the Act, in particular, has been invoked equally by proponents of a right to cure as by its antagonists. The section lays down the definitions of conditions and warranties, stating:

> Whether a stipulation in a contract of sale is a condition, the breach of which may give rise to a right to treat the contract as repudiated, or a warranty, the breach of which may give rise to a claim for damages but not to a right to reject the goods and treat the contract as repudiated, depends in each case on the construction of the contract.

It is nothing new for an English lawyer that a breach of condition should give rise to a right to reject and terminate—but should rejection automatically result in termination? Despite its ambiguities, it is thought that the provision leaves room for the opposite view. Thus, it does not, as suggested by Bridge, envisage a seamless transition from rejection to termination, 'leaving no room for the implication of some step, control, or constraint between those two actions of the buyer'.[47]

[46] *Kwei Tek Chao v British Traders & Shippers Ltd* [1954] 2 QB 459 (QBD) 480. Compare AG Guest (ed), *Benjamin's Sale of Goods*, 7th edn (London, Sweet & Maxwell, 2006) [12-028] fn 56.

[47] Bridge, *The Sale of Goods* (n 26 above) 199. The view that the transition is not seamless and that it leaves room for cure is supported by Goode, *Commercial Law* (n 44 above) 342–3, 376.

The wording of the section suggests that breach of a condition may give rise (i) to a right to reject, and (ii) to a right to terminate. However, it does not say that these two are inextricably linked. The fact that the 'right to reject the goods and treat the contract as repudiated' are mentioned consecutively should not be taken to mean that one seamlessly goes over into the other, for there is no indication as to the time at which either of these rights comes into being. The provision does not exclude the possibility that rejection may become available before the delivery date, but termination only afterwards, when the seller's obligation has become exigible.

On a side note, the fact that the provision uses the word 'breach' to define when rejection and termination become available does not stand in the way of interpreting it in this manner. What the provision implies is that a breach of condition may entitle a party to reject and to terminate, but it does not say that such a breach is always a repudiatory breach. Of course, by definition it will have to be if it gives the buyer a right to terminate. But it is not the same for rejection—any unsatisfactory performance may be regarded as a breach that gives the buyer the right to reject; it does not need to qualify as a repudiatory breach. For example, where goods are delivered before the due delivery date and turn out to be defective, this may be regarded as a breach of condition for which rejection is permitted. However, if the time for performance has not yet expired, in accordance with the principles set out earlier,[48] it is thought that the breach will not entitle the buyer to terminate if the seller is still willing to perform.

Another ground on which section 11(3) of the SGA may be said to support a right to cure is that it uses the word 'may' when it refers to termination. Thus, it suggests that the breach of a condition does not always automatically give rise to a right to terminate. This leaves open the possibility that a seller will be allowed to cure a defective performance. While it does not specify the circumstances in which cure may be allowed, if the right to withhold performance is the guiding principle before the due delivery date, cure should not be limited to defective tenders. There should also be room to reject goods without terminating the contract. After all, the seller's delivery obligation is not exigible before the contractual date for performance, and the buyer is therefore not entitled to terminate at this point in time. This is so regardless of whether defective goods have been tendered or actually delivered.

Counter-arguments put forward by Bradgate and White, supporting the view that a non-satisfactory delivery in itself amounts to a repudiatory breach, are unpersuasive. They state their argument as follows:[49]

> Although section 11(3) of the Act provides that a breach of condition only '*may*' give rise to a right to terminate the contract, we suggest that this is because where the

[48] See above, pp 153 ff.

[49] R Bradgate and F White, 'Rejection and Termination in Contracts for the Sale of Goods' in J Birds, R Bradgate and C Villiers (eds), *Termination of Contracts* (London, Wiley Chancery, 1995) 51 at 76.

contract is severable breach of condition does not automatically permit the buyer to treat the contract as repudiated. However, under a simple, non-severable contract, the seller has only one delivery obligation and the implied conditions that the goods supplied should correspond with the contract description, be of acceptable quality etc, go to the heart of that obligation and hence to the heart of the contract. We would argue that breach of those conditions, therefore, entitles the buyer to treat the contract as repudiated and to terminate it.

While the implied conditions of description, quality and fitness for purpose certainly go to the heart of the contract, it is not clear why these should be linked to the delivery obligation, especially where the time for performance has not yet expired. After all, at that point in time the seller is not actually *obliged* to deliver the goods—he does so of his own free will. Since the seller's performance is not exigible at this time, the buyer would not be entitled to enforce the implied conditions any more than he would be entitled to enforce the delivery obligation of the seller. Therefore, a delivery of defective goods cannot amount to a breach of condition for which termination would be allowed.

Nevertheless, while a case may be made for allowing cure before the due delivery date, it should be noted that the prevailing approach under English law, currently, is the one defended by Bradgate and White. Section 11(3) of the SGA, however, clearly does not give the definitive answer to the question of which approach should be favoured. In this light, perhaps legislative intervention may be called for to clarify the position of English law towards seller cure and, ideally, to bring it closer to other European systems.

4. Conclusion

Remedial contractual principles plead in favour of recognising a right of cure for the seller in cases where he still has time to perform. In these circumstances, the buyer will not be entitled to terminate but his sole remedy will be to withhold performance of his own obligations until the seller performs. This approach relies upon the view that a defective performance before the due delivery date does not automatically amount to a repudiatory breach, since the seller's performance is not normally exigible before this date—under Dutch and German law, the seller is not 'in default'. Thus, while the buyer may have a right to performance, it is not actionable and, unless the seller's behaviour amounts to an anticipatory breach, defective performance will not give him the right to terminate the contract. While English case law and statute law do not give an unambiguous answer as to whether a right to cure is recognised or not, it can be argued that English law operates under the same remedial principles as the Dutch and German systems. Therefore, there is scope for harmonisation of the systems.

The conclusion that seller cure should be generally available before the due delivery date is reflected in international rules applying to sale of goods transactions. For example, article 8:104 of the PECL and article 37 of CISG contain provisions to this effect.[50] The situation becomes more complicated when the focus is shifted to the possibility of cure *after* the due delivery date.

IV. CURE AFTER THE DUE DELIVERY DATE

Should the time period for cure be limited to the time before performance becomes due, or can it be extended to the time after the contractual delivery date? Some of the policy arguments that plead in favour of a right to cure before the due delivery date may also be valid after that date. For example, where a defective machine has been delivered, it may be more cost-effective for both seller and buyer to try repair before resorting to a different remedy, such as termination or damages.[51]

Nevertheless, the fact that the due delivery date has passed is significant—it is the turning point upon which entitlements come into force that the buyer could not rely upon before, but which may now limit the rights of the seller in relation to cure. Most importantly, the buyer may now be entitled to terminate the contract, for the seller is in breach of contract. He has breached the obligation—in English law, the condition—to deliver conforming goods. Most national laws recognise this as a ground on which the buyer may terminate, and thus as a limiting factor on the seller's right to cure. Moreover, apart from the implied conditions relating to the conformity of the goods, the seller is in breach of his obligation to deliver goods by the due delivery date. On this ground also, the buyer may be entitled to terminate and, inherently, the seller may be unable to cure.

However, while it may be right to say that the buyer should be entitled to terminate immediately and not await the seller's offer of cure where the due delivery date has passed, it is arguable that there should be some scope for allowing cure where the buyer has not lost anything as a result of the seller's breach. After all, economic considerations may be relied upon to justify a right of cure for the seller, as long as the performance interest of the buyer is sufficiently protected.[52] Hence, as long as untimely performance does not prevent the seller from giving the buyer what he contracted for, it is thought that he should be allowed to cure.

Therefore, it will be argued that the seller should have a limited right to cure after the due delivery date. This would fit in with the performance-oriented policy that may be discerned in several legal systems and that, moreover, forms the

[50] Note that the PECL speak of 'tender' rather than delivery. However, the commentary makes clear that the word is not used in the narrow English law sense, and that the provision must therefore be regarded as applying to cases of defective delivery as well as defective tender. Compare O Lando and H Beale (eds), *Principles of European Contract Law. Parts I and II* (The Hague, Kluwer Law International, 2000) 368, in particular Illustrations 1 and 2. See also art III.-3:202(1) of the DCFR.

[51] See above, p 150.

[52] *Ibid.*

basis of the theory adhered to in this thesis.[53] Breach of the conformity obligation after the due delivery date, therefore, should not be considered automatically to give the buyer a right to terminate. Nevertheless, time is an important consideration, especially in commercial sales. Therefore, it is thought that a distinction should be made between situations where time is of the essence and situations where it is not. The right to cure, arguably, should be more limited where time is of the essence, because in that case the seller's breach of the time clause is fundamentally at odds with the express intentions of the parties, to a greater degree than where time is not of the essence. The wrong committed by the seller, therefore, should be regarded as being of a more serious degree, and the right to cure should be limited accordingly.[54]

While both national sale of goods laws and international rules make a distinction between situations where time is of the essence and situations where it is not, there are differences in the scope that they allow for cure. Particularly where time is not of the essence, it is thought that certain approaches found in national laws provide a better model for harmonisation than the solutions found in CISG or the PECL.

1. Where Time is of the Essence

Where time is of the essence, the parties have made it clear that timely performance is essential to the contract. Therefore, it follows that any delay in performance should suffice to give the other party the right to terminate the contract, and that any possibilities of cure will be precluded. Such certainty is essential, especially in international commercial sales, where the stakes can be high.

In this respect, national and international sales laws draw one line—all of them generally deny the seller a right to cure where time is of the essence. Harmonisation of this aspect of the cure regime, therefore, should not pose too great a challenge. Perhaps the only thing that requires attention is the way in which the result is reached. It is arguable that some room should be left to enable cure where it would be a realistic option—for example where the buyer has suffered no detriment as a result of the seller's breach—and some regimes make greater allowance for this than others.

The English approach would seem too restrictive. If the parties stipulate that time is of the essence then it is,[55] regardless of whether the buyer has a true interest in performance by that date. For example, *Bowes v Shand* shows that, since

[53] Ch 3, pp 48 ff.

[54] Apart from restricting the scope where time is of the essence, limitations could also be that cure may only be effected if it can be done with minimal delay and inconvenience caused to the buyer. See ch 7, pp 192 ff.

[55] Provided that on proper construction of the contract, the time stipulation is intended to be of the essence; compare SGA s 10(2).

the failure of the seller to deliver on time is a breach of condition, the buyer may reject the goods even if he has suffered no loss as a result of the breach.[56] The result is that if the seller has failed satisfactorily to perform by the date fixed for performance the buyer will be entitled to terminate immediately. This appears to put too much of a restriction on the seller's option to cure, for by terminating the buyer may prevent all attempts at repair or replacement after the delivery date, even where these would still be possible and could provide a cost-effective solution for both parties. Moreover, there are concerns that a strict rule like this may allow buyers to escape from bad bargains purely on the basis of a technical breach of contract. Buyers may reject goods and terminate the contract not because they are really aggrieved by the early or late shipment but rather because the market has fallen.[57] This is not a policy generally condoned by English contract law, and it also does not do justice to the interests of the parties, in particular the seller. Rules that take account of the true interest that the buyer has in timely performance are thus to be preferred, though only if they can provide an adequate level of legal certainty.

It is submitted, therefore, that the less restrictive rules of the Dutch and German default regimes offer a preferable solution. In German law, § 323 II 2 *BGB* provides that a period of time does not have to be fixed if

> the obligor fails to perform by a date specified in the contract or within a specified period and, in the contract, the obligee has linked the continuation of his interest in performance to the punctuality of that performance.[58]

Dutch law contains a similar rule in article 6:83(a) *BW*, which provides that default commences without notice

> where the term set for performance lapses without the obligation having been performed, unless it appears that the term had another purpose.[59]

The German provision, especially, makes clear that it is not merely a question of the parties stipulating that timely performance is required, but also making clear *why* this is so. In other words, the buyer has to show that he has an interest in performance that is linked to the time stipulation. However, in putting the onus of proof on the buyer, the rule may be thought to be unfairly prejudicial to buyers, and in particular to consumers. To this extent, the Dutch rule may be

[56] *Bowes v Shand* (1877) 2 App Cas 455 (HL).

[57] Compare PS Atiyah, JN Adams and H MacQueen, *The Sale of Goods*, 11th edn (Harlow, Pearson, 2005) 133–4.

[58] In German: 'Die Fristsetzung ist entbehrlich, wenn der Schuldner die Leistung zu einem im Vertrag bestimmten Termin oder innerhalb einer bestimmten Frist nicht bewirkt und der Gläubiger im Vertrag den Fortbestand seines Leistungsinteresses an die Rechtzeitigkeit der Leistung gebunden hat'.

[59] Rather curiously, the translation in D Busch, EH Hondius, HJ van Kooten, HN Schelhaas and WM Schrama (eds), *The Principles of European Contract Law and Dutch Law—A Commentary* (Nijmegen, Ars Aequi Libri, 2002) 398 refers to 'a term which has been set for *payment*' (emphasis added). This would appear too narrow, for the provision relates to all obligations, not just those for payment. The Dutch text speaks of 'de verbintenis' (ie 'the obligation').

preferable, for while it takes account of the true interests of the parties in timely performance, it leaves it up to the seller to show that a fixed date for performance should not, in the circumstances of the case, prevent him from having an attempt at cure.[60]

Similar flexibility may be achieved by adopting the solution found in international regimes such as CISG and the PECL, which rely on a notion of 'fundamental breach'. Under these regimes, a right to cure is generally available subject to the possibility of termination.[61] While the right to terminate appears paramount, a buyer will only be allowed to terminate if the seller's breach is 'fundamental'—a flexible concept. CISG, article 25 defines it as follows:

> A breach of contract committed by one of the parties is fundamental if it results in such detriment to the other party as substantially to deprive him of what he is entitled to expect under the contract, unless the party in breach did not foresee and a reasonable person of the same kind in the same circumstances would not have foreseen such a result.

This definition leaves some room for interpretation, and may therefore allow cure in those exceptional situations where it would provide the better solution. For example, it may prevent buyers from getting out of a bad bargain merely on the ground that time was of the essence and the seller did not perform on time, even if they suffered no detriment as a result of the seller's breach. However, in comparison to national laws, it may be criticised for being unduly restrictive on the buyer's right of termination. By putting the burden on the buyer to prove that, in addition to the fact that time was of the essence, the breach has substantially deprived him of what he was entitled to expect under the contract, the scope for termination may be considerably limited. In cases where the buyer is unable to meet this burden of proof, he will simply lose his claim. This is at odds with the—better—solution adopted in Dutch and German law, and to an extent in English law, which recognises a general right of termination, limited only where the breach is too minor in nature.[62]

The solution found in CISG, nevertheless, appears preferable to that found in the PECL, for two reasons. First, similarly to English law, the PECL's definition of fundamental non-performance does not seem to leave much room for cure where it has been stipulated that time is of the essence. While article 8:103(b) contains a definition that is similar to CISG's definition of fundamental breach, which takes into account whether detriment has been suffered by the buyer,

[60] There is some debate in Dutch law as to the scope of art 6:83(a) *BW*. According to the Supreme Court (Hoge Raad), for the requirement of a default period not to apply, parties need to have *agreed* that a fixed time is of the essence (*Fraanje/Götte*, HR 4 oktober 2002, *NJ* 2003, 257). See also MAJG Janssen and MM van Rossum, 'Verzuim en ingebrekestelling bij schadevergoeding en ontbinding' [2004] *Nederlands Tijdschrift voor Burgerlijk Recht* 62 at 66; JB Londonck Sluijk, 'Verzuim en ingebrekestelling bij niet-nakoming van verbintenissen: een overzicht aan de hand van twee arresten' [2003] *Bedrijfsjuridische berichten* 50 at 52. The issue is not directly relevant to the current argument and it shall therefore not be discussed in more detail.

[61] CISG art 48; PECL art 8:104. Compare also art III.-3:202(2) of the DCFR.

[62] Compare art 6:265(1) *BW*, § 323 V *BGB*, and s 15A of the SGA. See also below, p 172.

article 8:103(a) deprives this provision of its effect where time has been made of the essence. It provides that non-performance of an obligation is fundamental to the contract if 'strict compliance with the obligation is of the essence of the contract'. According to the Commentary, if the parties have agreed that strict adherence to the contract is essential, the actual gravity of the breach is no longer a relevant factor in determining whether the breach justifies termination.[63] Therefore, there remains hardly any scope to consider the possibility of cure where time was of the essence.

Secondly, the PECL's provisions on termination appear to put too strict a curb on the right to cure. While a seller may have a right to cure under CISG even if his breach is fundamental, the PECL deny him this right if the breach relates to a delay in performance. Article 8:104 makes this clear by stating that the seller has a right to cure where 'the delay would not be such as to constitute a fundamental non-performance'. The result is that the seller does not have a right to cure, even if the buyer does not exercise his right to terminate.[64] In the light of, in particular, considerations of economic efficiency, this seems a very undesirable result. The practical significance of this restriction, however, is likely to be minimal. Even if the seller does not have the right to cure, he may still have the practical *opportunity* to repair or replace defective goods, as long as the buyer has not exercised his right of termination or claimed any other remedy that is inconsistent with performance.

In conclusion, Dutch law, German law and CISG appear to strike the balance between the interests of buyer and seller in the best place, leaving a little room for cure even where time is stipulated to be 'of the essence'. However, and this is true for all regimes under consideration, where the seller is in breach of contract by not observing the time clause, any right to cure can only exist subject to the buyer's right of termination. Therefore, once the buyer becomes entitled to terminate, the seller's right to cure is open to attack under any of the systems. This appears to be true for international instruments as much as for domestic sales laws.[65] Under the PECL, it is commonly accepted that the buyer's right of termination takes precedence over the seller's right to cure.[66] According to Yovel, 'in the context of the PECL . . . the power to terminate the contract is generally independent and effectively not contingent upon the right to cure'.[67] Likewise for CISG—arguably, where it has been established that the breach is

[63] Lando and Beale, *Principles of European Contract Law* (n 50 above) 364.

[64] Compare J Yovel, 'Cure after date for delivery: Comparison between provisions of the CISG (seller's right to remedy failure to perform: art 48) and the counterpart provisions of the PECL (arts 8:104 and 9:303)' in J Felemegas, *An International Approach to the Interpretation of the United Nations Convention on Contracts for the International Sale of Goods (1980) as Uniform Sales Law* (Cambridge, CUP, 2007) 381 at 390. See also art III.-3:203(a) of the DCFR.

[65] For English, Dutch and German law, see above, pp 152 ff.

[66] Yovel, 'Cure after date for delivery' (n 64 above) 390.

[67] *Ibid*. Yovel bases this conclusion on an analysis of the notice provisions of the Principles. These are outside the scope of this thesis; for a further discussion compare Yovel, 'Cure after date for delivery' (n 64 above); Lando and Beale, *Principles of European Contract Law* (n 50 above) 413 ff.

fundamental and the buyer is entitled to avoid, his right of avoidance appears to override the seller's right to cure. According to the official UNCITRAL Digest,

> it has been determined that it is for the buyer to decide whether or not the contract should be avoided. If a right to avoidance is established the buyer may exercise it without being restricted by the seller's right to cure.[68]

Though this interpretation of the Convention is not entirely undisputed, a number of cases back up the conclusion that the buyer's right to avoid prevails,[69] and it is also supported by article 48(2) according to which the seller must ask for the buyer's consent for cure.[70] The effect is that where a breach has been deemed fundamental despite the possibility of cure, the buyer may prevent any attempt at cure by the seller by terminating the contract.

2. Where Time is not of the Essence

Where time is not of the essence, it is arguable that the scope for seller cure can be wider than where time *is* of the essence, for the seller and the buyer find themselves in a situation that is largely similar to that where the time for performance has not elapsed. Time not being an essential element of the contract, it is likely that the seller is still able to provide the buyer with the performance that he contracted for.

There is a difference between the two situations, however, in that after the due delivery date the seller's performance has become exigible and a non-performance will thus constitute a breach of contract which may—possibly after a default period—entitle the buyer to terminate. On this ground, it is thought that the seller's right to cure after the due delivery date should be more limited than where the time for performance has not expired.

Within these general boundaries, there are several ways in which to determine the availability and scope of the seller's right to cure. In relation to the first point—the availability of cure—Dutch and German law take the default requirement as their starting point, under English law the time clause would seem to qualify as an 'innominate term', and CISG and the PECL rely on what may be called 'curability'. For reasons of legal certainty, it will be argued that the default regime of Dutch and German law should prevail. If so, there is still a question as to how long the time period for cure should be. The choice is

[68] UN Commission on International Trade Law, *UNCITRAL Digest of case law on the United Nations Convention on the International Sale of Goods—Article 48* (8 June 2004) 2, available at www.uncitral.org/uncitral/en/case_law/digests/cisg.html.

[69] ICC Arbitration No 7531 (1994) CLOUT case No 304; Bundesgerichtshof Germany (1997) CLOUT case No 235; Oberlandesgericht Oldenburg Germany (1995) CLOUT case No 165; Oberlandesgericht Frankfurt am Main Germany (1991) CLOUT case No 2; Pretura circondariale de Parma Italy (1989) CLOUT case No 90.

[70] *UNCITRAL Digest of case law on the United Nations Convention on the International Sale of Goods—Article 48* (n 68 above) 2.

between allowing a 'reasonable time' or allowing the seller to cure as long as the delay does not deprive the buyer of 'substantially the whole benefit which it was intended he should receive from the contract'.[71] It will be argued that, on balance, the interests of the buyer should weigh heavier than those of the seller and that, therefore, the solution most favourable to the buyer is opted for—which would appear to be the 'reasonable time' criterion. In order to minimise uncertainty that may arise from using a flexible concept like this, it will be argued that such a regime is most effective where the buyer is under an obligation to fix an additional period of time for performance before he becomes entitled to other remedies.

a) Basis of the Right to Cure

As seen above,[72] in Dutch law the seller is not automatically in default if the parties have not stipulated that time is of the essence. Thus, the buyer will have to take action if he wants to become entitled to terminate. According to article 6:82(1) *BW*,[73]

> [d]efault commences when the debtor is put into default by a written warning granting him a reasonable period for performance and when there is no performance within this period.

A similar requirement can be found in § 323 I *BGB*, which lays down the rule in German law that a buyer is not entitled to terminate until he has fixed to no avail an additional period of time for performance.

As an aside—it appears that Dutch law gives a limited entitlement to the seller to effect cure even once he has become in default. Article 6:86 *BW* provides:

> The creditor may refuse performance offered after the beginning of the default, so long as the offer does not also comprise the payment of damages which have, in the meantime, become due, as well as of costs.[74]

If this is meant to give the seller a right to cure even where he is in default, it is thought that the provision goes too far. The seller has had a second chance to perform during the additional period of time set by the buyer before the commencement of the default. If he did not make use of it, or if cure was unsuccessful, that is a risk that should fall on him rather than on the buyer. The buyer cannot be made to wait indefinitely for the seller to effect cure, and neither should the seller have an unlimited number of bites at the cherry.[75] The fact that

[71] Guest (ed), *Benjamin's Sale of Goods* (n 46 above) [8-025].

[72] See p 154.

[73] In Dutch: 'Het verzuim treedt in, wanneer de schuldenaar in gebreke wordt gesteld bij een schriftelijke aanmaning waarbij hem een redelijke termijn voor de nakoming wordt gesteld, en nakoming binnen deze termijn uitblijft'.

[74] Art 6:86 *BW*. In Dutch: 'De schuldeiser kan een na het intreden van het verzuim aangeboden nakoming weigeren, zolang niet tevens betaling wordt aangeboden van de inmiddels tevens verschuldigd geworden schadevergoeding en van de kosten'.

[75] As to how many chances the seller should have to effect cure, see ch 7, p 199.

default has commenced entitles the buyer to a number of other remedies (such as damages or termination) and he should be free to exercise these in his own time without having to wonder whether or not the seller will effect cure after all and take away the buyer's right to opt for a different remedy. Therefore, it is submitted that, once default has commenced, the buyer should be free to opt for the remedy he prefers and there should be no opening for the seller to 'surprise' him with a late cure.

An alternative approach to widening the scope of cure may be to take the 'curability' of a defect into account as a factor in determining whether a buyer has a right to terminate. If it is possible to remedy a defect in the goods, this could be seen as an indication that termination should not be allowed, at least until the seller has had a chance to effect cure. The approach found in CISG and the PECL, for example, provides a model that may take into account a notion of curability in determining whether the buyer is entitled to terminate. CISG makes the right of termination dependent on the seriousness of the breach—only a 'fundamental' breach will entitle the buyer to terminate.[76] Curability could be taken into account if it is accepted that a breach cannot be deemed fundamental if cure is possible. Such considerations may also, to a limited extent, be relevant in English law where innominate or intermediate terms are concerned. In cases where contractual terms have not been classified as either warranties or conditions, the rights arising on breach of such a term depend on the nature and consequences of that breach.[77] Curability could be an indication that a breach is not sufficiently serious to justify termination of the contract and that a term does therefore not qualify as a condition. However, the results in application are likely to be more limited than under CISG, since the SGA classifies the conformity obligations of the seller as implied conditions, breach of which will automatically give rise to a right of termination. Nevertheless, it may be relevant in relation to breach of a time stipulation in the contract, for such a provision may be classified as an innominate term if time is not of the essence.

However, it is submitted that as a model for future harmonisation, the default regime holds the better cards. While some criticism may be levied at the default regime, it appears to have clear advantages over the regimes of CISG and the PECL and, for that matter, English law. Its main advantage over a regime that relies on 'curability' is that it offers greater legal certainty. After all, only where performance has become impossible will the buyer be able to terminate instantly without setting an additional period for cure. 'Impossibility' is less flexible and should therefore be an easier concept to work with than fundamental breach or innominate terms. Fundamental breach, for example, does not necessarily

[76] CISG art 49(1)(a); PECL art 9:301(1). See also unreported, 31 January 1997 (Oberlandesgericht Koblenz), available at www.unilex.info.

[77] Compare *Hong Kong Fir Shipping Co Ltd v Kawasaki Kisen Kaisha Ltd* [1962] 2 QB 26 (CA) and *Cehave NV v Bremer Handelsgesellschaft mbH (The Hansa Nord)* [1976] QB 44 (CA). Also Guest (ed), *Benjamin's Sale of Goods* (n 46 above) [10-33].

require that performance has become physically impossible,[78] and therefore many more considerations need to be taken into account to determine whether the breach is fundamental. More factors mean greater scope for interpretation and, depending on the circumstances, sellers and buyers may thus not have a clear view of what their rights are. The default regime avoids such difficulties to a large degree, and therefore offers greater certainty.

It may be thought that these objections are mainly theoretical in nature. For example, as the Digest of CISG case law points out,[79] a breach is rarely fundamental when the failure of performance could easily be remedied. Thus, in many cases it will be clear that the buyer is not entitled to avoid and that the seller should have a right to cure. Furthermore, it may be thought that uncertainties can easily be overcome as long as the parties communicate and co-operate sufficiently with each other.[80] Article 48(2) and (3) may play a useful role in this respect, for if the seller offers performance under these provisions, the buyer is forced to state whether he opts for subsequent performance or for avoidance of the contract.[81] However, though these arguments may to some extent attenuate the uncertainty inherent in CISG's fundamental breach system, they do not cover all situations of breach. The default regimes in Dutch and German law, on the other hand, do apply generally to contractual dealings.

Furthermore, the qualification found in Dutch and German law that termination may not be allowed where the breach is of minor importance or immaterial[82] impinges to a lesser extent on legal certainty than a regime centred around fundamental breach does. Under these regimes, such a qualification is nothing more than an exception to the general rule that termination is available upon breach. The seriousness of the defective performance is not, as under CISG or the PECL, the main determinant for establishing breach. Thus, in the majority of cases it will be clear to buyers and sellers whether the buyer is entitled to terminate or not.

b) The Time Period for Cure

As to time, two possibilities present themselves: (i) the seller may be granted a reasonable time to perform, or (ii) the limit may be set where the delay would amount to a fundamental non-performance, or, equally, where it would deprive the buyer of substantially the whole benefit which he was intended to receive from the contract.

[78] Compare P Schlechtriem and I Schwenzer (eds), *Commentary on the UN Convention on the International Sale of Goods*, 2nd English edn (Oxford, Oxford University Press, 2005) 286–7.

[79] *UNCITRAL Digest of case law on the United Nations Convention on the International Sale of Goods—Article 48* (n 68 above) 2.

[80] Compare Schlechtriem and Schwenzer, *Commentary on the UN Convention on the International Sale of Goods* (n 78 above) 568.

[81] *Ibid.*

[82] Art 6:265(1) *BW*; § 323 V *BGB*. See also SGA s 15A—but note that this only applies to commercial sales.

The first is the approach adopted in Dutch law,[83] and possibly also in German law. Some uncertainty remains, in that § 323 I *BGB* lays down the default requirement for termination in German law, but the provision does not require the additional time period to be 'reasonable'. However, seeing that the provision was introduced in order to give effect to the Consumer Sales Directive, it may be inferred that the additional period has to be reasonable, at least to the extent that it applies to consumer purchases. Article 3(5) of the Directive, after all, states that the consumer can have the contract rescinded 'if the seller has not completed the remedy within a reasonable time'.[84]

The second approach has been adopted by CISG and the PECL, where it follows from the fundamental breach or fundamental non-performance requirements, and it can also be found in English law relating to innominate terms. It may lead to different results than the first approach, since unreasonable delay may not deprive the aggrieved party of substantially the whole benefit of the contract.[85] But does this mean that a seller should be allowed to cure even after a reasonable time has passed, simply because he may still be able to provide the buyer with the performance that he contracted for (or something not substantially less)?

It is submitted that with regard to the time period for cure the interests of the buyer should prevail. Since the seller is the party who is in the wrong, moral rights theory would appear to support a limitation of the right to cure where the interests of the buyer so demand.[86] It is thought that with regard to the time issue, a buyer is likely to have an interest in obtaining a remedy with as little delay and inconvenience as possible. Therefore, it is not enough merely to ensure that the buyer gets the performance that he contracted for, but the law should also provide that he obtains it within a reasonable time.

The 'reasonable time' criterion, moreover, would appear to find recognition in consumer and commercial sales alike. As said, the Consumer Sales Directive adopts it as the standard for consumer sales. CISG, applicable to commercial sales, ultimately relies upon the fundamental breach criterion—but while this may be a necessary requirement to trigger the buyer's right of termination, the reasonable time criterion does have a part to play in relation to cure. For example, article 48(1) provides that the seller has a right to cure if he can effect the remedy 'without unreasonable delay'. In other words, the seller may lose his right to cure even before the buyer becomes entitled to terminate if he does not manage to cure within a reasonable time. He may, of course, still have the *opportunity* to cure as long as the buyer does not invoke a remedy that is inconsistent with it (eg damages), but he cannot uphold a right to cure if the buyer prefers a different remedy. In practice, therefore, the seller's right to cure

[83] Art 6:82(1) *BW*; see above, p 170.

[84] Zimmermann does not question this interpretation of the provision; compare Zimmermann, *The New German Law of Obligations* (n 23 above) 108.

[85] Compare *Universal Cargo Carriers Corp v Citati* [1957] 2 QB 401 (QBD) 430, 432.

[86] Compare ch 3, pp 71 ff. See also ch 7, pp 193 ff.

extends only to a reasonable time after the due delivery date, as it does in Dutch and—arguably—German law.

c) Notice or No Notice?

In German law, § 323 I *BGB* provides that a promisee may terminate the contract 'if he has fixed, to no avail, an additional period of time for performance'. Dutch law, in article 6:82(1) *BW*, also lays down the requirement that written notice is sent to the defaulting promisor, granting him extra time to perform. It may be thought that the buyer's right to terminate is unduly restricted by this requirement—if he does not set an extra time for performance, he does not become entitled to terminate, even if a reasonable time has passed after the due delivery date and the seller has failed to cure.

However, the requirement of notice of default has advantages which appear to outweigh the arguments against it. In particular, it minimises uncertainty, for the seller will be aware of the buyer's intention to terminate the contract if cure is not effected within a reasonable time. In other words, he has a pre-warning and may thus be encouraged to attempt cure within the time set. In systems where notice of default is not a requirement for termination, on the other hand, the seller may be unsure as to if and when the time for cure may be cut off by the buyer's termination. For example, in English law the buyer may decide to terminate the contract at any time once the delay has become such as to deprive the buyer of substantially the whole benefit of the contract. But when is this? It may be very hard for sellers to determine when their right to cure has come to an end and when they may expect termination by the buyer. Moreover, while the buyer may become entitled to terminate the contract, it is not guaranteed that he chooses to do so—he may be willing to hold on for a little while longer in order to obtain performance by the seller. However, the seller needs to be aware of this. It is fundamental to the successful remedying of a defective performance that the parties communicate with each other. In this respect, the requirement of notice of default may serve a useful function, for it forces buyers and sellers to make their intentions clear to the other party.

Furthermore, legal certainty is served by the fact that a concrete date for performance is fixed. The seller will know that he has until that date to make an attempt at cure, while the buyer will have the certainty that he may terminate on that date if the seller does not succeed in doing so. The default regime, in this respect, is preferable to a regime which focuses on curability without the requirement of notice.

Finally, it may be doubted whether the buyer would truly be disadvantaged if he had omitted to send out a default notice or to set an additional period of time for performance. Even if a reasonable time had elapsed after the due delivery date without the seller performing, nothing would prevent the buyer from setting a time limit then. Since some time would have passed by then, it is likely that the seller would be granted less time to effect cure. The 'reasonable' time requirement, thus, leaves room for flexibility. For example, it may be taken into account that the seller has had time to perform within the time set by the original contract and that an additional period of time, therefore, is likely to be shorter.[87] If the buyer had given notice before, but had merely omitted to fix a time, the new time period likewise may be very short.

Nevertheless, the default regime is not the only possibility—there are other ways in which notice procedures may be applied in order to achieve cure. However, these appear inferior to the default regime. One alternative is available in the doctrine of *Nachfrist*, derived from the German law of obligations and also adopted by CISG and the PECL.[88] It stipulates that a party who does not receive the performance that he contracted for may set an extra time for the other party to perform. If the aggrieved party decides to fix an additional period of time for performance, he will be allowed to terminate the contract only after this period,[89] usually a 'reasonable' period of time.[90] Though the concept of *Nachfrist* may appear similar to the default requirement, it is submitted that the latter is preferable since it provides a much greater degree of legal certainty.

The uncertainty of *Nachfrist* derives from the fact that, unlike the default regime, it does not give the seller a *right* to cure. The crucial distinction is that *Nachfrist* will only apply at the discretion of the buyer—he is not obliged to set an extra period of performance for the seller. If he prefers another remedy, such as damages in lieu of performance, he is free to choose this option. Nevertheless, there are circumstances in which the buyer may have incentives to refer to *Nachfrist*, and where the regime will thus give the seller an opportunity to cure. For example, in cases of delay, the regime may have an entitlement-creating function. If the delay is not sufficiently serious to constitute a fundamental breach, the buyer will not be entitled to terminate. However, upon expiration of the extra period of time set for performance, if the seller has not satisfactorily cured the defect, the buyer *then* becomes entitled to terminate.[91] Thus, the buyer may be tempted to invoke article 47(1) of CISG where the breach is not fundamental. *Nachfrist* may, in this way, create a limited possibility for sellers to cure a delay in performance. However, no matter how strong the incentives may be, there is no *obligation* on the buyer to fix an extra period for performance. As a consequence, the seller may face a delay where the buyer has not yet made up his mind whether to try *Nachfrist* or to opt for another remedy. This uncertainty would be avoided under the default regime, where the seller would automatically have a reasonable time to cure.

[87] Compare Schlechtriem and Schwenzer, *Commentary on the UN Convention on the International Sale of Goods* (n 78 above) 556–7.

[88] CISG art 47; PECL art 8:106.

[89] Compare CISG art 49(1)(b) and 49(2)(b)(ii).

[90] Compare CISG art 47(1).

[91] Other systems, such as Dutch law, function in a different way. Though it may sometimes be allowed to set an additional period of time, it is not possible for a party to bring into life a right of termination where none existed previously. Compare Busch, Hondius, van Kooten, Schelhaas, and Schrama, *The Principles of European Contract Law and Dutch Law—A Commentary* (n 59 above) 339.

3. Conclusion

The fact that the due delivery date has passed, thus, does not have to preclude the availability of a right to cure for the seller. What sets the situation apart from cure before the due delivery date is that, here, the seller is in breach of contract. This may to some extent limit the possibilities for cure after the due delivery date, since the seller's breach may entitle the buyer to certain remedies that were not available to him earlier. If the buyer exercises a remedy inconsistent with performance, the seller's right to cure automatically comes to an end.

However, a way around this is to put the buyer's remedies on hold, at least for a while, to enable the seller to make an attempt at cure. National and international sales laws appear favourable to such a solution, though to different degrees. On grounds of legal certainty, it is thought that a default regime, such as found in Dutch and German law, on balance offers the best solution for both sellers and buyers.

V. INFORMAL ATTEMPTS AT CURE

The previous sections dealt with situations in which a right to cure may be recognised for the seller. Instead of giving him a *right* to cure, however, an alternative approach could be to encourage informal attempts at cure. This could be defendable from a policy point of view, for it may engender similar economic benefits to those brought by a general right to cure, avoiding the economic waste associated with immediate termination of contracts upon breach. It is also the approach adopted in English law under the SGA. Section 35(6), in particular, was introduced with an eye to encouraging sellers and buyers to try repair before rejecting the goods and terminating the contract.[92] The provision states that the buyer is not deemed to have accepted the goods merely because 'he asks for, or agrees to, their repair by or under an arrangement with the seller'. Not having accepted the goods, the buyer remains entitled to reject and rescind should the attempted cure fail. With this safeguard, buyers may be encouraged to give sellers an opportunity to attempt cure.

Nevertheless, section 35(6) of the SGA operates under the presumption that rejection and termination are two sides of the same coin, ie that a buyer's rejection of defective goods may immediately be followed by termination of the contract. As was seen earlier, this approach does not fit in with the fundamental principles that underlie the remedial scheme in contract law: the right to withhold performance and the right to terminate. The correct view would seem to be that rejection is a sub-form of the right to withhold performance, not of the right

[92] The provision was introduced on the basis of recommendations made by the Law Commissions in their report on *Sale and Supply of Goods* (Law Com No 160, Scot Law Com No 104 (May 1987)) [5.27]–[5.29].

to terminate, so that a rejection before the time of delivery may still leave time for the seller to cure. It is submitted, therefore, that it is not sufficient for a remedial scheme merely to encourage attempts at cure. What is needed is a system that gives the seller a right to cure, at least for the time period before the delivery date.

The case law shows that two deficiencies in particular limit the possibilities for successful attempts at cure under section 35 of the SGA. First, there is some debate as to whether the time taken for cure may be taken into account as a factor in establishing the limits of the buyer's right to reject. For the purposes of section 35(5), does the clock start ticking when negotiations about repair are entered into, or only when more concrete steps have been taken towards repair? Secondly, it is unclear whether a buyer is under a duty to accept repaired goods if an agreement to cure has been entered into with the seller. If any general guidelines may be gleaned from the case law, they show that English courts are reluctant to loosen the tightly held grip that the law allows buyers to have on the exercise of remedies leading to cure. An explanation may be that the cases in issue mostly deal with situations of cure after the original time for performance has passed, in which case a narrower basis exists for the recognition of a right to cure.[93] Still, section 35 does not distinguish between cases of cure before or after the due delivery date. To the extent that the courts' interpretation of the provision limits the functioning of cure in the former situation, it is submitted that a re-evaluation of the rule is called for.

1. The Time Period for Cure

Under an informal cure regime, the seller's option to cure depends entirely on the decision of the buyer. If the buyer is in a position where the delivery of defective goods is regarded as a breach that entitles him to reject the goods and terminate the contract, he has a strong bargaining tool to wield against the seller. Non-performance means the end of the game. The buyer may, however, have an incentive to allow cure, for example where this would be convenient or relatively inexpensive. He may be inclined to take this route if he can keep his right of termination pending, so that in the circumstance that the seller fails satisfactorily to remedy the defect, he has not lost this remedy. Section 35(6) of the SGA gives a buyer this opportunity by making clear that an agreement to repair does not automatically imply acceptance of the goods. However, it does not make clear for how long a period of time the buyer is able to delay rejection of the goods without losing his right to reject and terminate. This period of time is of course not going to be indefinite—the seller should at some point be able to know where he stands. But where does the cut-off point lie?

[93] See above, pp 164 ff.

Perhaps not surprisingly, the test found in section 35 of the SGA is one for a 'reasonable' period of time.[94] This appears similar to the requirements found in other systems in relation to cure after the delivery date, such as in article 48 of CISG and article 6:82(1) *BW*. However, while the time stipulations in these provisions refer to a period of time where the seller is guaranteed an opportunity to cure, section 35 does the opposite—it guarantees a time period for the buyer during which his right to reject and terminate remains alive, regardless of whether this is before or after the due delivery date. As a result, the seller is likely to be unsure about his opportunities to cure in either situation. In this light, it is submitted that section 35 of the SGA is inadequate in the extent that it seeks to encourage informal attempts at cure. After all, depending on the circumstances, the seller may be left in suspense for a considerable amount of time, not knowing whether the buyer will decide to reject the goods and terminate, or whether he will accept cure. Thus, sellers are likely to face a significant measure of uncertainty, which, in turn, may put them off attempting cure.

The point is proven by case law indicating that, especially in consumer sales, the buyer may have a substantial period of time in which to consider rejecting the goods and terminating the contract. A good example of such a case is *Clegg v Andersson*,[95] which concerned a defective yacht. The finding that the keel of the ship was too heavy led to a prolonged correspondence between the seller and the buyer as to the possibility of fixing the defect. After more than five months from the time of purchase of the yacht, it became clear that the seller could not offer a satisfactory solution to the problem, and three weeks after this the buyer rejected the yacht for non-conformity. The Court of Appeal held that the buyer had been entitled to do so. Apart from section 35(6) of the SGA, the Court also relied on section 35(5), which provides that amongst the factors that are material in determining what is a reasonable time to retain the goods before rejecting is whether the buyer has had a reasonable opportunity of examining the goods to determine their conformity with the contract. Applying these provisions to the facts of the case, it was held that the buyer had not lost his right to reject by seeking information which the seller had agreed to supply which would enable him to make a properly informed choice between acceptance, rejection or cure.[96]

Had the case been decided under a system such as the Dutch or the German, the seller would have been in a better position. Under these systems, he would have been entitled to attempt cure and, seeing that no date for delivery had been agreed on, he would have been given a reasonable time to do so.[97] He would thus have had the certainty that repairs would be accepted by the buyers during this period of time, as long as they sufficed to make the yacht of satisfactory quality. The latter requirement may not have been fulfilled in *Clegg*, and the

[94] SGA s 35(4).
[95] *Clegg v Andersson* [2003] EWCA Civ 320, [2003] 1 All ER (Comm) 721.
[96] *Ibid*, [75].
[97] See p 170 above.

outcome of the case may therefore not have been any different. However, this does not change the fact that this approach generally gives sellers a much greater incentive to attempt repairs, simply by the fact that it offers greater certainty of cure being accepted.

The position under English law, however, may be somewhat less harsh on sellers than *Clegg* suggests, for it is not a rule of law that time taken for repair cannot count towards establishing what is a reasonable time for the purposes of section 35(5) of the SGA. Whilst on the facts of *Clegg* the time for obtaining information that enabled the buyer to make an informed choice on whether to reject the defective yacht could easily be deemed 'reasonable', the question remains one of fact,[98] and there may well be situations in which the time taken for repair does count for the purposes of section 35(5). Such was the case in *Jones v Gallagher*.[99] The case concerned the design, supply and installation of a hand-made fitted pine kitchen, which was to match 'existing dresser cabinet, cabinets, surfaces etc'.[100] A week after the installation was completed, the buyers wrote to the sellers, raising various issues and complaints about aspects of the installation, including that the colour of the new units did not match that of the existing dresser as required. A lengthy correspondence followed and several attempts at repair were made, but, although the colour problem was not consistently raised, it was never satisfactorily resolved. An intermittent correspondence between the sellers and the solicitors then hired by the buyers also led to nothing, and eventually the buyers brought proceedings seeking reimbursement of the price of the kitchen plus damages. The Court of Appeal regarded this as a different factual situation from *Clegg*, taking into account that the buyer complained of a series of defects, bringing up new ones as negotiations progressed, and that there were long periods without contact. Therefore, whereas the sellers in *Clegg* ought reasonably to have known that the buyers had not finally accepted the yacht, the suppliers in *Jones* may perhaps reasonably have believed that the buyers had accepted their kitchen.[101]

Nevertheless, while this decision limits the possibilities for the buyer to keep the seller on a string for a prolonged period of time, it still leaves room for considerable uncertainty. Since the question is one of fact, it will depend on the circumstances of the case whether the court decides that the buyer has lost the right to reject or not. However, the case law leaves a large measure of flexibility and it may therefore not be clear to either seller or buyer whether the decision is likely to be in their favour.

[98] SGA s 59.

[99] *Jones v Gallagher* [2004] EWCA Civ, [2005] 1 Lloyd's Rep 377, especially [33]–[35].

[100] *Ibid*, [2].

[101] *Ibid*, [21]–[23]. Compare R Bradgate, 'Remedying the Unfit Fitted Kitchen' (2004) 120 *Law Quarterly Review* 558 at 561.

2. Acceptance of Repaired Goods

A further point of uncertainty relates to the obligation of the buyer to accept repaired goods. If he does not reject defective goods, but instead agrees to an attempt at cure, does this prevent him from rejecting the goods further down the line? If it did, the seller's position with regard to cure would be considerably strengthened, for the risk that repairs will be carried out in vain would be reduced. A recent Scottish case, *J&H Ritchie Ltd v Lloyd Ltd*,[102] suggests that, in certain circumstances, section 35(6) of the SGA does not stand in the way of such an approach. However, significant inroads may be made on this rule—as in the case itself—on the basis of a neglect of information duties on the part of the seller.[103] More importantly, elements of uncertainty remain which, it is submitted, render the cure regime of the SGA inadequate for Scots as well as English law.

The factual situation of *Ritchie* is fairly straightforward. Defective farm equipment was delivered to the buyers who, after becoming aware of a malfunctioning in the goods, returned them to the sellers. The sellers offered repair, and also provided a replacement harrow so that the buyers could finish the seeding that they had started. When the sellers tried to re-deliver the repaired equipment to the buyers, they refused to accept the goods. The arguments on which they relied were that the defect could have had a knock-on effect in damaging other parts of the equipment and, furthermore, that they had been refused an engineer's report from the sellers as to the quality of the goods after repair. Moreover, the buyer thought it likely that he would not be able to test the machine until the following springtime and expressed concern as to the effect of this delay on the manufacturer's guarantee period.

Having been paid only minor attention in the proceedings in the Scottish courts, the sellers' refusal to supply information relating to the repair of the harrow became the main focus in the House of Lords decision, and also the ground on which the final victory went to the buyers. In the words of Lord Rodger,

> I am satisfied that business efficacy required the implication of a term that, if asked, the respondents would tell the appellants what their inspection had shown to be wrong with the harrow and what they had done to put it right. The respondent's outright refusal to supply that information constituted a material breach of the inspection and repair agreement, entitling the appellants to rescind it and refuse to collect the harrow, even though . . . it had actually been repaired to a factory gate standard.[104]

[102] *J&H Ritchie Ltd v Lloyd Ltd* [2007] UKHL 9; [2007] 1 WLR 670 (*rev'ng* [2005] CSIH 3, 2005 SLT 64). See also V Mak, 'Repair and Loss of the Right to Reject—A Remedial Dilemma in Sale of Goods Law' [2006] *Lloyd's Maritime & Commercial Law Quarterly* 163; WCH Ervine, 'Cure and Retender Revisited' [2006] *Journal of Business Law* 799; A Barron, 'Section 35(6) of the Sale of Goods Act 1979—Loss of the Right to Reject and Rescind' 2005 SLT 17.

[103] See V Mak, 'Missing Bearings—Information Duties of the Seller under Section 35 of the Sale of Goods Act 1979', note on *J&H Ritchie Ltd v Lloyd Ltd* [2007] UKHL 9, [2007] 1 WLR 670, (2007) 70 *Modern Law Review* 1002.

[104] *J&H Ritchie Ltd v Lloyd Ltd* [2007] UKHL 9, [2007] 1 WLR 670 at [37].

Nevertheless, Lord Hope—in a judgment of similar thrust—concedes that these circumstances 'cannot be assumed to apply in every case'.[105] Thus, while the outcome of the case hinged on the neglect of certain information duties by the seller, other elements of the judgment throw more light on the court's stance with regard to the general usefulness of section 35 as a mode of promoting informal attempts at cure. In these, it can be seen that the court acknowledges a broader interpretation of the section that strengthens the seller's opportunity to cure. Still, it falls short of giving the seller an actual *right* to repair or replace defective goods and in this respect, it is submitted, it shows the weakness of the informal cure regime laid down in the SGA.

The encouraging element of the Lords' judgments is found in their approval of the proposed effect of section 35(6), in combination with section 35(2) of the SGA, in the interpretation of Lord Hamilton and Lord Philip in their judgments for the Inner House of the Court of Session. The Law Lords go along with the suggestion of the Scottish judges that the fact that the buyers had not opted for rejection and termination after the original delivery of goods but instead agreed to investigation of the defect and, if possible, repair meant that they would normally be bound to accept the repaired goods.[106] In these circumstances,

> [i]t may then be said that a buyer who . . . allows the seller to incur the expense of repair is under an implied obligation to accept and pay for the goods once the repair has been carried out. His right to resile will be lost when the repair has been completed. The buyer's protection is the reasonable opportunity to examine the goods after delivery which he is given by section 35(2) of the 1979 Act.[107]

While there is some divergence in the analysis of the relevant SGA provisions in this context, there does not seem to be a substantial difference between the positions as adopted by the different Law Lords. Lord Hope's decision builds directly on the contentions of Lord Hamilton and Lord Philip in the Inner House decision, which stated that the fact that the buyers did not reject and terminate after the initial discovery of the defect meant that the contract remained in existence.[108] As a result, the sellers were bound to deliver and the buyers to accept the goods on the basis of section 27 of the SGA. By contrast, Lord Rodger and Lord Brown assert that, while the contract of sale remained alive, the sellers did not exercise any rights of theirs under this contract when taking away the harrow for repair. Instead, a separate agreement for inspection and repair was made between the parties and it is from this that an (implied) obligation arises for the buyers to accept the repaired goods. According to Lord Rodger,

> if, in accordance with the terms of that agreement, the respondents eventually repaired the equipment to the proper standard and duly made it available to the appellants, the

[105] *Ibid*, [19].

[106] *Ibid*, at [15], [34], [44] and, more tentatively, Lord Mance at [54]. Lord Scott concurs with the other judgments.

[107] *Ibid*, Lord Hope at [15].

[108] *Ritchie v Lloyd* [2005] CSIH 3, 2005 SLT 64 at [45] and [53]. See Lord Hope at [11] and [15].

> appellants would not be entitled to rescind the contract of sale and reject the equipment because of the original breach. A term to this effect would have been necessary to give the inspection and repair agreement business efficacy.[109]

From an English law perspective, this view may have greater merit than the one adopted by Lord Hope, seeing that repair is not generally recognised as a form of (specific) performance and would therefore not automatically come within the scope of the original contract of sale. To what extent the same is true for Scots law is hard to say. It may be that repair fits more neatly into the notion of specific implement, in which case the position adopted by Lord Hope would be more accurate. Nevertheless, regardless of which analysis is the correct one, the effect in both cases is the same—if the sellers succeed in repairing the goods to a satisfactory standard before the buyers exercise their right to rescind, the buyers are obliged to accept the repaired goods.

The objection to this approach remains, however, that it does little to promote a general right to cure for the seller, even on an informal basis as envisaged by the Law Commissions.[110] Even if the buyer has agreed to an attempt at repair by the seller, it seems that he may still at any time decide to exercise his right of termination and thus preclude the completion of any repairs by the seller. At least, this conclusion must be drawn from the judgments of Lord Hamilton and Lord Philip, which, on this point, found little resistance in the House of Lords. The only suggestion of possible relief comes from Lord Rodger who states that

> it must have been an implied term of the inspection and repair agreement that, so long as the respondents were duly performing their obligations under it, the appellants were not to exercise the right to rescind the contract of sale.[111]

This seems a fair inference that would benefit legal certainty in informal cure agreements.[112] The point was not in issue on the facts of the case, however, with the main focus of the proceedings shifting to the sellers' refusal to give information on the nature of the defects. The other judgments, therefore, do not deal with this point and it remains an open question whether such a limitation may indeed be placed on a buyer's entitlement to reject the goods and terminate the contract during the seller's attempt at cure.[113]

In brief, apart from the fact that *Ritchie* does not provide authority for extending the inroads to section 35(6) of the SGA further than is suggested by Lord Philip and Lord Hamilton and now (at least partially) approved by the House of Lords, it leaves intact the main criticism of informal cure regimes: the

[109] *Ritchie v Lloyd* (n 104 above) at [34]. Compare Lord Mance at [43]–[44].

[110] Above, p 176.

[111] *Ritchie v Lloyd* (n 104 above) at [34].

[112] Another possibility would be to invoke a personal bar which would prohibit the buyers from exercising their right to reject if they had not definitely intimated such intention to the sellers. See Mak, 'Repair and Loss of the Right to Reject' (n 102 above) 165. Seeing that the question relates to a statutory code and its consequences, the court may nevertheless prefer to find the solution in an implied term; compare *Ritchie v Lloyd* (n 104 above), Lord Hope at [15].

[113] Compare *Ritchie v Lloyd* (n 104 above), Lord Brown at [44].

discretionary nature of the remedy. In order to have a chance at cure, the seller is entirely at the buyer's mercy—if he does not agree to repair, there will be no cure. Thus, from a viewpoint of promoting cure, the regime remains inferior to systems that give the seller a right to cure.

3. Rejection and Termination Revisited

A cure for the deficiencies of the informal cure regime endorsed by section 35 of the SGA may be found in the adoption of a different stance towards rejection and termination. If, in line with the principles set out earlier,[114] it is accepted that rejection is not a sub-form of termination but rather of the right to withhold performance, section 35 may give a much more balanced expression to the rights of the buyer and the seller. Moreover, this may be done in a way that supports the seller's right to cure, at least before the contractual time for performance has expired.

With regard to the question of whether or not the time taken for cure counts towards the 'reasonable time' requirement of section 35(4) and 35(5), a mechanism that makes rejection a right that can be exercised independently from termination may prove to be beneficial for the buyer as well as the seller. In this situation, if the buyer rejects defective goods without at the same time terminating the contract, the seller would have the possibility to cure—or, if the time for performance has not yet expired, even a right to cure.[115] Moreover, since the buyer explicitly rejects the goods, it is clear to both parties which positions they are taking and this may serve to prevent misunderstandings and subsequent disputes as to whether or not goods were accepted and whether cure was sought. At the same time, the buyer would retain the strong bargaining power that the right of termination gives him. The concern for this was a major consideration for the Law Commission in its dismissal of a cure regime,[116] but if proper limits are set it is hard to see how a right to cure would have a negative effect on the buyer's position in the way that the report suggests. The buyer's right to terminate may indeed set such a limit. It would enable the buyer to end attempts at cure once the contractual time for performance had expired and the seller had not managed to bring the goods up to the contractual standard. Also, it would enable the buyer to reject any possibility of cure offered after this date.

A similar conclusion may be drawn with regard to the question whether the buyer should be obliged to accept repaired goods if he has agreed to an attempt at cure. If the attempt took place within the time for performance, there would be no question but that the buyer would be so obliged should the seller succeed in his attempt. In the alternative situation, where the time period for performance has expired, the buyer would be able to wield his right of termination and

[114] Above, pp 152 ff.
[115] *Ibid.*
[116] Law Commissions, *Sale and Supply of Goods* (n 92 above) [4.14].

thus to limit the seller's possibilities of cure, pursuant to the interpretation of section 35 of the SGA as set out in *J&H Ritchie Ltd v Lloyd Ltd.*[117] However, especially in the first situation, the separate role attributed to rejection in relation to termination emphasises that while the buyer may denounce the goods, he may only terminate if the seller has not succeeded in re-tendering satisfactory goods by the date agreed for performance. In other words, where the time for performance has not yet lapsed, the seller has a right to cure.

VI. CONCLUSION

A right to cure would give the seller an adequate answer to the buyer's strong arsenal of remedies, in particular the right of termination. By allowing the seller to repair or to replace defective goods, economic waste can be avoided whilst the performance interest of the buyer remains protected. Thus, a balance can be struck within the remedial regime for sale of goods that does justice to the interests of sellers as well as buyers.

Harmonisation of the cure regimes of European sale of goods laws, however, is unlikely to come about easily. It is problematic to fix the scope that a right to cure should have, especially in relation to the time period within which it is to be effective. In this respect, it seems more difficult to reach agreement on the scope for cure after the delivery date than before that date. After all, whereas legal principle limits the possibilities for the buyer to terminate before the due delivery date, it appears that a right to cure can only exist after the delivery date subject to the buyer's right of termination. It is a matter of policy, and up to the legislator to decide, whether inroads should be made into the right of termination that permit the seller to cure if the time for delivery has expired. Currently, there is no consensus in European sale of goods laws, such as the Dutch, the German and the English, as to whether cure should be allowed after the delivery date. Considerations of market regulation, in particular the lowering of the costs of remedies, nevertheless, plead in favour of extending the scope of the right.

Furthermore, it appears preferable to have a statutory regime for cure rather than an informal regime under which attempts at repair or replacement are 'encouraged' but where the seller has no legal means to ensure a possibility for cure. An informal regime is unlikely to provide a level playing field for sellers and buyers since it places the choice for cure entirely at the buyer's discretion. It can be criticised, therefore, for not allowing the seller to insist upon cure against the buyer's wishes, even where repair or replacement would be a more appropriate remedy than damages. In order to provide an effective right to cure, therefore, it is necessary to have a statutory regime on which the seller can rely. Even if the parties choose to depart from this, as they may in commercial sales, such

[117] Above, p 181.

a regime will strengthen the bargaining position of the seller and emphasise the importance of keeping the contract alive with an eye to the avoidance of economic waste.

Thus, despite controversy, an argument may be made in favour of a right to cure for the seller. To some extent the right may in fact mirror the buyer's entitlement to specific performance, for it gives the seller a similar possibility to enforce performance. However, that the position of the seller is after all different will be seen in the next chapter, which deals with the potential boundaries that the seller may face in exercising his right to cure.

7

Cure: Enforcement, Limitations and the Hierarchy of Remedies

I. INTRODUCTION

IN AN EARLIER chapter, the seller's right to cure was called the mirror image of the buyer's entitlement to specific performance.[1] Instead of giving preference to the buyer's request for performance, cure focuses on situations in which it is the seller who may insist on performance even where the buyer desires a different remedy. The previous chapter filled in part of this image by setting out the justifications for a right to cure, and by assessing its scope, in particular in relation to the buyer's right to terminate. No mention was made, however, of the seller's possibilities of enforcing his right to cure—Is he entitled to a court order that obliges the buyer to accept the goods delivered in the attempted cure, in the same way that the buyer is entitled to a court order that obliges the seller to perform? Furthermore, as there are limitations to the buyer's entitlement to specific performance, so it is assumed that there will be limits to the seller's right to cure—but do these mirror the restrictions on specific performance? In order to complete the reflection, this chapter will examine the enforcement of, and the limits to the seller's right to cure.

As to the first part, it is important that the seller can enforce his right to cure. In order to ensure that he is able to insist upon cure, the seller needs to know that there is an obligation on the buyer to accept the repaired goods or replacement goods. In the absence of such an obligation, the right would lack the necessary strength, for a buyer would be able to reject a second delivery, thus making the seller's attempt at cure altogether pointless. The argument proposed here is that the best way forward is to put an obligation on the buyer to take delivery, combined with an adequate enforcement mechanism. This enforcement mechanism could take the form of an entitlement to specific performance for the seller, thus completing the mirror image analogy between the rights of the buyer and those of the seller.

The second strand of the argument relates to situations in which the seller's right to cure is limited in the light of justified interests of the buyer. As explained in chapter three, the circumstance that, on grounds of his failure to perform, the

[1] Ch 6, p 149. Specific performance is used here in the wider sense, which includes repair and replacement. See ch 5, pp 120 ff.

seller should be regarded as the wrongdoer may be of some relevance in determining the scope of the right to cure.[2] On the basis of moral rights reasoning, arguably, by failing satisfactorily to perform the contract the seller has committed a wrong. This chapter seeks to determine to what extent the seller's right to cure may be limited as a result of this. It will be argued that, since he is the wrongdoing party, the seller's right to cure should be under stricter limitations than the buyer's entitlement to specific performance.

Finally, another connection may be made between cure and specific performance. As hinted at earlier, a case may be made for a hierarchy of remedies that places performance-oriented remedies at the top.[3] An example of this may be found in the remedial scheme of the Consumer Sales Directive.[4] The argument proposed in this chapter is that the basis for such a hierarchy should be sought in the protection of the interest of the seller to provide the remedy that is most cost-effective. At the same time, it is suggested that the interests of the buyer, while benefited by the general availability of performance-oriented remedies, seem less influenced by the existence or non-existence of a hierarchy. It is submitted, in other words, that the hierarchy stems from a policy of market regulation and not, as may be thought, from one of consumer protection.

II. ENFORCEMENT OF THE RIGHT TO CURE

Whilst it is a prerequisite that the buyer is prevented from terminating the contract for a certain period of time, this alone is not enough to give the seller a *right* to cure. It gives him breathing space and the opportunity to perform a second time, but it lacks one important feature—it does not oblige the buyer to *accept* this performance. Thus, one may wonder, would it be possible for the buyer simply to refuse this performance and terminate the contract when he is entitled to do so?

The answer to this question is not as straightforward as it may seem. In particular, it should be noted that the point relates not only to the enforcement of cure, but also to the initial delivery of goods under the contract. It would seem logical, in both situations, to put an obligation on the buyer to take delivery, and to give the seller a means of enforcing this obligation. This would strengthen the possibilities of achieving performance of the contract, which could be beneficial to both parties from a viewpoint of avoiding economic waste. In relation to cure, it would ensure that repair or replacement by the seller does not occur in vain, but that satisfactory attempts at cure will be accepted by the buyer.

However, while this may be the 'best' solution, it requires a policy change in European sale of goods laws—currently only the UN Convention on Contracts

[2] See p 74.

[3] See p 123.

[4] Directive 99/44/EC of the European Parliament and of the Council on certain aspects of the sale of consumer goods and associated guarantees [1999] OJ L171/12 (Consumer Sales Directive).

for the International Sale of Goods (CISG) adopts this approach.[5] While German law adopts a similar approach, neither English nor Dutch law currently shares this solution. Thus, whether the CISG approach can be transposed directly onto national sale of goods laws is questionable. It will be argued, however, that there is a need for a stronger enforcement mechanism against the buyer, especially in relation to cure. The main argument for this is that it would put the seller in a more equal position in relation to the buyer, who has a much bigger arsenal of remedies at his disposal than the seller. This imbalance is likely to lead to situations in which sellers are left to grapple with losses flowing from an unsuccessful attempt at performance—costs that might have been diminished, or altogether avoided, had the seller been able to enforce a right to cure.

Concerns that a strengthening of the seller's position in relation to cure may negatively affect the position of the buyer, it will be argued, are largely unfounded. After all, safeguards may be built in that protect the interests of buyers, and some of these can already be found in domestic sale of goods laws. For example, common conditions for acceptance are that the goods are in conformity with the contract and that the buyer has had a chance to inspect the goods before accepting them.

1. The Buyer's Obligation to Take Delivery

Article 62 of CISG states that the seller 'may require the buyer to . . . take delivery'. This remedy is in a sense the counterpart of the buyer's remedy under article 46 to 'require performance by the seller'. While there is no guarantee of actual enforcement through specific performance in either case,[6] these provisions do indicate that, at least within the context of the Convention, the seller's interest in cure is taken as seriously as the buyer's right to obtain performance. This makes sense, especially in relation to attempts at cure before the delivery date, where the seller is not technically in breach. In these circumstances, why should he be put in a worse position than the buyer merely because his first attempt at performance was unsuccessful? Even after the due delivery date, there may well be circumstances in which the buyer should not be free to refuse acceptance of goods that have either been repaired or that are tendered in replacement of a defective delivery. For example, where the seller has re-delivered the goods to an agreed place, high costs may be involved with taking back the goods and transporting them back to the premises of the seller. In those circumstances, it may be more beneficial from an economic point of view to oblige the buyer to take delivery of the goods.

[5] UN Convention on Contracts for the International Sale of Goods (adopted 11 April 1980, entered into force 1 January 1988) 1489 UNTS 3 (CISG).

[6] Art 28 of CISG leaves it open to national courts to refuse specific performance if they would not do so under their own law.

It is submitted that the CISG approach is preferable to that found in English law, but only because of the possibilities for enforcement that it offers. The English system does, to a certain extent, offer the seller a counterweight to the remedies of the buyer in the form of an obligation on the buyer to take delivery. If he breaches it, the seller will be entitled to remedies that are similar to the buyer's remedies for breach, eg he may sue the buyer for damages for non-acceptance.[7] Nevertheless, there is no mechanism that enables the seller to compel the buyer to accept the delivery of the goods, in the form of specific performance or a related remedy.[8] In this respect, the English approach offers weaker protection to the seller than CISG does. However, English law's commitment to specific performance as a remedy for the buyer is also less than whole-hearted, so at least there appears to be a balance between the interests of both parties. Furthermore, whilst the bare obligation—ie an obligation that is not backed up by a performance remedy—on the buyer to take delivery does not protect the seller's interest in performance in the way that specific performance can, it should be regarded as the next best thing. At least it offers the seller the possibility of full monetary compensation for the losses suffered as a result of the buyer's refusal to take delivery.

The position under Dutch law, however, appears to give less support to the seller's enforcement of his right to cure. Mainly a remnant from an earlier era, the system does not regard it as a given fact that the seller's remedies should be as strong as the buyer's. Thus, there is no obligation on the buyer to take delivery. However, the view that a debtor (eg a seller) only has obligations but no rights no longer seems valid in the current day and age.[9] Especially in the light of market integration in Europe, consideration needs to be given to the economic interests of sellers and the risk-allocation between actors involved in sale of goods transactions. An indication that the systems may be open to a different approach can, for example, be gleaned from the fact that civilian systems are to a certain extent letting go of the notion of fault as a requirement for liability. German law, for instance, has abandoned the requirement of fault on the part of the debtor as a condition for termination.[10] The system, thus, is moving away from fault-based liability and instead is relying on a scheme that best allocates the risks between debtor and creditor. In accordance with this, the fact that the seller is the non-performing party does not necessarily lead to the conclusion that the remedies available to him should automatically be more limited in nature than the buyer's.

In this light, the current enforcement mechanism for cure found in Dutch law would appear too weak. Apart from the possibility of including an express

[7] PS Atiyah, JN Adams and H MacQueen, *The Sale of Goods*, 11th edn (Harlow, Pearson, 2005) 311.

[8] A Vaquer, 'Tender of Performance, Mora Creditoris and the (Common?) Principles of European Contract Law' (2002) 17 *Tulane European and Civil Law Forum* 83 at 86.

[9] Compare AJ Feenstra, 'Nakoming door de terkortschietende verkoper en de macht van de koper' [1997] *Nederlands Tijdschrift voor Burgerlijk Recht* 243.

[10] R Zimmermann, *The New German Law of Obligations* (Oxford, Oxford University Press, 2005) 71.

obligation to take delivery in the terms of the contract, the mechanism of *mora creditoris*[11] operates to protect the interests of the seller.[12] However, whilst it protects the interests of the seller to a certain extent, it is thought that the doctrine is too narrow to ensure a fully effective right of cure.

Article 6:58 *Burgerlijk Wetboek* (*BW*) provides that a creditor (in this case the buyer) comes into default where the performance of an obligation is prevented because of a lack of cooperation on his side, or because of another impediment on his part.[13] This provision, and the related rules laid down in articles 6:59–6:72 *BW*, regulate the doctrine of *mora creditoris*. Similar rules can be found in §§ 293 ff of the German *Bürgerliches Gesetzbuch* (*BGB*). Under German law, however, the doctrine is available only as an additional enforcement mechanism besides the general right to specific performance under § 241 I *BGB* that the seller may invoke to enforce the buyer's obligation to take delivery under § 433 II *BGB*. In Dutch law, on the other hand, the provisions fill in a gap in the cure regime caused by the absence of a general duty of the buyer to take delivery of goods tendered. *Mora creditoris* enables the seller to coerce the buyer to take delivery. As long as the buyer does not accept the goods, he remains in default and he will be liable to pay damages to the seller for losses caused as a result of his non-acceptance. In addition, to ensure that the seller completely discharges his obligation to deliver, the *BW* provides that the seller may deposit the goods with a public tribunal.

It is thought that the doctrine of *mora creditoris* does not adequately protect the interests of the seller.[14] To begin with, the scheme is of a coercive nature only and it does not entitle the seller actually to compel the buyer to take delivery. He may still end up with a monetary remedy only. Moreover, an award of damages may not represent the full extent of the seller's interests. The buyer's liability in damages only extends to the costs incurred by the seller in relation to a deposit of goods made pursuant to the provisions of the *BW*, or for costs otherwise attributable to the default.[15] In this respect, it is more limited than English law, where non-acceptance may be treated as a repudiation and damages will be assessed on the basis of the general rules.[16]

[11] In Dutch: *schuldeisersverzuim*, which can be translated as 'default by the creditor'.

[12] It also features in other systems; compare Vaquer, 'Tender of Performance, Mora Creditoris and the (Common?) Principles of European Contract Law' (n 8 above) 87.

[13] In Dutch: 'De schuldeiser komt in verzuim, wanneer nakoming van de verbintenis verhinderd wordt doordat hij de daartoe noodzakelijke medewerking niet verleent of doordat een ander beletsel van zijn zijde opkomt, tenzij de oorzaak van verhindering hem niet kan worden toegerekend'. Translation taken from D Busch, EH Hondius, HJ van Kooten, HN Schelhaas and WM Schrama (eds), *The Principles of European Contract Law and Dutch Law—A Commentary* (Nijmegen, Ars Aequi Libri, 2002) 318. Compare also arts 7:30 ff of the *BW* (on *mora creditoris* in sale of goods law).

[14] Cf Feenstra, 'Nakoming door de terkortschietende verkoper en de macht van de koper' (n 9 above) 245.

[15] Art 6:63 *BW*.

[16] Sale of Goods Act 1979 (SGA) ss 50(2) and (3), 54. See R Goode, *Commercial Law*, 3rd edn (London, LexisNexis, 2004) 402.

The doctrine of *mora creditoris* thus offers only a limited recourse for the seller. Two possible solutions may be suggested. First, a duty to take delivery could be imposed on the buyer, as is done in other legal systems. Alternatively, the doctrine of *mora creditoris* could be widened to put a greater range of remedies at the seller's disposal, so as to put him in a more equal position as against the buyer. From a viewpoint of harmonisation, the first option is likely to be preferable, for it would be closest in line with the approaches found in CISG, and in German and English law.

2. Safeguards for the Buyer

Would the buyer be disadvantaged to a disproportionate degree if the seller's opportunities to enforce cure were strengthened? The answer would appear to be 'no'. All sale of goods regimes contain provisions that protect the position of the buyer. For example, common requirements for acceptance are that goods are in conformity with the contract and—to a lesser or greater degree, depending on the legal system—that the buyer has had an opportunity to examine the goods to ensure that they are satisfactory. In general, these apply equally to every delivery of goods, including those relating to repaired or substitute goods.[17] Provisions to this effect can be found in sections 35(2) and 48F of the Sale of Goods Act 1979 (SGA), article 7:17 *BW*, and § 459 *BGB*. The interests of the buyer, therefore, are safeguarded to the same extent for attempted repairs or replacements as they are for deliveries of goods in the first place. Moreover, the seller is not allowed to attempt cure indefinitely, nor for an infinite number of times.[18] Accordingly, there is little risk that the buyer will be kept on a string by the seller and that he will be forced to accept goods of substandard quality.

III. LIMITATIONS TO THE RIGHT TO CURE

Both article 37 and article 48 of CISG limit the seller's right to cure to situations where the seller can effect it without causing the buyer 'unreasonable inconvenience or unreasonable expense'. Article 48, which relates to cure after the contractual delivery date, goes even further by implying that, not only should the buyer not be made to suffer unreasonable expense, but also, the seller should be obliged to compensate the buyer for expenses suffered because of the exercise of

[17] For an example of the application of the rules in practice, compare *J&H Ritchie Ltd v Lloyd Ltd* [2007] UKHL 9; [2007] 1 WLR 670 (rev'ng [2005] CSIH 3; 2005 SLT 64); see also V Mak, 'Missing Bearings—Information Duties of the Seller under Section 35 of the Sale of Goods Act 1979', note on J&H Ritchie Ltd v Lloyd Ltd [2007] UKHL 9, [2007] 1 WLR 670, (2007) 70 *Modern Law Review* 1002; KFK Low, 'Repair, rejection and rescission: an uneasy resolution' (2007) 123 *Law Quarterly Review* 536 at 539. Contrast M Bridge, 'A second tender: J&H Ritchie Ltd v Lloyd Ltd' [2007] *Journal of Business Law* 814 at 819. Further ch 6, pp 180–83.

[18] See p 173, and below, p 199.

the right to cure.[19] Moreover, each of the provisions stipulates that the buyer retains any right to claim damages under the Convention, which would include any costs incurred by the buyer in connection with the exercise of the seller's right to cure.[20]

These appear to be fairly strict limitations on the seller's right to cure. The question is whether restrictions on the seller's right to cure should be this tight, especially in comparison to the restrictions on the buyer's entitlement to specific performance. CISG does not provide a definitive answer to this question, seeing that it leaves it up to domestic courts to decide whether or not to make a specific performance order. A comparison with other systems may shed more light on the matter. As an earlier comparison of the functioning of the remedy in several national systems showed, courts may refuse to make an order for specific performance if to do so would be disproportionate, ie would cause severe hardship on the seller. Similar limitations apply to repair and replacement.[21] While these restrictions follow from efficiency-based considerations, it may be thought that the restrictions on the seller's right to cure are of a different nature. The question is not so much whether cure would put *disproportionate* costs on the buyer, but rather whether, at all, the buyer should be made to bear the costs related to the exercise of the seller's right to cure, or any other losses suffered by him as a result of the initial defective performance and the subsequent cure. On the basis of moral rights reasoning, it will be argued that such expenses should fall on the seller. After all, it was the seller who was in the wrong by not performing satisfactorily in the first place. Moreover, it will be argued that the standard of 'unreasonable inconvenience' should be interpreted in a stricter way with regard to cure than with regard to specific performance. The fact that the seller was the wrongdoer suggests that stronger limitations should be imposed on the scope of cure than on the scope of the buyer's right to specific performance.

1. Limitations—Cure Compared with Specific Performance

The seller, having committed the wrong of failing to perform his contractual obligation to deliver conforming goods, may be subject to some sort of sanction. As was made clear in chapter three, the way in which this is administered is generally through the entitlements of the buyer. Thus, where the buyer has become entitled to certain remedies to fix the non-performance or defective performance, the scope of these remedies may be influenced by a desire to punish the wrongdoer, ie the seller. In the words of Birks, quoted earlier: '[t]he label

[19] This addition was made following a proposal by UNCITRAL; see 'UNCITRAL: Preparation of the 1977 UNCITRAL "Sales" Draft' in J Honnold (ed), *Documentary History of the Uniform Law for International Sales* (Deventer, Kluwer, 1989) 338.

[20] P Schlechtriem and I Schwenzer (eds), *Commentary on the UN Convention on the International Sale of Goods*, 2nd English edn (Oxford, Oxford University Press, 2005) 444.

[21] Ch 4, pp 98 ff; ch 5, pp 130 ff.

'wrong' operates as a licence to the law to mistreat the wrongdoer. The entitlements which the law can accord to the victim of the wrong are, so to say, at large'. The entitlements of the buyer, thus, are seen to have a basis in moral rights reasoning. However, Birks attenuates the statement by adding: 'at least until the range has been narrowed by authority, statutory or otherwise'.[22] Thus, it is acknowledged that the buyer's entitlements may be limited, and not necessarily by considerations of a moral nature. Considerations of efficiency, for example, may also be of relevance. An argument to this effect has been made in chapters four and five. It was argued that the entitlements of the buyer might take the shape of performance-oriented remedies such as specific performance, repair and replacement. Moreover, it was argued that these remedies should be of general availability (to this extent they could be seen as 'at large'), but accompanied by appropriate restrictions to safeguard the position of the seller (in other words, factors that narrow the entitlements of the buyer).

It is thought that an analogy may be drawn with the seller's right to cure, at least to the extent that it can be regarded as the mirror image of specific performance. In particular, the mirror image analogy comes shining through with regard to the right to cure *after the due delivery date*. Here, it is submitted, justifications for the right may be found in considerations of efficiency, whereas moral rights reasoning may lay down the limits of the right. As such, the right to cure mirrors specific performance, where justifications are provided by moral rights theory, while efficiency considerations mark the boundaries to its scope.

A slightly different view, it is thought, should be taken with regard to cure before the due delivery date, at least where the *basis* of the right is concerned. As seen in chapter six, the seller's right to cure at this time follows from the contract itself.[23] In this respect, the basis of the right is similar to that of the buyer's entitlement to specific performance. Nevertheless, it is thought that the *limitations* to the seller's right to cure before the due delivery date are of the same nature as those applying to cure after that date. If the seller performs unsatisfactorily before the due delivery date, he has committed a wrong, for he has not given the performance that he contracted to give. Even if there is still time to make good the initial substandard performance, the fact remains that any extra costs related to the exercise of the right to cure, or losses suffered as result of it, follow from the fact that the seller performed unsatisfactorily in the first place. Therefore, it is thought that the restrictions on the seller's right to cure before the due delivery date share a basis in moral rights reasoning similar to that of the restriction on the right to cure after the due delivery date.

Since considerations of a different nature underlie the limitations to the seller's right to cure and the buyer's entitlement to specific performance, it could be argued that the restrictions on the rights are divergent in scope. Efficiency may set a different standard than moral rights reasoning. For example, where

[22] P Birks, 'Rights, Wrongs and Remedies' (2000) 20 *Oxford Journal of Legal Studies* 1 at 33. See ch 3, p 73.

[23] Ch 6, pp 152 ff. See also ch 3, p 59.

'unreasonable expense' is invoked as a limitation with regard to specific performance, a fairly objective balance may be struck between the rights of the seller and of the buyer. Factors to be taken into account could include the value of the goods and the significance of the lack of conformity, both of which can to a certain degree be quantified in monetary terms.[24] Moreover, while specific performance may be denied in cases where interests of the seller other than economic ones are at stake, the significance of this limitation appears less great than the restriction based on economic considerations. Thus, while the buyer's entitlement to specific performance may potentially be limited by a consideration that it would cause 'unreasonable inconvenience' for the seller—a factor which may be less easily quantifiable—this restriction would seem to be of limited relevance. After all, in sales cases, the seller's main interests will generally be of an economic nature; his interest is in obtaining the contract price and making a profit. Concerns with regard to specific performance orders, therefore, will generally be limited to the monetary sphere (eg additional costs that the seller may have to incur in the performance, which will limit his profit margin). Hence, since the limitations to the right are essentially based on considerations of economic efficiency and since these, to a great extent, are easily quantifiable, they set fairly clear limits to the buyer's right of specific performance.

2. Limitations to Cure Based on Moral Rights Reasoning

It is more difficult, however, to get a firm grasp on moral rights, and there may therefore be less guidance available for determining the boundaries of the seller's right to cure.[25] Moral rights reasoning may be of relevance on two levels: first, in determining to what extent the costs incurred in the exercise of the right to cure should be regarded as the responsibility of the seller; and secondly, in determining whether the exercise of the remedy would cause 'unreasonable inconvenience' to the buyer. It is submitted that, in both respects, moral rights reasoning may support the proposition that limitations to the seller's right to cure should be stricter than those to the buyer's entitlement to specific performance.

a) 'Unreasonable Expense'

The first issue appears fairly straightforward. Since the seller is the wrongdoer who has not (satisfactorily) performed his part of the contract, it is arguable that he should be made to bear the additional expense incurred with regard to cure.[26]

[24] Compare ch 5, p 139–40.

[25] Moral rights reasoning is thought to be of relevance even where the duties of the seller with regard to conformity are strict; see ch 3, p 71.

[26] Goode speaks of an 'implied collateral duty' of the seller not to make an invalid tender, breach of which would entitle the buyer to compensation for loss suffered and expenses needlessly incurred in collecting the goods. See Goode, *Commercial Law* (n 15 above) 345.

In this respect, he would be in a similar position to that if an order for specific performance were made against him; if extra expense has to be incurred in order to effect performance, there is no question that the seller will have to bear the burden of it.[27]

The best example of a sales law that supports the view that the seller should be made to carry the costs related to the exercise of cure is CISG. As seen above, it obliges the seller to reimburse the buyer for expenses incurred, and it stipulates that the buyer retains any right to claim damages (which could cover such costs).[28] Other laws also support this view, though not always in the same express manner. For example, while German law does not contain a specific rule to this effect, § 439 II *BGB* may lend support to the rule that expenses should fall on the seller. It provides that '[t]he seller must bear all expenditure required for the purposes of supplementary performance, in particular carriage, transport, labour and material costs'. While, technically, the provision applies to requests made by the buyer for repair or replacement, the principle appears to be the same where it is the seller who insists on supplementary performance. Since other remedies only become available after an additional time for performance has lapsed to no avail, the buyer is initially limited to requesting repair or replacement. To the extent that the seller in this way is given a right to cure, the requirement that the remedies are provided free of charge would seem to apply equally.

Dutch law also supports the rule that the seller must bear the costs of cure. Article 6:86 *BW* stipulates that the seller is obliged to offer payment of damages and/or costs if he wants to exercise his right to cure in this situation. However, the provision deals only with cure after the commencement of default. Thus, since the desirability of permitting cure after the commencement of default was called into question in chapter six,[29] the support that it lends to a rule that obliges the seller to pay costs is questionable. However, a general rule similar to the German one may be derived from article 7:21(2) *BW*. It provides that the costs of repair and replacement should not be charged to the buyer. Since, as in German law, the remedies are the principal remedies of the buyer, it is thought that in a similar way an obligation to pay costs related to cure may be inferred from the provision.

However, while various sales laws may support the principle that it should be the seller who carries the burden of the extra costs involved with cure, it remains unclear whether they apply it equally to cure *before* as well as *after* the due delivery date. In the Principles of European Contract Law (PECL), under which the right to cure is effectively limited to the time before the due delivery date,[30] no obligation of the seller to pay damages or costs is spelt out in the relevant

[27] Proof of this can, for example, be found in art 3(4) of the Consumer Sales Directive; see also art 7:21(2) *BW* and § 439 II *BGB*.

[28] See p 192 above.

[29] See ch 6, p 171.

[30] See for example p 168.

provision (article 8:104). While Dutch law recognises a right to cure before and after this date, it appears that the stipulation regarding damages and costs made in article 6:86 *BW* applies, for practical purposes, only to the time after the due delivery date. After all, the provision is limited to situations where the seller is 'in default', which he will not generally be before the time for performance has arrived.[31]

It does not make sense, however, to oblige the seller to pay damages or costs related to cure after the due delivery date, but not to do the same in cases where cure is offered before the due delivery date. As said earlier,[32] at least from a viewpoint of moral rights reasoning, the seller is equally wrong in not performing satisfactorily before that date as he is afterwards. While it is true that different consequences may be attached to the seller's failure to perform depending on whether the delivery obligation had become exigible or not, this does not affect the circumstance that the failure was the seller's responsibility, and not the buyer's. It was the seller who performed unsatisfactorily, and thus caused both the need for cure and the expenses related to it. On this ground, there seems to be equal ground for holding the seller accountable for costs made in relation to cure before the due delivery date as after this date.

The solution found in CISG, therefore, appears preferable. It is submitted that this should be the approach followed in future instruments aimed at harmonising European sales laws. The seller should only be permitted to cure his defective or non-performance if he offers to pay for damages and extra costs made in relation to this.

b) 'Unreasonable Inconvenience'

The second issue appears to pose some more difficult questions, however. When does the exercise of the right to cure cause 'unreasonable inconvenience' for the buyer? There is no obvious way to quantify the limits that moral rights may set on the right to cure in this respect. Inconvenience, after all, could include more than the monetary consequences felt by the buyer as a result of the exercise of the seller's right to cure. It may include situations in which, during the time that the seller has taken the goods away for repair, the buyer suffers inconvenience by not having a substitute. For example, a student who hands in a computer for repair may be unable to work for the time that he does not have the computer at his disposal. Also, the repair of domestic appliances (eg washing machines, dish washers) may cause inconvenience to the buyer who is deprived of the equipment during the time of its repair.

Nevertheless, there seems to be a case for applying this limitation in a broad manner. Since the seller was the wrongdoing party, it is submitted that the 'unreasonable inconvenience' exception should be interpreted in a way that

[31] Unless the non-performance or defective performance amounts to an anticipatory breach, see p 153.

[32] Above, p 194.

favours the buyer rather than the seller. To this extent, it is similar to the inconvenience objection that the buyer may invoke in order to by-pass the disproportionality factor that may render a particular form of specific performance unavailable to him.[33] With regard to cure, however, the term appears to have a wider function—not only does it protect the buyer against having to accept a particular type of cure, it may be interpreted in such a way as to negate entirely the seller's right to cure. For example, where the buyer requests a performance-oriented remedy, he may do so even if it would cause him a certain degree of inconvenience. What matters is that this remedy would be less inconvenient to him *in comparison* to the other available remedies (eg repair compared to replacement). Where this is the case, the buyer is free to leave the more inconvenient remedy out of consideration and to choose the other remedy. It is up to the buyer to decide whether he is willing to go ahead with this remedy, even if that causes him some inconvenience. To this extent, thus, it is in the hands of the buyer to decide what level of inconvenience he considers 'unreasonable'. When it comes to cure, however, it is thought that the 'unreasonable inconvenience' standard should be interpreted in a stricter way. Since the seller is the wrongdoing party, it is thought that it should not be left to him to set the standard for 'unreasonable inconvenience'. In order to protect the interests of the buyer, a stricter standard should apply that not only asks whether the seller may insist on providing the form of cure that would cause least inconvenience to the buyer, but rather whether the seller should be entitled to insist on cure at all if it causes a certain degree of inconvenience. It is submitted that, as a consequence of the seller's wrong, the standard should be stricter than with regard to specific performance. Therefore, if offered by the seller to give effect to his right to cure, repair or replacement may sooner be thought unreasonably inconvenient than if the buyer had opted for either as performance-oriented remedies.

Thus, it is thought that in relation to cure the term 'unreasonable inconvenience' should be interpreted broadly. Concerns that such a wide interpretation of the exception may lead to uncertainty or that it may unduly deprive sellers of opportunities to cure could be countered on the ground that the inconvenience limitation is likely to apply only in a minority of cases. After all, because of the predominance of economic interests at stake in sale of goods cases, parties are more likely to turn to the other exception, ie 'unreasonable expense'. This may be especially true in commercial sales. Take, for example, an illustration given by Schlechtriem of extra costs incurred for transportation with regard to a delivery of goods as part of cure (whether through repair, replacement, or simply delivery where no goods had been delivered in the first place).[34] The buyer would be entitled to reject such a delivery. While the refusal of the delivery could be explained on grounds of inconvenience caused to the buyer by being faced with unexpected costs, the real concern appears to be with the fact that these

[33] See pp 141–2.

[34] Schlechtriem and Schwenzer, *Commentary on the UN Convention on the International Sale of Goods* (n 20 above) 444.

costs were not part of the initial contract. Thus, the question is not so much one of inconvenience, as one of unreasonable expense suffered by the buyer—'unreasonable' here referring to costs that should not be considered the responsibility of the buyer.

Situations in which the 'unreasonable inconvenience' limitation may be of particular relevance are those where the seller's first attempt at cure was unsuccessful and he seeks to make a second (or even a third or fourth) attempt at it. In these cases, the inconvenience caused to the buyer may be a ground on which to limit the seller's right to cure. For example, take the case of the purchase of furniture by a consumer-buyer. After delivery, the buyer notices several defects in the goods: the glass on the cupboard is scratched, a hole in the table has been covered up, or the cushions do not fit properly on the chairs.[35] The seller offers replacement of the goods, but the goods offered in place of the original ones also show defects. In this situation, a buyer should not be obliged to give the seller another opportunity to cure the lack of conformity. The inconvenience caused is such that another attempt at replacement would be disproportionate.

The inconvenience exception thus lends support to the rule that a seller should not have an unlimited number of chances to effect cure. This is also reflected in the fact that existing sales laws limit the number of attempts that the seller has at cure. For example, in German law, § 440 *BGB* provides that

> [a] repair is deemed to have failed after two unsuccessful attempts, unless, having regard in particular to the nature of the thing or of the defect or the other circumstances, a different conclusion is appropriate.

The provision is meant to give a guideline only; whether two attempts or more are permitted is a question of interpretation of the provision in the light of the Consumer Sales Directive, in which it finds its origin.[36] A similar rule applies in Dutch law.[37] Also, to the extent that a right to cure has been recognised in English law, it is conceded that 'several imperfect tenders would obviously expose the seller to an allegation that he has repudiated'.[38] In other words, after several failed attempts at cure, the buyer may well become entitled to terminate the contract or to invoke other remedies.

3. Conclusion

In conclusion, it is thought that moral rights reasoning may in two respects impose stronger limitations to the seller's right to cure than those that efficiency

[35] These were the complaints of the buyer in *Van Hout/Zijderveld*, Hof Den Bosch, 1 november 1993, PRG 1994, 4040.

[36] O Jauernig (ed), *Bürgerliches Gesetzbuch Kommentar*, 11th edn (München, CH Beck, 2004) 552.

[37] Geschillencommissie Thuiswinkel, 17 juni 2005 [2005] *Tijdschrift voor Consumentenrecht* 232–3, with commentary MBM Loos.

[38] Goode, *Commercial Law* (n 16 above) 345.

reasons prescribe with regard to the buyer's right of specific performance. First, whereas an order for specific performance would only be denied if it were disproportionate on the seller, it is thought that the seller's right to cure should be denied where it imposes any costs at all on the buyer. The seller, therefore, will have to offer compensation in order to be permitted to effect cure. Secondly, the seller's right to cure should be denied where it would cause unreasonable inconvenience to the buyer. This limitation relates to interests not caught by the first exception, in other words, to those that are not of an economic nature. Since the seller's interests generally do not extend to interests of a non-economic nature, it is of little relevance as a restriction to the buyer's right of specific performance. In relation to cure, however, it may act as a barrier to the seller's right to effect cure—since the seller committed a wrong in the first instance, it is thought that he should only be permitted to exercise his right to cure if he can do so without causing inconvenience to the buyer.

IV. CURE AND THE HIERARCHY OF REMEDIES

A final link between cure and specific performance may be discerned in the hierarchy of remedies. The previous chapter argued that, after the due delivery date, the seller only becomes in default after an additional period of time for performance has lapsed to no avail.[39] The buyer's entitlements to claim damages or termination, as a result, are postponed until after the expiration of such an extra time period. The practical effect of this is that the only remedies initially available to the buyer upon the seller's breach are the performance-oriented remedies. Thus, the default requirement may have the side-effect of imposing a hierarchy in which performance-oriented remedies are the primary recourse of the buyer upon the seller's breach of contract. The buyer will be forced first to try and obtain performance, and only if this fails will he be permitted to invoke another remedy, such as damages or termination. It is thought that this approach may be defended on grounds of policy.

The policy that may underlie a hierarchy in which performance-oriented remedies are placed at the top appears to be related to the protection of the interests of the seller. Seeing that the default requirement is a feature of the proposed cure regime, rather than a necessary prerequisite for specific performance, the hierarchy of remedies appears to find its origin in a desire to protect the interests of the seller, rather than those of the buyer. By limiting the buyer's choice initially to performance-oriented remedies, the seller is guaranteed an extra period of time for performance, which may allow him to provide a more cost-effective remedy. The buyer, in the meantime, does not seem to gain or lose anything from the imposition of a hierarchy. He does not gain anything, assuming

[39] There are a few exceptions to this rule, for example that performance has become impossible. See in more detail ch 6, p 171.

that he has a general entitlement to specific performance, repair or replacement, and thus would have been able to obtain any of these remedies anyhow.[40] At the same time, he does not lose anything, since performance-oriented remedies by definition are assumed to give him the performance that he contracted for.

Applying this reasoning to the remedial regime of the Consumer Sales Directive, it is submitted that, rather than furthering the EU policy of consumer protection, the instrument is actually inspired by considerations of market efficiency. What the Directive seeks to do by restricting the buyer's choice of remedy initially to repair and replacement is to protect the interests of the seller. In essence, the rule is about reducing the costs of remedies.[41] There may be some uncertainty as to the place of damages in this hierarchy, seeing that they fall outside the scope of the Directive. However, it appears that national legal systems should not permit the damages remedy to interfere with the availability of the performance-oriented remedies.[42] Therefore, repair and replacement are thought to remain at the top of the hierarchy, ensuring a right to cure. The emphasis thus being on cure, it is thought that the Directive should be regarded as a mechanism of market regulation that enables sellers to provide the most cost-effective remedies. From this perspective, a hierarchy of remedies may be a useful tool in sale of goods law.

Finally, it is thought that the hierarchy may be extended to commercial sales, as is the case for example in Dutch and in German law. Damages and termination, in these systems, only become available to the buyer once an additional period of time for performance has lapsed to no avail.[43] The effect of this is similar to the hierarchy of remedies in consumer sales—it places performance-oriented remedies at the top. While this may not be the most appropriate remedy in all types of commercial sale transactions, it is thought that the exceptions to the default requirement build in sufficient safeguards to ensure that performance-oriented remedies can be avoided where another remedy, such as damages, would be more appropriate. For example, the parties may stipulate that time is of the essence, in which case a breach of contract will entitle the buyer to terminate or to claim damages immediately, without first having to set an additional time for performance. At the same time, there may be other types of cases in which a performance-oriented remedy is the most appropriate option for both seller and buyer. For example, in cases where the transaction relates to complicated equipment that is of high value, which the buyer needs to have at

[40] A counterargument stating that specific performance is not generally available in all legal systems (the most notable exception being English law) does not appear to affect the argument made with regard to the hierarchy. After all, such systems do not show a great commitment to performance-oriented remedies and, in accordance with this, do not adhere to a hierarchy of remedies that places these remedies at the top.

[41] Compare S Grundmann, 'Consumer Law, Commercial Law, Private Law: How can the Sales Directive and the Sales Convention be so Similar?' [2003] *European Business Law Review* 237 at 243. See also pp 150–51.

[42] Compare ch 5, pp 132–4.

[43] See pp 170 ff.

its disposal (eg if it is used in a factory) or for which a substitute is not immediately available in the market, repair may be the most appropriate remedy. It gives the buyer the performance that he contracted for, and it is likely to be the most cost-effective remedy for the seller to provide. As long as time has not been made of the essence, the default requirement will apply and repair will be the principal remedy for the buyer, ie the seller will be permitted to cure. In this way, the hierarchy of remedies would appear to be of use in commercial sales as well.[44]

V. CONCLUSION

It can be seen that the mirror image analogy between cure and specific performance does not cover the rights completely. While there are similarities with regard to the possibilities of enforcement, as well as with regards to the limits to the scope of the rights, in general stricter limitations apply to cure than to specific performance. This may be justified with regard to the limits to the scope of cure, but it is questionable whether the seller's possibilities to enforce his right to cure should be this restrictive.

In order for a cure regime to be effective, it is essential for it to contain some opportunities for enforcement. First, to give the seller the certainty that attempts at cure will not be in vain, the right should be accompanied by a duty on the buyer to take delivery of the goods after repair or replacement. Secondly, it is thought that this should be backed up by an entitlement to specific performance of this obligation for the seller. This will prevent the buyer from rejecting goods where the seller has duly performed cure and has succeeded in bringing the goods up to a satisfactory standard. In this respect, the seller should thus be put in an equally strong position as the buyer, who—it has been argued—should have a general right to specific performance of the seller's obligation to deliver conforming goods. Nevertheless, the only instrument that currently contains an enforceable obligation on the buyer to take delivery is CISG. To this extent, it may be the best model for future harmonisation of sale of goods laws in Europe.

With regard to the limits to cure, a case may, however, be made for imposing stricter limitations than those that apply to the buyer's right to specific performance. Moral rights reasoning suggests that the seller, being the wrongdoing party, should bear the burden of the non-performance or defective performance. Accordingly, it is thought that the seller should be made to compensate the buyer for any expenses related to the exercise of his right to cure, as well as for any losses suffered in this respect. Moreover, the seller's right to cure may be denied where it causes unreasonable inconvenience to the buyer—a limitation that appears to have little bearing on its mirror image, specific performance.

[44] It should be noted, however, that the scope of cure may be influenced by a stipulation that makes time of the essence. It could thus provide a mechanism for the buyer to limit the seller's right to cure, as long as the seller agrees to the time stipulation.

Finally, a link between cure and specific performance becomes apparent in the existence of a hierarchy of remedies. The hierarchy enables the seller to insist on cure, whilst (temporarily) limiting the buyer's freedom of choice of remedy to performance-oriented remedies. At this point, where performance is the only option for both seller and buyer, the mirror images appear to merge.

8

Conclusion

ON THE BASIS of the observations made in the preceding chapters, it will have become clear that it will be no mean feat to create an EU regime for remedies in sale of goods law that is acceptable for all of the Member States. Nevertheless, it is thought that there are similarities in the underlying principles that shape the different systems, which may provide a basis for future harmonisation. Without repeating all of the arguments made in the preceding chapters, I will use the remaining pages to draw together the main threads of the discussion and, on the basis of this, to make some suggestions as to the future of sales law in Europe. Three elements of the main question will be focused on: (i) the buyer's entitlement to a performance-oriented remedy; (ii) the seller's right to cure, and its apparent effect on the hierarchy of remedies; and (iii) the relevance of the commercial or consumer nature of the sale transaction.

I. THE BUYER'S ENTITLEMENT TO A PERFORMANCE-ORIENTED REMEDY

According to the theory proposed in chapter three, performance-oriented remedies should be generally available (i) because contractual obligations are binding and they give the promisee—in sales cases the buyer—an enforceable interest in performance, and (ii) because the best way to protect this performance interest is through a remedy that takes the form of performance by the seller, rather than through an award of damages. Support for this view, it has been argued, may also be found in the remedial regimes of domestic sales laws, as well as in uniform instruments of international origin. These rules are shaped by two countervailing policies: on the one hand to protect the performance interest of the buyer, and on the other hand to achieve the result that is most beneficial for both parties from a viewpoint of economic efficiency. It is thought that, even if different regimes currently attach different weight to these policies, it is possible to reach a compromise that may reflect common law and civil law attitudes towards performance-oriented remedies. As far as the remedies of the buyer are concerned, the following guidelines may be formulated for the future harmonisation of European sale of goods laws.

First, as a starting point, the buyer should be free to choose the remedy that he prefers. This ensures the best protection of the performance interest, since the buyer will usually be in a better position than the seller to determine which remedy is able to give him the performance that he contracted for. This approach, moreover, is in accordance with national laws, which generally allow the buyer to choose his remedy, subject to certain limitations that protect the interests of the seller.[1]

Secondly, in order to ensure that the buyer is able to enforce his performance interest through a performance-oriented remedy if he so prefers, it is necessary for those remedies to be generally available. In other words, the buyer should be entitled to specific performance, or to repair or replacement, in all cases of breach by the seller of the obligation to deliver conforming goods. Support for this view can be found in civil law systems, which give the buyer a general entitlement to these remedies. While the solution is foreign to the English common law system, the courts are beginning to show a tendency towards a wider scope for specific performance. Even if it is unlikely that an overnight change in attitude will occur, the courts' tentative recognition of a wider scope for specific performance may indicate a willingness gradually to give greater recognition to the performance interest. This development, moreover, may gain impetus from the introduction of the related remedies of repair and replacement in consumer sales as a result of the Consumer Sales Directive.[2] These remedies, it has been argued, could be regarded as sub-forms of specific performance. If English law accepts them as remedies for non-conformity that are of generally available to consumer-buyers, the diminished significance of the 'inadequacy of damages' test in this context could potentially have an impact on the scope of specific performance. Moreover, a wider, or even general, availability of specific performance and (its sub-forms) repair and replacement would be in accordance with international instruments such as the UN Convention on Contracts for the International Sale of Goods (CISG),[3] the Principles of European Contract Law (PECL) and the Unidroit Principles of International Commercial Contracts (PICC). Nevertheless, considering the fact that the latter two are non-binding in nature, and that CISG leaves the authority to order or to deny specific performance in the hands of national courts, less weight may be attached to the solutions adopted therein than to those of national laws.

Thirdly, in order to ensure that the protection of the buyer's interests is not at the expense of the seller's legitimate interests, a number of restrictions need to be in place to limit the scope of specific performance, repair and replacement. While limitations found in national systems do not overlap completely, they appear similar in nature. The seller may find a defence in impossibility, as well as in factors such as good faith, severe hardship or disproportionality, which in sale of goods cases appear mainly to relate to considerations of economic efficiency.

[1] On which, see p 207 below.

[2] Directive 99/44/EC of the European Parliament and of the Council on certain aspects of the sale of consumer goods and associated guarantees [1999] OJ L171/12 (Consumer Sales Directive).

[3] UN Convention on Contracts for the International Sale of Goods (adopted 11 April 1980, entered into force 1 January 1988) 1489 UNTS 3 (CISG).

II. THE SELLER'S RIGHT TO CURE AND THE HIERARCHY OF REMEDIES

The interests of the seller can also be protected in another manner: through a right to cure. It has been argued that, before the contractual delivery date, the seller has a right to perform which is not lost until the time for performance has lapsed. Thus, as long as the seller still has time to perform, he will be entitled to remedy a defective performance made before the due delivery date. Furthermore, even after this date a limited right to cure may be defended on the basis of policy considerations. It is thought that performance will often be a more cost-effective solution for the seller and the buyer than immediate termination of the contract would be.

The seller's right to cure, to some extent, also links in with the hierarchy of remedies that the buyer may encounter when choosing his remedy. In order to ensure a right to cure for the seller after the due delivery date, an argument has been made in favour of a default regime similar to that found in Dutch and German law. This regime establishes that a buyer may only claim damages or terminate the contract after an additional period of time set for performance has lapsed to no avail. Apart from securing a time for cure for the seller, a side-effect of this regime is that it limits the buyer's initial choice of remedy to performance-oriented remedies. After all, performance must be requested before damages or termination become available. While there are a few exceptions to this rule—in particular where performance has become impossible or where the time for performance was 'of the essence'—the default requirement essentially creates a hierarchy of remedies with performance-oriented remedies at the top. Specific performance, repair and replacement in this regime are thus made the principal remedies of the buyer.

It should be stressed that the hierarchy of remedies is regarded merely as a by-product of the seller's right to cure. The thesis does not seek to argue that performance-oriented remedies, by definition, are always preferable over damages or termination. While they appear to offer the fullest possible protection of the buyer's performance interest, it is not suggested that other remedies may not, in appropriate circumstances, also protect this interest. Especially where the buyer has a strong preference for another remedy, such as damages, it could be assumed that he regards it as a full equivalent of performance. Therefore, the only inspiration for making performance-oriented remedies the principal remedies of the buyer stems from the desire to protect the interests of the seller. On the basis of such reasoning, it could be argued that the remedial regime laid down in the Consumer Sales Directive should be regarded as a measure of market regulation, rather than one of consumer protection.[4]

[4] Compare S Grundmann, 'Consumer Law, Commercial Law, Private Law: How can the Sales Directive and the Sales Convention be so Similar?' [2003] *European Business Law Review* 237 at 243; see also ch 7, p 201.

III. COMMERCIAL AND CONSUMER SALES

If considerations of market regulation, rather than a policy of consumer protection, form the main basis for the remedial scheme of the Consumer Sales Directive, it follows that the increased emphasis on performance-oriented remedies resulting from the Directive may not be limited to the consumer sphere. While the power balance between seller and buyer may be different in commercial sales, otherwise the interests at stake are very similar to consumer sales. The buyer has an interest in performance, and the seller has an interest in providing performance in the manner that is most cost-effective (and thus gives him the maximum profit). To this extent, the conclusions reached with regard to the availability and scope of performance-oriented remedies appear to apply equally to commercial and to consumer sales.

Nevertheless, in some respects commercial buyers may have very different interests from consumer-buyers. For example, whereas the consumer may have an interest in purchasing a particular type of goods, a commercial buyer may be interested only in the profit that he will be able to make from selling the goods on to a sub-buyer. Thus, where the consumer may prefer a performance-oriented remedy if goods turn out to be defective, a commercial buyer may prefer an award of damages which enables him swiftly to move on and make a cover purchase in the market, even if the goods so obtained are not of exactly the description or quality that was originally contracted for. However, it is thought that the proposed regime for performance-oriented remedies can also do justice to these interests of the buyer. After all, not only the performance-oriented remedies, but also damages and termination are generally available. Moreover, the fact that the default requirement may prevent those remedies from being available immediately upon the seller's breach appears to be of somewhat less relevance in the commercial context. In these type of contracts, the parties will usually have stipulated that timely performance is of particular significance, as a result of which the default requirement will not apply. Therefore, if the seller has not satisfactorily performed by the due date, the buyer will be free to choose from the entire range of remedies. Thus, the remedial regime makes provision for commercial buyers who prefer a performance-oriented remedy, but also for those who prefer a remedy in damages.

IV. THE FUTURE OF EUROPEAN SALES LAW

What does the future look like for European sale of goods law? As seen in chapter two, the ultimate destination of the harmonisation process remains unclear, at least for the moment. While the creation of a European Civil Code has proved much too ambitious a goal, the current programme for harmonisation has proposed a number of rather more low-key alternatives to further the approximation of the private laws of the Member States. The creation of a Common Frame of Reference (CFR) may to some extent provide a framework for establishing greater coherence in European legislation. An optional instrument, furthermore, may provide a relatively low-risk testing ground for harmonised rules. Since it does not impose rules, parties will be drawn to it only when it provides them with a better solution than domestic laws do. The creation of an alternative set of rules may therefore stimulate competition between legal rules, which may give some answers as to which rules offer the best solutions for intercommunity trade in Europe.[5] However, the effect of these instruments on harmonisation of European contract law remains to be seen. The question of harmonisation is mainly a political one, related to the market policy of the European Union, and it will therefore be for the European legislator to decide on further steps to be taken in this direction. Moreover, the more radical the proposed measures, the more difficult it will be to attain the required level of support from the Member States to enact the legislation.

Nevertheless, it has been argued that there is currently a greater basis for harmonisation in sale of goods law than there is in the general law of contract. The relatively dense level of harmonisation already achieved in this field provides a starting point for further developments and gives sales law a head start over other areas of contract law. In this light, sales law is likely to play a key role in future projects towards harmonisation of European contract law.[6] It is hoped that the current book may contribute to this process, or at least provide a signpost as to future directions that it may take.

[5] Compare J Smits, 'A European Private Law as a Mixed Legal System' (1998) 5 *Maastricht Journal of European and Comparative Law* 328 at 336–7. See also ch 2, p 24.

[6] Current projects recognise this; see for example the Green Paper on the Review of the Consumer Acquis COM(2006) 744 final (8 February 2007) 8.

Bibliography

J Adams and R Brownsword, 'The Ideologies of Contract Law' (1987) 7 *Legal Studies* 205

A Apps, 'The right to cure defective performance' [1994] *Lloyd's Maritime & Commercial Law Quarterly* 525

PS Atiyah, *The Rise and Fall of Freedom of Contract* (Oxford, Clarendon Press, 1979)

—— *Promises, Morals, and Law* (Oxford, Clarendon Press, 1981)

—— *An Introduction to the Law of Contract*, 5th edn (Oxford, Clarendon Press, 1995)

PS Atiyah, JN Adams and H MacQueen, *The Sale of Goods* (Harlow, Pearson, 2005)

HG Bamberger and H Roth, *Kommentar zum Bürgerlichen Gesetzbuch* (München, Beck, 2007)

A Barron, 'Section 35(6) of the Sale of Goods Act 1979—Loss of the Right to Reject and Rescind' 2005 SLT 17

P Bassenge, G Brudermüller and others (eds), *Palandt Kommentare zum Bürgerliches Gesetzbuch*, 66th edn (München, Beck, 2007)

H Beale, *Remedies for Breach of Contract* (London, Sweet & Maxwell, 1980)

—— 'English Law Reform and the Impact of European Private Law' in S Vogenauer and S Weatherill (eds), *The Harmonisation of European Contract Law* (Oxford, Hart Publishing, 2006) 31

MC Bianca and MJ Bonell (eds), *Commentary on the International Sales Law. The 1980 Vienna Sales Convention* (Milan, Giuffrè, 1987)

MC Bianca and S Grundmann (eds), *EU Sales Directive: Commentary* (Antwerp, Intersentia, 2002)

P Birks, 'Rights, Wrongs and Remedies' (2000) 20 *Oxford Journal of Legal Studies* 1

G Bitter and E Meidt, 'Nacherfüllungsrecht und Nacherfüllungspflicht des Verkäufers im neuen Schuldrecht (2001) 22 *ZIP-Zeitschrift für Wirtschaftsrecht* 2114

R Bradgate, 'Remedying the Unfit Fitted Kitchen' (2004) 120 *Law Quarterly Review* 558

R Bradgate and C Twigg-Flesner, *Blackstone's Guide to Consumer Sales and Associated Guarantees* (Oxford, Oxford University Press, 2003)

R Bradgate and F White, 'Sale of Goods Forming Part of a Bulk: Proposals for Reform' [1994] *Lloyd's Maritime & Commercial Law Quarterly* 315

—— 'Rejection and Termination in Contracts for the Sale of Goods' in J Birds, R Bradgate and C Villiers (eds), *Termination of Contracts* (London, Wiley Chancery, 1995) 51

M Bridge, *The Sale of Goods* (Oxford, Oxford University Press, 1997)

—— 'The Vienna Sales Convention and English Law: Curing Defective Performance by the Seller' in LL Andersen, J Fejø and R Nielsen (eds), *Festskrift til Ole Lando* (Copenhagen, Gadjura, 1997) 83

—— *The International Sale of Goods. Law and Practice* (Oxford, Oxford University Press, 1999)

—— 'What is to be Done about Sale of Goods?' (2003) 119 *Law Quarterly Review* 173

M Bridge, 'A second tender: *J&H Ritchie Ltd v Lloyd Ltd*' [2007] *Journal of Business Law* 814

T Burns 'Better Late than Never: the Reform of the Law on the Sale of Goods Forming Part of a Bulk' (1996) 59 *MLR* 260

AS Burrows, 'Specific performance at the crossroads' [1984] *Legal Studies* 102

A Burrows, *Remedies for Torts and Breach of Contract*, 3rd edn (Oxford, Oxford University Press, 2004)

D Busch and others (eds), *The Principles of European Contract Law and Dutch Law—A Commentary* (Nijmegen, Ars Aequi Libri, 2002)

J Calais-Auloy, 'Un code européen de la consommation?' in F Osman (ed), *Vers un code européen de la consommation. Codification, unification et harmonisation du droit des États-membres de l'Union européenne/Towards a European Consumer Code. Codification, unification and harmonisation of European Union Member States law* (Bruxelles, Bruylant, 1998) 399

A Chamboredon, 'The Debate on a European Civil Code: For an "Open Texture" ' in M Van Hoecke and F Ost (eds), *The Harmonisation of European Private Law* (Oxford, Hart Publishing, 2000) 63

Commission follow-up Communication to the Green Paper on EU Consumer Protection COM(2002) 289 (11 June 2002)

Communication from the Commission to the Council and the European Parliament on European Contract Law COM(2001) 398 final (11 July 2001) (Communication on European Contract Law)

Communication from the Commission to the European Parliament, the Council, the Economic and Social Committee and the Committee of the Regions, 'Consumer Policy Strategy 2002–2006' [2002] OJ C137/2

Communication from the Commission to the European Parliament and the Council, 'A more coherent European contract law—an action plan' COM(2003) 68 final (12 February 2003) ('Action Plan')

Communication from the Commission to the European Parliament and the Council, 'European Contract Law and the revision of the *acquis*: the way forward' COM(2004) 651 final (11 October 2004) ('The Way Forward')

R Cooter and T Ulen, *Law and Economics*, 3rd edn (Reading MA, Addison-Wesley, 2000)

Council of the European Union, Interinstitutional File 2005/0261 (COD) (3 December 2007)

R Craswell, 'Contract Law, Default Rules, and the Philosophy of Promising' (1989) 88 *Michigan Law Review* 489

G De Geest, *Economische analyse van het contracten- en quasi-contractenrecht. Een onderzoek naar de wetenschappelijke waarde van de rechtseconomie* (Antwerpen, MAKLU, 1994)

Lord Devlin, 'The Treatment of Breach of Contract' [1966] *Cambridge Law Journal* 192

U Drobnig, 'Scope and General Rules of a European Civil Code' (1997) 5 *European Review of Private Law* 489

WCH Ervine, 'Cure and Retender Revisited' [2006] *Journal of Business Law* 799

AJ Feenstra, 'Nakoming door de terkortschietende verkoper en de macht van de koper' [1997] *Nederlands Tijdschrift voor Burgerlijk Recht* 243

F Ferrari, 'Specific Topics of CISG in the Light of Judicial Application and Scholarly Writing' (1995) 15 *Journal of Law and Commerce* 1

C Fried, *Contract as Promise* (Cambridge MA, Harvard University Press, 1981)
D Friedmann, 'The Performance Interest in Contract Damages' (1995) 111 *Law Quarterly Review* 628
R Goode, *The Concept of Good Faith in English Law* (Roma, Centro di Studi e Ricerche di Diritto Comparato e Straniero, 1992)
—— *Commercial Law*, 3rd edn (London, LexisNexis, 2004)
Green Paper on guarantees for consumer goods and after-sales services COM(1993) 509 final (15 November 1993)
Green Paper on European Union Consumer Protection COM(2001) 531 final (2 October 2001)
Green Paper on the Review of the Consumer Acquis COM(2006) 744 final (8 February 2007)
and Report on the Outcome of the Public Consultation on the Green Paper on the Review of the Consumer Acquis (9 October 2007)
DG Health and Consumer Protection, 'Preparatory Work for the Impact Assessment on the Review of the Consumer Acquis' (6 November 2007)
S Grundmann, 'Consumer Law, Commercial Law, Private Law: How can the Sales Directive and the Sales Convention be so Similar?' [2003] *European Business Law Review* 237
S Grundmann and A Hoerning, 'Leistungsstörungsmodelle im Lichte der ökonomischen Theorie—nationales, europäisches und internationales Recht' in T Eger and H-B Schäfer (eds), *Ökonomische Analyse der europäischen Zivilrechtsentwicklung* (Tübingen, Mohr Siebeck, 2007) 420
AG Guest (ed), *Benjamin's Sale of Goods*, 7th edn (London, Sweet & Maxwell, 2006)
D Harris, A Ogus and J Phillips, 'Contract Remedies and the Consumer Surplus' (1979) 95 *Law Quarterly Review* 581
DR Harris, 'Specific Performance—a Regular Remedy for Consumers?' (2003) 119 *Law Quarterly Review* 541
AS Hartkamp, *Asser IV(I) Verbintenissenrecht. De verbintenis in het algemeen*, 12th edn (Deventer,WEJ Tjeenk Willink, 2004)
AS Hartkamp and others (eds), *Towards a European Civil Code*, 3rd revised edn (The Hague, Kluwer Law International, 2004)
MW Hesselink, 'The Principles of European Contract Law: Some Choices Made by the Lando Commission' in MW Hesselink and GJP de Vries, *Principles of European Contract Law* (Deventer, Kluwer, 2001) 9
—— *Contractenrecht in Perspectief* (Den Haag, Boom Juridische Uitgevers, 2004)
J Hijma, *Asser V(I) Bijzondere overeenkomsten. Koop en ruil*, 6th edn (Deventer, WEJ Tjeenk Willink, 2001)
OW Holmes, 'The Path of the Law' (1897) 10 *Harvard Law Review* 457
E Hondius, *Consumer Guarantees: Towards a European Sale of Goods Act* (Roma, Centro di Studi e Ricerche di Diritto Comparato e Straniero, 1996)
E Hondius, V Heutger and C Jeloschek, *Principles of European Law. vol 5. Sales Contracts* (Munich, Sellier, 2007)
JO Honnold, *Uniform Law for International Sales*, 3rd edn (The Hague, Kluwer Law International, 1999)
P Huber, 'Der Nacherfüllungsanspruch im neuen Kaufrecht' [2002] *Neue Juristische Wochenschrift* 1004
MAJG Janssen and MM van Rossum, 'Verzuim en ingebrekestelling bij schadevergoeding en ontbinding' [2004] *Nederlands Tijdschrift voor Burgerlijk Recht* 62

O Jauernig (ed), *Bürgerliches Gesetzbuch Kommentar*, 11th edn (München, CH Beck, 2004)
A Johnston and H Unberath, 'Law at, to or from the Centre? The European Court of Justice and the Harmonization of Private Law in the European Union' in F Cafaggi (ed), *The Institutional Framework of European Private Law* (Oxford, Oxford University Press, 2006) 149
G Jones and W Goodhart, *Specific Performance*, 2nd edn (London, Butterworths, 1996)
M Kandler, *Kauf und Nacherfüllung* (Bielefeld, Gieseking, 2004)
I Kant, *Metaphysische Anfangsgründe der Rechtslehre* (Königsberg, Nicolovius, 1798)
WCA Ker (ed), *Benjamin on Sale*, 6th edn (London, Sweet & Maxwell, 1920)
D Kimel, *From Promise to Contract. Towards a Liberal Theory of Contract* (Oxford, Hart Publishing, 2003)
P Klik, *Koop en Consumentenkoop* (Deventer, Kluwer, 2004)
T Koopmans, 'Towards a European Civil Code?' (1997) 5 *European Review of Private Law* 541
AT Kronman, 'Specific Performance' (1978) 45 *University of Chicago Law Review* 351
W Krüger (ed), *Münchener Kommentar zum Bürgerlichen Gesetzbuch*, vol 2, 5th edn (München, CH Beck, 2007)
T Krummel and R D'Sa, 'Sale of consumer goods and associated guarantees: a minimalist approach to harmonised European Union consumer protection' (2001) 26 *European Law Review* 312
M Kuneva, 'Healthy markets need effective redress' (Conference on Collective Redress, 2007)
Y-M Laithier, *Étude comparative des sanctions de l'inexécution du contrat* (Paris, LGDJ, 2004)
—— 'Comparative Reflections on the French Law of Remedies for Breach of Contract' in N Cohen and E McKendrick (eds), *Comparative Remedies for Breach of Contract* (Oxford, Hart Publishing, 2005) 103
H Lando and C Rose, 'The Myth of Specific Performance in Civil Law Countries', *American Law & Economics Association Annual Meetings* (paper 15, 2004)
O Lando, 'My life as a lawyer' [2002] *Zeitschrift für Europäisches Privatrecht* 508
O Lando and H Beale (eds), *Principles of European Contract Law. Parts I and II* (The Hague, Kluwer Law International, 2000)
O Lando and others (eds), *Principles of European Contract Law. Part III* (The Hague, Kluwer Law International, 2003)
L Landy, 'Le consommateur européen: une notion éclatée' in F Osman (ed), *Vers un code européen de la consommation. Codification, unification et harmonisation du droit des États-membres de l'Union européenne/Towards a European Consumer Code. Codification, unification and harmonisation of European Union Member States law* (Bruxelles, Bruylant, 1998) 57
Law Commissions, *Sale and Supply of Goods* (Law Com No 160, Scot Law Com No 104 (May 1987))
—— *Sale of Goods Forming Part of a Bulk* (Law Com No 215, Scot Law Com No 145 (July 1993))
P Legrand, 'Against a European Civil Code' (1997) 60 *Modern Law Review* 44
MA Leijten 'Tekortkoming: nakoming of schadevergoeding?' [2001] *Bedrijfsjuridische berichten* 43
JB Londonck Sluijk, 'Verzuim en ingebrekestelling bij niet-nakoming van verbintenissen: een overzicht aan de hand van twee arresten' [2003] *Bedrijfsjuridische berichten* 50

MBM Loos, *Consumentenkoop* (Kluwer, Deventer 2004)
M Loos, *Spontane harmonisatie in het contracten- en consumentenrecht* (Den Haag, Boom, 2006)
KFK Low, 'Repair, rejection and rescission: an uneasy resolution' (2007) 123 *Law Quarterly Review* 536
HL MacQueen, 'Remedies for Breach of Contract: the Future Development of Scots Law in its European and International Context' (1997) 1 *Edinburgh Law Review* 200
—— 'Scots law in Europe: the case of contract' in HL MacQueen, A Vaquer and S Espiau Espiau (eds), *Regional Private Laws and Codification in Europe* (Cambridge, Cambridge University Press, 2003) 102
HL MacQueen and LJ Macgregor, 'Specific Implement, Interdict and Contractual Performance' (1999) 3 *Edinburgh Law Review* 239
HL MacQueen and J Thomson, *Contract Law in Scotland* (Edinburgh, Butterworths, 2000)
C Mak, 'Aansprakelijkheid voor afgebroken onderhandelingen: een vergelijking tussen Nederlands recht en de Principles of European Contract Law' (2002) 51 *Ars Aequi* 62
V Mak, 'Repair and Loss of the Right to Reject—A Remedial Dilemma in Sale of Goods Law' [2006] *Lloyd's Maritime & Commercial Law Quarterly* 163
—— 'The seller's right to cure defective performance—a reappraisal' [2007] *Lloyd's Maritime & Commercial Law Quarterly* 409
—— 'Missing Bearings—Information Duties of the Seller under Section 35 of the Sale of Goods Act 1979', note on *J&H Ritchie Ltd v Lloyd Ltd* [2007] UKHL 9; [2007] 1 WLR 670 (2007) 70 *Modern Law Review* 1002
BS Markesinis, 'Why a code is not the best way to advance the cause of European legal unity' (1997) 5 *European Review of Private Law* 519
BS Markesinis, H Unberath and A Johnston, *The German Law of Contract*, 2nd edn (Oxford, Hart Publishing, 2006)
U Mattei, 'A Transaction Costs Approach to the European Code' (1997) 5 *European Review of Private Law* 537
—— 'Hard Code Now!' (2002) 2 *Global Jurist Frontiers* 1
WW McBryde, *The Law of Contract in Scotland*, 3rd edn (Edinburgh, W Green, 2007)
E McKendrick, 'Specific Implement and Specific Performance—a Comparison' 1986 SLT 249
—— 'Good Faith: A Matter of Principle?' in ADM Forte, *Good Faith in Contract and Property* (Oxford, Hart Publishing, 1999) 39
—— 'The Common Law at Work: the Saga of *Alfred McAlpine Construction Ltd v Panatown Ltd*' (2003) 3 *Oxford University Commonwealth Law Journal* 145
—— *Contract Law*, 6th edn (Basingstoke, Palgrave Macmillan, 2005)
—— *Contract Law: Text, Cases and Materials*, 2nd edn (Oxford, Oxford University Press, 2005)
—— 'Harmonisation of European Contract Law: The State We Are In' in S Vogenauer and Stephen Weatherill (eds), *The Harmonisation of European Contract Law* (Oxford, Hart Publishing, 2006) 5
R Michaels, 'The Functional Method in Comparative Law' in M Reimann and R Zimmermann (eds), *The Oxford Handbook of Comparative Law* (Oxford, Oxford University Press, 2006)
CJ Miller and others (eds), *Benjamin's Sale of Goods. Special Supplement to the 6th Edition: Sale and Supply of Goods to Consumers Regulations* (London, Sweet & Maxwell, 2003)

PM North and JJ Fawcett, *Cheshire and North's Private International Law*, 13th edn (London, Butterworths, 1999)
E Peden, 'Policy Concerns Behind Implication of Terms in Law' (2001) 117 *Law Quarterly Review* 459
E Peel (ed), *Treitel on the Law of Contract*, 12th edn (London, Sweet & Maxwell, 2007)
Proposal for a Regulation of the European Parliament and the Council on the law applicable to contractual obligations (Rome I) (presented by the Commission) COM(2005) 650 final (15 December 2005)
J Raz, 'Book Review: Promises in Morality and Law' (1982) 95 *Harvard Law Review* 916
—— *The Morality of Freedom* (Oxford, Clarendon Press, 1986)
WHM Reehuis and EE Slob, *Parlementaire Geschiedenis van het Nieuwe Burgerlijk Wetboek, Invoering Boeken 3, 5 en 6, Boek 7, Bijzondere Overeenkomsten* (Deventer, Kluwer, 1991)
D Reinicke and K Tiedtke, *Kaufrecht* (München, Luchterhand, 2004)
L Reurich, 'Risico en proportionaliteit' in WH van Boom and others (eds), *Koop! BW-krant jaarboek 1998* (Deventer, Gouda Quint, 1998) 59
F Reynolds, 'A Note of Caution' in P Birks (ed), *The Frontiers of Liability* (Oxford, Oxford University Press, 1994)
H-B Schäfer and C Ott, *Lehrbuch der ökonomischen Analyse des Zivilrechts*, 4th edn (Berlin, Springer, 2005) 464–7
P Schlechtriem, 'Some Observations on the United Nations Convention on Contracts for the International Sale of Goods' in P Birks (ed), *The Frontiers of Liability* (Oxford, Oxford University Press, 1994)
P Schlechtriem and I Schwenzer (eds), *Commentary on the UN Convention on the International Sale of Goods*, 2nd English edn (Oxford, Oxford University Press, 2005)
A Schwartz, 'The Case for Specific Performance' (1979) 89 *Yale Law Journal* 271
H Sivesand, *The Buyer's Remedies for Non-Conforming Goods: Should there be Free Choice or are Restrictions Necessary?* (Munich, Sellier, 2005)
A Smith, 'Specific Implement' in K Reid and R Zimmermann (eds), *A History of Private Law in Scotland. Vol 2. Obligations* (Oxford, Oxford University Press, 2000) 195
L Smith, 'Understanding Specific Performance' in N Cohen and E McKendrick (eds), *Comparative Remedies for Breach of Contract* (Oxford, Hart Publishing, 2005) 221
SA Smith, 'Performance, Punishment and the Nature of Contractual Obligation' (1997) 60 *Modern Law Review* 360
—— *Contract Theory* (Oxford, Oxford University Press, 2004)
J Smits, 'A European Private Law as a Mixed Legal System' (1998) 5 *Maastricht Journal of European and Comparative Law* 328
—— 'Naar een nieuw Europees consumentenkooprecht: Over de Europese richtlijn verkoop van en garanties voor consumentengoederen in het Nederlandse recht' [2000] *Nederlands Juristenblad* 1825
—— *The Making of European Private Law. Towards a Ius Commune Europaeum as a Mixed Legal System* (Antwerp, Intersentia, 2002)
JM Smits, 'De toekomst van het Europees privaatrecht: Gemeenschappelijk Referentiekader, optionele code en implementatie van richtlijnen' in AS Hartkamp, CH Sieburgh and LAD Keus, *De invloed van het Europese recht op het Nederlandse privaatrecht* (Deventer, Serie Onderneming en Recht, deel 42-I, Kluwer, 2007) 281

ICF Spry *Equitable Remedies*, 6th edn (Sydney, LBC Information Services, 2001)

D Staudenmayer, 'The Directive on the Sale of Consumer Goods and Associated Guarantees—a Milestone in the European Consumer and Private Law' (2000) 8 *European Review of Private Law* 547

—— 'The Commission Communication on European Contract Law and the Future Prospects' (2002) 51 *International Comparative Law Quarterly* 673

H Stoll, 'Abschied von der Lehre von der positiven Vertragsverletzung' (1932) 136 *AcP* 257

MM Stolp, *Ontbinding, schadevergoeding en nakoming. De remedies voor wanprestatie in het licht van de beginselen van subsidiariteit en proportionaliteit* (Deventer, Kluwer, 2007)

Study Group on a European Civil Code/Research Group on EC Private Law (Acquis Group) (eds), *Principles, Definitions and Model Rules of European Private Law. Draft Common Frame of Reference (DCFR). Interim Outline Edition* (Munich, Sellier, 2008).

RJ Tjittes, 'Het recht op nakoming' (2001) 162 *RM Themis* 161

GH Treitel, *Remedies for Breach of Contract. A Comparative Account* (Oxford, Clarendon Press, 1988)

C Twigg-Flesner and R Bradgate, 'The EC Directive on Certain Aspects of the Sale of Consumer Goods and Associated Guarantees—All Talk and No Do?' (2000) *Web Journal of Current Legal Issues*

TS Ulen, 'The Efficiency of Specific Performance: Toward a Unified Theory of Contract Remedies' (1984) 83 *Michigan Law Review* 341

J Ulph 'The Sale of Goods (Amendment) Act 1995: Co-ownership and the Rogue Seller' [1996] *Lloyd's Maritime & Commercial Law Quarterly* 93

H Unberath, *Die Vertragsverletzung* (Tübingen, Mohr Siebeck, 2007)

'UNCITRAL: Preparation of the 1977 UNCITRAL "Sales" Draft' in J Honnold (ed), *Documentary History of the Uniform Law for International Sales* (Deventer, Kluwer, 1989) 338

United Nations Commission on International Trade Law, *UNCITRAL Digest of case law on the United Nations Convention on the International Sale of Goods—Article 48* (8 June 2004) 2

A Vaquer, 'Tender of Performance, *Mora Creditoris* and the (Common?) Principles of European Contract Law (2002) 17 *Tulane European and Civil Law Forum* 83

RHJ van Bijnen, 'Naar een wederzijds voordelige remedie bij teleurstellende contracten' [2003] *Weekblad voor Privaatrecht Notariaat en Registratie* 710 and 735

R Van den Bergh, 'Forced Harmonisation of Contract Law in Europe: Not to be Continued' in S Grundmann and J Stuyck (eds), *An Academic Green Paper on European Contract Law* (The Hague, Kluwer Law International, 2002) 249

W van Gerven, 'Codifying European private law? Yes, if . . .!' (2002) 27 *European Law Review* 156

—— 'A Common Law for Europe: The Future Meeting the Past?' (2001) 4 *European Review of Private Law* 485

M Van Hoecke, 'The harmonisation of private law in Europe: some misunderstandings' in M Van Hoecke and F Ost (eds), *The Harmonisation of European Private Law* (Oxford, Hart Publishing, 2000) 1

S Vogenauer, 'Eine gemeineuropäische Methodenlehre des Rechts' [2005] *Zeitschrift für Europäisches Privatrecht* 234

S Vogenauer and S Weatherill, 'The European Community's Competence to Pursue the Harmonisation of Contract Law—an Empirical Contribution to the Debate' in S Vogenauer and S Weatherill (eds), *The Harmonisation of European Contract Law* (Oxford, Hart Publishing, 2006) 105

S Watterson, 'Consumer Sales Directive 1999/44/EC—The Impact on English Law' [2001] *European Review of Private Law* 197

S Weatherill, *EC Consumer Law and Policy*, 2nd edn (Cheltenham, Edward Elgar, 2005)

C Webb, 'Performance and Compensation: An Analysis of Contract Damages and Contractual Obligation' (2006) 26 *Oxford Journal of Legal Studies* 41

S Whittaker, *Liability for Products* (Oxford, Oxford University Press, 2005)

S Whittaker and R Zimmermann, 'Coming to Terms with Good Faith' in R Zimmermann and S Whittaker (eds), *Good Faith in European Contract Law* (Cambridge, Cambridge University Press, 2000) 669

J Yovel, 'Cure after date for delivery: Comparison between provisions of the CISG (seller's right to remedy failure to perform: Article 48) and the counterpart provisions of the PECL (Articles 8:104 and 9:303)' in J Felemegas (ed), *An International Approach to the Interpretation of the United Nations Convention on Contracts for the International Sale of Goods (1980) as Uniform Sales Law* (Cambridge, Caambridge University Press, 2007) 381

R Zakrzewski, *Remedies Reclassified* (Oxford, Oxford University Press, 2005)

R Zimmermann, *The New German Law of Obligations* (Oxford, Oxford University Press, 2005)

K Zweigert and H Kötz, *Introduction to Comparative Law*, 3rd revised edn (Oxford, Oxford University Press, 1998)

Index